Direct Democracy Worldwide

Challenging the common assumption that models of direct democracy and representative democracy are necessarily at odds, *Direct Democracy Worldwide* demonstrates how practices of direct and representative democracy interact under different institutional settings and uncovers the conditions that allow them to coexist in a mutually reinforcing manner. Whereas citizen-initiated mechanisms of direct democracy can spur productive relationships between citizens and political parties, other mechanisms of direct democracy often help leaders bypass other representative institutions, undermining republican checks and balances. The book also demonstrates that the embrace of direct democracy is costly, may generate uncertainties and inconsistencies, and in some cases is easily manipulated. Nonetheless, the promise of direct democracy should not be dismissed. Direct democracy is much more than a simple, pragmatic second choice when representative democracy seems not to be working as expected. Properly designed, it can empower citizens, breaking through some of the institutionalized barriers to accountability that arise in representative systems.

David Altman received his Ph.D. in political science from the University of Notre Dame and is Associate Professor of Political Science at the Pontificia Universidad Católica de Chile. Born in Uruguay, he works on comparative politics with an emphasis on the quality of democratic institutions, mechanisms of direct democracy, and executive-legislative relations. He is an associate researcher for the Uruguayan National Agency for Research and Innovation, was the winner of a Junior Post-Doctoral Scholars in the Study of Democracy Competition of the Woodrow Wilson Center and the Ford Foundation, and has previously held a Fulbright-LASPAU fellowship. He also was Guest Research Assistant Professor at the Helen Kellogg Institute for International Studies. His recent work has appeared in *Electoral Studies*, *Party Politics*, *Democratization*, *Journal of Legislative Studies*, *Canadian Journal of Political Science*, *The Developing Economies*, *Política y Gobierno*, *Revista de Ciencia Política*, *Swiss Political Science Review*, and *Journal of Developing Economies*.

Direct Democracy Worldwide

DAVID ALTMAN
Pontificia Universidad Católica de Chile

CAMBRIDGE
UNIVERSITY PRESS

CAMBRIDGE
UNIVERSITY PRESS

32 Avenue of the Americas, New York NY 10013-2473, USA

Cambridge University Press is part of the University of Cambridge.

It furthers the University's mission by disseminating knowledge in the pursuit of education, learning and research at the highest international levels of excellence.

www.cambridge.org
Information on this title: www.cambridge.org/9781107427099

First published 2011
First paperback edition 2014

A catalogue record for this publication is available from the British Library

Library of Congress Cataloguing in Publication data

Altman, David, 1968–
Direct democracy worldwide / David Altman.
    p.   cm.
Includes bibliographical references and index.
ISBN 978-1-107-00164-0 (hardback)
1. Direct democracy.   2. Comparative government.   I. Title.
JC423.A5165   2010
321.8 – dc22   2010029360

ISBN 978-1-107-00164-0 Hardback
ISBN 978-1-107-42709-9 Paperback

To Ro, Naomi, and Mati

Contents

Tables

Figures

Preface and Acknowledgments

I remember exactly how I became interested in the study of political science. It was about thirty years ago, during the spring of 1980, in Uruguay, the country where I was born. At that time, Uruguay was under military rule and the military attempted to ratify – via a plebiscite – a new constitution that sought to establish a new order in the country, essentially a militarily protected democracy. A few days before the plebiscite, I asked my father how he was planning to vote. With no knowledge of the political leanings of my schoolmates' parents (and perhaps fearful that they were members of the military regime), he sat me on his lap. Softly and calmly, he told me that he and my mother were voting against the military, but that I could not tell anyone ... ANYONE! When I asked why they were voting "no," he explained that sometimes the "bad guys" govern, and that he and my mother did not want that kind of future for Uruguay. My intuition then pushed me to ask why, if they were the bad guys, they were governing, when *of course* the good guys should be governing the country. I do not remember what my father told me then, but I do recall the perplexed look on his face. My confusion was later exacerbated in my search for an answer as to why the military accepted their disastrous defeat.

After the transition to democracy in Uruguay had been completed and democratic rulers were governing the country, I decided to study political science at the Hebrew University of Jerusalem. During my years in Israel, I lived in a kibbutz in the north of the country, Kibbutz Yehiam. Participating in several of the members' assemblies on Saturday nights at the collective dining room, I was inspired by a completely new democratic experience. It was then that I experienced the most obvious and clear example of a participative, deliberative, direct democracy that I could ever image. But I soon realized that the kibbutz was not Israel and that a democracy could not exist only in meetings on Saturday nights. Something else must be in place.

By that time, political science had already become my obsession, and later I pursued a Ph.D. at the University of Notre Dame. Though it was not to be my dissertation topic, my very first paper was on the subject of direct democracy.

From that time forward, I developed a secret intellectual love affair with direct democracy. When I returned to Latin America to begin my professional career, the constant search for improvements to democracy forced me to make, more often than not, new dates with my old intellectual love. Those dates formed the prelude to this book.

Since that time, I have become immeasurably indebted to those who have supported me in my intellectual pursuits – indeed, they are too numerous to acknowledge here. Yet, at the risk of forgetting someone, I cannot start to express my gratitude to my professors at the University of Notre Dame: Michael Coppedge, Robert Fishman, Andrew Gould, Scott Mainwaring, Guillermo O'Donnell, and Benjamin Radcliff. They taught me not only to organize scattered ideas but also to think. Yet I would not be exaggerating if I said that, in certain regards, I learned more from my classmates than from anyone else: Dan Brinks, Rossana Castiglioni, Andreas Feldmann, Carlos Guevara-Mann, and Aníbal Pérez-Liñán, who were, and in a way still are, an informal working team.

In pursuing field research and writing this manuscript, several people offered insightful advice, invaluable information, and constant opportunities to exchange ideas. My colleagues at the Catholic University of Chile (*Pontificia Universidad Católica de Chile*), where I now work, were bombarded almost daily with questions in search of advice: Tomás Chuaqui, Arie Epstein, Oscar Godoy, Renato Lewin, Juan Pablo Luna, Rodrigo Mardones, Anthony Pezzola, Alfredo Rehren, and Miguel Vatter, and also my students Germán Bidegain, Piru Farías, Pili Gianini, Mauricio Morales, Rafael Piñeiro, Roody Reserve, Fernando Rosenblatt, and Sergio Toro.

In Uruguay, field work was performed in stages, yet behind the scenes; Daniel Buquet, Gerardo Caetano, Antonio Cardarello, Fonzy Castiglia, Daniel Chasquetti, and Fito Garcé were always there. The presidents of Uruguay, Jorge Batlle, Luis Alberto Lacalle, and Julio María Sanguinetti; the ministers of the Electoral Court, Rodolfo González-Rissotto, Washington Salvo, and Carlos Urruty; and legislators of the Parliament of the republic provided vital assistance in completing my research on Uruguay.

In Switzerland, interactions with Andreas Auer, Fernando Méndez, Uwe Serdült, Vasiliki Trigka, Yanina Welp, and Jonathan Wheatley were critical for discussing some of the ideas of this manuscript. This research also benefited from other colleagues: Evaristo Thomas Acuña, Angel Alvarez, Santiago Basabe, Anita Breuer, Rolf Büchi, Ernesto Calvo, Maxwell Cameron, Luis Caravacho, John Carey, Miguel de Luca, Jørgen Elklit, Claudio Fuentes, Jael Goldsmith, Andreas Gross, Simon Hug, Kestutis Jankauskas, Bruno Kauffmann, Herbert Kitschelt, Algis Krupavicius, Larry LeDuc, Marcelo Leiras, Andrés Malamud, Wilfried Marxer, Joe Mathews, Juan Pablo Morales, Vicky Murillo, Jennifer Pribble, Adam Przeworski, Daniela Rivera, Theo Schiller, Maija Setälä, Peter Siavelis, Palle Svensson, Fredrik Uggla, Pier Vincenzo Uleri, Jorge Vargas-Cullel, Andreas Vatter, Greg Weeks, and Kurt Weyland.

Many institutions and programs provided me with significant and influential milieus: the Political Science Institute at the Catholic University of Chile;

the Political Science Institute at the University of the Republic in Uruguay; the Department of Political Science and the Helen Kellogg Institute for International Studies at the University of Notre Dame; the Fulbright Commission – LASPAU; the National Commission for Scientific and Technological Research of Chile (Grants 1040920, 1060749, and 1090294); the Junior Post-Doctoral Scholars in the Study of Democracy Competition of the Latin American Program of the Woodrow Wilson Center for Scholars and the Ford Foundation; and the Centre for Research on Direct Democracy (C2D) at the University of Zurich.

Special thanks go to my colleague Gerardo Munck, who constantly encouraged me to work on this project and read several drafts of it. His advice was absolutely essential. I am also indebted to John Londregan and Luis Andrés Herskovic for their helpful comments and suggestions on Chapter 3, as well as to John Sonnet and Charles Ragin for their suggestions on Chapter 7. Philip Pettit provided me with a helpful sounding board to test the reasonableness of the central arguments of the book. Hethba Fatnassi did a wonderful job editing and proofreading the manuscript. And, at Cambridge University Press, Lew Bateman was a helpful interlocutor who very professionally oversaw the review and publication of this book.

Last, but not least, my family: my parents, Lea and Ruben, and my sister, Janine; without them I could have not started this beautiful journey; my wife, Rossana, for her encouragement and support; and my kids, Naomi and Matías, who make everything have sense. This book could not have been written whatsoever without their inspiration. Wishing that Naomi and Matías never have to ask the same question I asked thirty years ago . . . here it goes!

Permission to use the following materials from previously published articles is gratefully acknowledged: Passages of Chapter 2 are based on "Assessing the Quality of Democracy: Freedom, Competitiveness, and Participation in 18 Latin American Countries" published in *Democratization* (2002), co-authored with Aníbal Pérez-Liñán. Chapter 6 draws on "Collegiate Executives and Direct Democracy in Switzerland and Uruguay: Similar Institutions, Opposite Political Goals, Distinct Results," published in the *Swiss Political Science Review* (2008), and on "Popular Initiatives in Uruguay: Confidence Votes on Government or Political Loyalties?" in *Electoral Studies* (2002).

Also, I would like thank EFE for the picture reproduced in Figure 1.3, the Communal Archives of Rottenburg for letting me use the ballot displayed in Figure 4.1, and Pablo La Rosa for the picture reproduced in Figure 7.1.

Abbreviations

AFAP	Administradora de Fondos Previsionales (Administrator of Pension's Savings Funds), Uruguay
ANCAP	Administración Nacional de Combustibles, Alcohol y Portland (Nacional Fuels Company), Uruguay
ANTEL	Administración Nacional de Telecomunicaciones (National Telecommunications Company), Uruguay
AUTE	Sindicato de Trabajadores de UTE (Workers' Union of UTE), Uruguay
CAFTA	Central America Free Trade Agreement
CFU	Commercial Farmers Union, Zimbabwe
CI-MDD	citizen-initiated mechanism of direct democracy
GDP	Gross Domestic Product
LPI	legislative popular initiative
LPP	Ley de Participación Popular (Law of Popular Participation), Bolivia
MAS	Movimiento al Socialismo (Movement toward Socialism), Bolivia
MDD	mechanism of direct democracy
MPP	Movimiento de Participación Popular (Popular Participation Movement), Uruguay
OECD	Organisation for Economic Co-operation and Development
OLS	ordinary least-squares analysis
ONAJPU	Organización Nacional de Jubilados y Pensionistas del Uruguay (National Organization of Pensioners), Uruguay
OSE	Obras Sanitarias del Estado (National Water Supply Company), Uruguay
PIT-CNT	Plenario Intersindical de Trabajadores-Convención Nacional de Trabajadores (Inter-Union Workers Plenary–National Workers Convention), Uruguay
PPP	purchasing power parity
QCA	qualitative comparative analysis

SUTEL	Sindicato Único de Trabajadores de las Telecomunicaciones (Workers' Union of the National Telecommunications Company), Uruguay
TD-MDD	top-down mechanism of direct democracy
TDP	Turkmenistan Democratic Party
TSCS	time-series cross-sectional
UTE	Administración Nacional de Usinas y Transmisiones Eléctricas (National Electricity Company), Uruguay
ZANU	Zimbabwe African National Union
ZANU-PF	Zimbabwe African National Union–Popular Front
ZAPU	Zimbabwe African Peoples Union

I

Direct Democracy at the Turn of the Century

Direct Democracy Worldwide addresses the relationship between direct and representative democracy and uncovers the specific conditions under which both can coexist in a mutually reinforcing way. It demonstrates that direct democracy is Janus-faced: Some mechanisms of direct democracy look forward in an attempt to democratize politics whereas others look backward, enhancing the power of politicians who deliberately use them. From this latter perspective, instead of *giving power to the people, other times it subjects the people to the powerful. Direct Democracy Worldwide* fills a lacuna in our understanding on the uses of mechanisms of direct democracy in the contemporary world, paying special attention to how direct and representative democracies interact under different institutional circumstances.

This book reevaluates how citizens acquire power to abide by public decisions and whether they have the right to take part equally and fairly in the *entire process* that generates these decisions, which naturally fall beyond national elections and the twelve or thirteen times we exercise sovereignty in our lives. It does not debase the importance of free and fair elections – to the contrary. Free and fair elections are a sine qua non constitutive element of democracy, and without them everything collapses. However, the time elapsed between elections may be agonizingly long for citizens whose preferences are systematically unheard, and these interelection spaces constitute the weakest link of current democracies. They tend to be left aside as an empty space filled with horizontal – but not vertical – accountability in a manner that eliminates the most important component of the first polyarchy transformation (Dahl 1989).

Any constitutive part of democracy, such as freedom of expression, is expected to be fulfilled at any time and indefinitely in the future. This must hold true for popular sovereignty as well – and it should not be limited to just one day every few years. Thus, this book attempts to revitalize something that is intrinsically one of the backbones and leitmotivs of the democratic tradition: popular sovereignty as a way of addressing the demands of citizens and the dependence of public policies on their preferences. The question is: How can current democracies translate popular sovereignty into working institutions adapted for the twenty-first century?

This book answers this question in relatively simple terms. I claim that there are some institutions that deserve a closer look and, depending on certain prerequisites, should be given a chance. These institutions comprise the citizen-initiated mechanisms of direct democracy (CI-MDDs). Yet this assertion of CI-MDDs should not be understood as a romanticized version of participatory or deliberative democracy. I simply claim that these are control mechanisms to be potentially used by citizens, and this does not imply voting every week, the steamrolling of minorities through majority rule, or the substitution of party politics by citizens. More important, CI-MDDs are not intended to supplant representative democracy but rather to serve as intermittent safety valves against perverse or unresponsive behavior of representative institutions and politicians. Citizen-initiated mechanisms of direct democracy are not simply about a blind use of majority rule, and those understanding them as mere votes on a certain issue are ignoring possibly the most crucial part of the direct democratic game: the process itself, which is arguably more important than the outcome of the ballots themselves.[1]

Citizen-initiated mechanisms of direct democracy are a subtype of mechanisms of direct democracy (MDDs) in general and, by definition, not every MDD has to be initiated by citizens gathering signatures, as is usually the case. Some MDDs are initiated by chief executives (e.g., presidents) or by a well-defined group of individuals (e.g., legislators), and sometimes by both. These "top-down" MDDs often have no other intention than the erosion of the power of other state institutions or simply bypassing institutions and procedures when the political aims of the initiator do not match with the other power. Thus, some MDDs could be characterized as strongly eroding crucial aspects of representative democracy, minimizing the exchange of ideas, and evading the political battles that characterize representative liberal democracies.

Direct democracy involves many complex factors and is most certainly not a monolithic concept. Any assessment of direct democracy in general must be undertaken with extreme caution. In large part, the debate surrounding the topic has been based on stereotypes of representative and direct democracy; consequently, the literature repeatedly asks the wrong questions and, thus, provides the wrong answers. Portraying direct democracy as inherently *good* or *bad* for representative democracy does not seem to be a very good starting point for a productive and wise research agenda, yet this is where much of the literature begins.

Not every concern about direct democracy is based on stereotypes; however, as the reader will witness, the discussion about direct democracy is plagued with normative and empirical tensions, many of which have a palpable influence in our daily life. This book captures the negative side of direct democracy, provides

---

[1] On the value of processes in and of themselves, see Ackerman and Fishkin (2004), Elster (1998), Sen (1997), Tyler (1997), Benhabib (1996), Fishkin (1991), and Pateman (1970).

a balanced treatment of the subject, and fairly vents the considerable skepticism that has emerged about these mechanisms. For example, it would not be risky to acknowledge that these institutions have often been manipulated by elites; this is very damaging to representative democracy.[2]

Nonetheless, and despite their potential misuses, it would be unwise not to seriously consider CI-MDDs and their potential positive synergy with representative democracy. Indeed, parliaments, elections, and even basic freedoms have also been repeatedly misused, yet their normative value had not decreased – in fact, our efforts for improving them are constantly increasing. The words of a president who faced several national CI-MDDs during his administration (and lost most of them) are eloquent:

All institutions have their own weaknesses, including those mechanisms of direct democracy. It has been the situation with all institutions and it had always been so. But so what? Will we then have to remove the mechanism because it could be deformed? Oh no! Extrapolating that, we might even think that we are to eliminate national elections because they could warp, because people could use them demagogically.... No, no, no.... (Interview with Jorge Batlle, February 2008)[3]

In broader terms, this book deals with the distribution and exercise of power in our states – the *power* of making binding decisions that affect our lives. Who is in charge of making such binding decisions – the powerful or the numerous? What types of decisions are made, and are all included? What about overriding those decisions – who does that? All these questions remain open despite having been considered for thousands of years and having perhaps one of the longest traditions – in what we today call "the social sciences" – engaged in the constant search for the best form of government. From Herodotus' time – and not omitting Aristotle – we have compared the virtues and deficiencies of contemporary governments. Nowadays, for normative and practical reasons, we are convinced more than ever that representative democracy is the best regime of all possible, or at least the lesser evil.

Since its very millenarian origins, democracy has been always under enormous pressure for renewal – a renewal that becomes inexorable.[4] If the beginnings of the twentieth century were marked by demands for extending citizenship and ensuring fair representation, contemporary democracies face different challenges, such as transparency, access, and accountability. Phases of democratic transformation are a persistent matter throughout history, and demands for adjustments "in one direction often wane as new problems and new possibilities surface" (Cain, Dalton, and Scarrow 2003: 3). Indeed, I am positive there is at least a minimum consensus in political science: There are no

---

[2] As becomes clearer in Chapter 2, this does not parallel the populist paradox, as Gerber titles her book, which is based on the belief that economic interest groups manipulate direct legislation against other interests (Gerber 1999: 6).

[3] Jorge Batlle, president of Uruguay from March 2000 until March 2005.

[4] The study of democracy has been one of the most prolific areas of interest in comparative politics. If truth be told, most of us agree on many of the diagnoses of current democracies, yet consensus has not been reached in terms of the prognosis.

magic formulas that will ensure us a "high-quality" democracy. All institutional settings are the product of a delicate balance, often between conflicting choices. Although there are no neutral institutional arrangements, the status quo implies a deliberate policy choice.

Yet representative democracy remains far from perfect, presenting numerous problems and shortcomings. A great consensus exists on the contemporary challenges of current democracies (high levels of civic disaffection, distrust of political parties, and in general, animosity toward the democratic game), and one of the most tricky aspects of our democracies lies in the direct and daily relationship between citizens and the state (O'Donnell 2004a: 57). Indeed, the warning given by Dunn about representative democracy is rather illustrative: "[O]ne day's rule every four years has very much the air of a placebo" (1979: 16). Evidently, we all want a greater involvement of the citizenry in public affairs, a greater sensitivity of the state with regard to weaker sectors of society, and a greater redistributive justice of markets, among other numerous and noble aspirations. This discussion focuses on how best to achieve these goals.

A number of forces have been devoted to improving democratic institutions; electoral systems have excelled among these democracy-improving institutions despite the tradeoffs implied by this choice (e.g., representation versus efficiency). Elections usually become the focus of analysis, which leads scholars to overlook what occurs in the period between elections. Nonetheless, some scholars with a more sophisticated vision warn us that "the development of democracy is much more than the perfection of its electoral system" (O'Donnell 2004a: 49). The basic problem of democracy goes beyond simple institutional improvements: "Democracy, once again in favor, is in need of conceptual renewal. Although the traditional concerns of democratic theory with state-centered institutions remain importantly crucial and ethically central, they are increasingly subject to the limitations we should expect when nineteenth-century concepts meet twenty-first century realities" (Warren 2001: 226).

Democracy, as we understand it today, is the long fusion, and sometimes confusion, of political traditions at least centuries long. Athenian democracy, despite its highly restrictive (by today's standards) enfranchisement rules, demonstrated the fairest imaginable distribution of power among its agents. It also exemplified the value of a political milieu that excels through the *equality* and *sovereignty* of its (few) members. With Republicanism – first Roman and then Florentine – came the concept of mutual *control* as the means for citizens to be free from state domination and arbitrary misbehaviors. A sophisticated net of institutions was established to control each other, and these operated under known rules of the game, establishing a key concept: the rule of law. Finally, liberalism, from which we borrow the idea that individuals are *free,* emerges; individuals are thus perceived as autonomous and responsible (à la Kant) and know what is best for themselves (à la Hobbes), their peer community, and their society as a whole (à la Rousseau or Locke).

Thus, democracy today can be fit under four umbrella concepts: freedom, equality, sovereignty, and control. All democracies have a flavor of each, but the concepts are combined in different shapes and sizes, and an even combination is hardly – if ever – attained. I argue, however, that in current definitions of democracy, one concept is systematically minimized but must be refreshed and invigorated: Popular sovereignty, galvanized in the twentieth century, must be revitalized in the form of binding CI-MDDs.

Current democracies are indisputably far from the ideal representative democracy that theory promises us. It could be claimed that democracy today more closely resembles an oligarchy with the façade of democracy rather than the ideal, prototypical, representative democracy about which we teach our students every year. According to Walzer, "[G]overnment is in principle democratic, in (liberal) theory mixed, and in practice oligarchic" (2004: 25).[5] How many of us genuinely are potentially elected officials in our community? Of course, it is not that we do not have the proper conditions or vocation to do or be so; it is simply that in real terms, we do not have the effective right to be elected despite that we assume, believe, and have collectively decided we are all legally entitled to stand for election if we so choose. In practice, only a small group of people actually run for office.

Even assuming, for the time being, a positive institutional assemblage of the state, wherein the legislature, the executive, and the administration relate to each other in institutionalized patterns of behavior under the umbrella of what we call the *democratic rule of law*, the infamous "corridors of power" generate incentives for perverse interests and behaviors (Pettit 2003).[6] But this is not terribly new: Already, Michels (1999 [1911]), in his *Iron Law of the Oligarchy*, and the writings about the circulation of elites of Mosca, Pareto, and even Weber, later reevaluated by the literature on party cartelization (Cox and McCubbins 1993; Katz and Mair 1995; Koole 1996), account for these tendencies. Contemporary democracies must provide tools for controlling these behaviors both horizontally (by other institutions) and vertically (by citizens).

An almost Schumpeterian, electoralist conceptualization of democracy would tell us that citizens regularly exert control in national elections, activating their sovereignty, punishing misbehaviors and rewarding others. Nevertheless, "the chances to exercise vertical accountability, however, are only periodic and, in some cases, citizens must wait several years for the next election" (Morlino 2004: 19) – when, sometimes, the misdeeds are already done, the window for justice has passed, and our desires and preferences are ignored. The implications of these rather scattered flashes of popular sovereignty for the crafting of controlling institutions are evident. If the people's interest is

---

[5] In this regard, Rousseau's disrespect for elected representation is noteworthy: "The English people believes itself to be free; it is gravely mistaken; it is free only during the election of Members of Parliament; as soon as the Members are elected, the people is enslaved; it is nothing. In the brief moments of its freedom, the English people makes such a use of that freedom that it deserves to lose it" (Rousseau, *The Social Contract*, bk. III, chap. 15).

[6] By corridors of power, I loosely imply those obscure places where the elite can impose their own will in how they interpret and implement policy without public scrutiny (e.g., bureaucracy, cabinet, courts, police force).

undermined or ignored, it is incumbent on them to activate their democratic power – their sovereignty – to force a change in the status quo or ensure its maintenance in keeping with their preferences. Maintenance activities take the shape of *referendums* (trying to stop certain measures going against the general preferences), whereas status quo shifts often manifest as *popular initiatives* (trying to push forward certain measures that, otherwise, the establishment would not consider of its own volition).[7]

Direct democracy now has entered the game, and it is unlikely that use of its mechanisms will decrease because of its theoretical and practical tensions with representative democracy. Despite the importance and growing impact of these institutions worldwide, we still lack a comprehensive understanding of these mechanisms. There are two reasons that can explain the relatively low intensity of the cross-national study of MDDs. One stems from the belief that direct democracy has a marginal role in contemporary politics. Indeed, some colleagues argue that "referendums are relatively rare events in politics of most democratic nations" (LeDuc 2003: 13; see also Qvortrup 2002: 2). Yet I have collected information on more than seventeen hundred MDDs at the national level alone since 1900. A total of 5,342 state-level *direct popular votes* in the United States have been on the ballot between 1904 (when the first one went before voters in Oregon) and 2008;[8] this figure increases exponentially if we include MDDs at the county level, which number literally in the tens of thousands. Between 1970 and 2003, a total of 3,709 cantonal popular votes were held in Switzerland, and Bavaria alone held more than one thousand popular ballots since their constitutional introduction in 1995. It seems evident that the intermittency claim regarding the use of MDDs is, at least, questionable.

The second reason often given for the as-yet minimal cross-national study of MDDs is the disorder that still exists in terms of a common language to deal with this multifaceted factor in contemporary politics. Evidently, some clarification of the concept of direct democracy is required and urgently needed given the terminological confusion that exists in constitutional texts (e.g., what is called a *referendum* in one country is termed a *plebiscite*, or even a *popular initiative*, in another). Furthermore, it is not the case that in each country there is at least a systematic use of the definitions and wording of MDDs; rather, concepts such as "initiatives," "plebiscites," and "referendums" are actually used as synonyms within the very same piece of legislation! To aggravate this problem, scholars have demonstrated relatively low elasticity in trying to

[7] I define measures as a complete range of political actions that could perfectly oscillate between practical policy implications (on taxes, subsidies, alcohol, and even sex education) to discursive and even symbolic ones (e.g., anthems and flags).

[8] It has to be noted that despite that, the first popular initiative was held in Oregon in 1904; the first state to adopt the initiative and the referendum on a statewide level was South Dakota in 1898. Since then, of the 5,342 popular direct votes, 3,285 (61.5 percent) were initiated by the executives or legislatures and 2,057 (38.5 percent) initiated by citizens. Based on Initiative & Referendum Institute (2007), The National Conference of State Legislatures (2008), and the author's calculations.

find criteria that can travel relatively easily from one place to another. Some colleagues fall into the temptation of studying MDDs from a purely formal perspective, based on the names that constitutional texts provide for direct democracy, but research may only proceed if we eschew this and do not become entangled in semantic confusion.

It is important to note that this volume does not purport to be a book on democratic theory, despite having theoretical, conceptual, and empirical implications. I will not elaborate a justification of representative democracy because there is a large literature on the topic. I begin with the assumption that current representative democracy is given yet perfectionable in both realistic and conceptual ways. In so doing, I follow Morlino, explicitly acknowledging two liberal assumptions that cross evenly through this research. First, people are able to accurately perceive their own needs. Second, "either alone or as part of a group, people are the only possible judges of their own needs [...] this is to say, no third party can decide those needs" (Morlino 2004: 13–14).

1. What Constitutes Direct Democracy? Definition and Typology

I define an MDD as a publicly recognized institution wherein citizens decide or emit their opinion on issues – other than through legislative and executive elections – directly at the ballot box through universal and secret suffrage. Therefore, a sine qua non characteristic of all MDDs is the vote itself, where we are all equal, delivering our Rousseauean $1/n$ power.[9] From this perspective, MDDs are composed of those mechanisms through which, after the representatives and the government are elected, the citizenry continues to be – voluntarily or involuntarily, explicitly or implicitly – a veto actor or a proactive player in the political process.[10] Here, it is theoretically reasonable to exclude legislative popular initiatives from the realm of direct democracy and to treat nonbinding MDDs as populist placebos (I return to this point in due course).

Direct democracy constitutes a broad category that incorporates diverse resources, such as referendums, plebiscites, recalls, and popular initiatives.[11] The literature offers several typologies of MDDs, each one stressing a different aspect of these mechanisms. Because one of my major interests is conducting

---

[9] From a Rousseauean perspective, each citizen has a $1/n$ share of "sovereign authority," where n is the total number of citizens.

[10] According to Tsebelis, veto players are individual or collective actors whose agreement (by majority rule for collective actors) is required for a change of the status quo (Tsebelis 1995: 289).

[11] A more orthodox perspective on the matter would refer to this group of institutions as expressions of "semidirect" instead of "direct" democracy." The latter term is reserved for those citizens' assemblies where issues were brought up, discussed, and decided directly without any institutional intermediation. Examples include New England town hall meetings and the modern-day remnants of the Swiss *Landsgemeinde* in Obwalden and Nidwalden, where voting is done by show of hands. This also applies to citizens' assemblies in classical Greece. Because a consensus on terminology is difficult to attain, I will adhere to its simplest form, "direct democracy."

an empirical study on direct democracy at different levels of democracy, the typology I provide should travel relatively easily along the democratic continuum. The first dichotomy I use to classify MDDs refers to whether the mechanism considered is regulated by law (or the constitution). In other words, are MDDs *mandatory* or *facultative* (also termed *regulated* or *unregulated* in the literature)?

A second dimension involves whether the resolution of an MDD is absolute in a given discourse or if another institution has the final say on that topic. The literature refers to this dichotomy as *binding* versus *consultative* MDDs. The third criterion refers to the intention of the MDD, which could be either *proactive* or *reactive*. Simply put, does the MDD attempt to alter or sustain the status quo? The fourth and final criterion concerns the main trigger of the MDD: Did it derive from the political establishment (e.g., the executive power or the legislature – whether a majority or a minority), in which case the event is labeled *top-down*? Or, rather, was it derived from a group of citizens, in which case the event is labeled *bottom-up* or *citizen-initiated*? From this last dichotomy (establishment versus citizens), we can derive a third group of MDDs, which refers to constitutionally mandatory MDDs, sometimes called "obligatory referendums."

For this research, I built a typology that travels relatively easily from one place to another. It also fits rather well within the categories used by the most prodigious employer of MDDs worldwide: Switzerland.[12] The adoption of these categories has nothing to do with Swiss terminological imperialism; it is simply a matter of practicality. I do not see the point of forcing rather marginal categories based on ad hoc criteria instead of using the categories employed by the country that, in one way or another, serves as a focal point in the study of direct democracy. In other words, if the same "animal" is called "cow" 85 percent of the time, "spotted grass-eater" 10 percent of the time, and "methane maker" 5 percent of the time, we should simply call it "cow."

Nonetheless, the Swiss terminology is not exhaustive enough to cover, in a systematic way, most of the "animals" that fit within the basic criteria of this study. Many but not all types of MDDs exist in Switzerland and, as a result, the terminological names of these other types must be obtained elsewhere. The questions are where and how.

If we agree that a typology should help to aggregate MDDs in clusters, a question remaining is how many levels of disaggregation are required for traveling far enough while remaining adequately profound. A typology – a nominal measurement – has to fulfill certain conditions; namely, it must be exhaustive

---

[12] Switzerland occupies a unique and prominent position in the literature of direct democracy not only because it is the most experienced country on earth with these institutions, but also because it is an ideal case scenario for comparative research given its huge variations in how direct democracy is practiced and institutionalized at and within its different levels (federal, cantons, communities). Moreover, the late Stein Rokkan once called Switzerland a microcosm of Europe because of its cultural, religious, and regional diversity (Linder 1994: xii).

and its categories mutually exclusive. In other words, categories should include all of the possibilities for the measure, and they should be differentiated in such a way that a case will fit into one, and only one, category. Of course, in the case of institutions, the creation of a typology can be a complex task. For instance, it is still open for debate what type of regime exists in Switzerland. For those who emphasize executive formation, Switzerland is a truly pure hybrid regime (Klöti 2001; Lüthi 2007); however, for those who highlight government business and daily life, it behaves more like a presidential one (Kriesi 2001). As a matter of fact, in terms of government survival, Switzerland resembles a "pure" presidential regime in the sense that once the executive is appointed by the Federal Assembly, councilors cannot be removed and there is no possibility of dissolution of the legislature by the executive (Cheibub 2007: 36). Thus, if the question that motivates research is government survival, the inclusion of the Swiss case, along with other parliamentary regimes of Western Europe, would distort the research, unless we want to explain how different regimes affect government survival.[13]

Because my interest is to examine how direct and representative democracies interact while keeping my typology relatively simple, I consider it crucial to determine who initiates the MDD, what its purposes are, and whether the MDD is the final word on an issue. Each of the three criteria is then further divided. With regard to initiators, I found three major alternatives: citizens (through signature gathering), political establishment (executives, legislators, or both), and the legal or constitutional regulations existing in a country. With regard to the purposes of MDDs, we find two very large groups: those that maintain the status quo and those that alter it. Finally, the issue of whether the MDD is the last word (i.e., it becomes law) or can simply be ignored is important (this is the differentiation between binding and nonbinding MDDs). This typology thus allows for conceptualization comprising twelve categories (three types of instigators times two possible purposes times two potential legal statuses). Although these are all theoretically possible combinations, not all of these combinations exist, as we will see.

On many occasions, colleagues have told me that "this particular MDD held in that particular country" was rather special and thus could not fit properly into any of the twelve categories I have created. Rather, we should create a special box for "this type of case." My answer is simple: I do not continue disaggregating this typology because my theory does not require it. I simply note that this typology could be disaggregated further, even to the extreme of generating a typology with as many categories as the number of MDDs that exist. In other words, given that no two MDDs are exactly equal, we could expand our typologies to capture a minor difference between two extremely similar MDDs. The question, however, is whether this practice is

---

[13] Vatter (2008) has shown how difficult it is even to locate Switzerland within just one continuum (majoritarian-consensus) and how stressing different characteristics of this continuum would produce rather different locations for a single case.

useful either for research or theory building. For example, if technical nuances on how a vote was held are of interest for the researcher, it would be logical to include whether the vote was an e-vote (electronic in some way) or if ballots were cast at physical polling stations. Otherwise, including that distinction would not be theoretically relevant and would be, for practical reasons, inconvenient.[14]

Figure 1.1 describes the typology of MDDs using the criteria delineated in the previous paragraphs. Note that the second row deals with the initiators and the third row considers whether the MDD is binding. The bottom row indicates the political purposes of MDDs in terms of the status quo. Before moving on to the figure and describing each category, I elucidate a few points.

We must be extremely careful in dividing the waters between MDDs into categories. In this typology, I make the division between those that are "citizen-initiated" (or "bottom-up") and those initiated from above, "top-down." This differentiation is crucial because top-down MDDs usually represent plebiscitary means either for bypassing other representative institutions, disengaging from the responsibility of tough policies, or simply as mobilization/legitimization populist tools. As Kaufmann and Waters state,

[I & R (initiatives and referendums)] have to be clearly distinguished from plebiscites. These are votes on issues implemented from above by a government, without support from or influence of the citizens. Plebiscites have nothing to do with I&R; on the contrary, they are often used by governments who want to get a special legitimacy on their policies by bypassing existing laws and constitutional rules (Kaufmann and Waters 2004: xix).

Here, the terminological differences between the continental and American literatures are evident. Whereas the previous quotation notes a clear

---

[14] The literature offers a wide menu of typologies that link mechanisms of direct democracy and democracy types, such as those presented by Vatter (2009) or that of Hug and Tsebelis (2002). These typologies include certain aspects not covered by my typology, including "decision rules" (particularly with parliamentary-minority initiated MDDs). Vatter's typology (and, for this matter, also the typology offered by Hug and Tsebelis) is an extremely useful cognitive map of different types of mechanisms of direct democracy in the context of developed democracies. However, I have reservations about how useful it would be to extrapolate it to non-European countries because it does not necessarily travel smoothly to the southern regions of the globe. For example, unlike most Western developed countries (Vatter's universe of cases), all Latin American countries are typical presidential regimes, where the executive party is usually the largest minority within the legislature and sometimes even a small minority within it (as the cases of Brazil and Ecuador illustrate best; many countries in Africa also present this configuration). In this context, although it is possible to identify MDDs triggered by the gathering of citizens' signatures that favor or go against the status quo, it is extremely difficult to assess if legislators pushing for a particular MDD belong or not to the executive's legislative-coalition in that particular time in a broader cross-regional comparison. By the own nature of regimes, assessing the "ruling majority" in a multiparty presidential regime is far more complicated than doing so in parliamentary regimes (Chasquetti 2001). In other words, I am more concerned about the applicability of Vatter's typology to my universe of cases (all countries of the world) and its fit with the objectives of my research than with the typology itself.

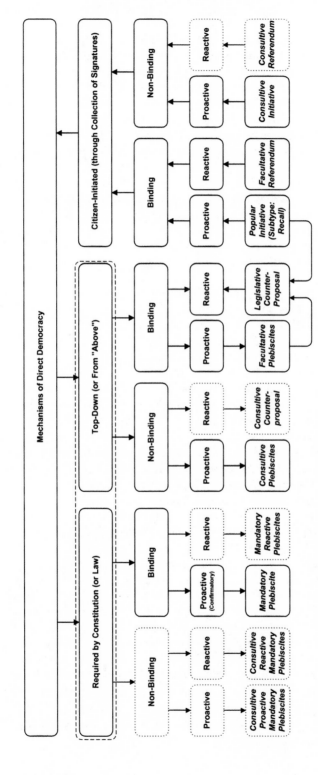

FIGURE 1.1. Procedural Typology of Mechanisms of Direct Democracy.[15]

[15] The dashed box denotes the current debate of whether MDDs required by constitution and top-down MDDs are strictly discernible families of MDDs. Dotted boxes represent theoretically plausible configurations but with no correlates in real life.

differentiation between *initiatives* and *referendums* on the one hand and *plebiscites* on the other, in the American vocabulary, the differentiation is the following: "The *initiative* allows voters to propose a legislative measure (statutory initiative) or a constitutional amendment (constitutional initiative) by filing a petition bearing a required number of valid citizen signatures. A *referendum* refers a proposed or existing law or statute to voters for their approval or rejection. Some state constitutions require referendums; in other states, the legislature may decide to refer a measure to the voters" (Cronin 1999: 2).

The differentiation (in the second row) among the initiators addresses the mechanics of triggering an MDD and how this process takes place rather than the content of the proposal. We must be aware that although the great majority of MDDs that come "from below" are truly citizen-activated weapons, this is not necessarily always the case. This differentiation could be blurred by the fact that in some countries (e.g., those in Latin America), a given president could ask a group of loyalists to start gathering signatures for an "MDD from below." These cases are extremely rare, and usually presidents pursue routes for advancing their interests other than mobilization of their constituents. Indeed, the unique case of an executive pushing for an MDD from below is exemplified by the Colombian reelection movement under the presidency of Uribe at the time this manuscript was published. Evidently, Uribe is rather fond of the initiative, but undoubtedly there is also a legitimate social movement pushing the measure forward. It is highly unlikely that this movement is simply a consequence of presidential desires (see Chapter 5).

However, in an extremely weak democracy that needs to maintain a legalistic façade, presidents have resorted to artificial, even forced signature gathering. Maybe the most evident case is that of Ukraine in 2000, when more than 4 million signatures were gathered in record time. Many of the signatures were adulterated, some even faked to boost presidential powers vis-à-vis parliament (Wheatley 2008). Technically, the mechanism was "citizen initiated" but, of course, it was supported by all-encompassing executive power. The good news is that in these cases, it is rather easy to find out when there is something suspicious occurring by examining the level of correspondence between the MDD and the executive's desires.

Now I briefly describe the most important characteristics of each of these institutions, starting with those for which there are cases and then moving to those where – despite theoretically possible alternatives – no cases are found. As described, Figure 1.1 shows three large subgroups of MDDs: a) those required by the constitution, b) top-down (or from "above"), and finally, c) citizen-initiated through collection of signatures (or from "below)." Each of these groups is divided into two subgroups, binding and nonbinding, which are subsequently divided into two other additional subgroups, proactive and reactive. In the bottom row, each box denotes the highest level of disaggregation considering these criteria. Note that there are some boxes drawn with dots; these are theoretically plausible combinations but for which no correlate "in real life" has been found.

Starting from the left on Figure 1.1, the first family of MDDs we find are those required by the legal apparatus of a country. This family has only one combination with empirical correlates, *mandatory plebiscites* (the European literature sometimes refers to these as *obligatory referendums*). A mandatory plebiscite does not depend on the wishes of an individual because they are determined by law and, most of the time, by the constitution of a country. Usually, this type of institution accompanies constitutional reforms.[16] This type of plebiscite is binding; it has the power to oblige whatever is decided becomes law. By their very nature, these are proactive MDDs; they are mandated popular votes that are sought to gather support for a major constitutional reform or political alteration of the status quo.

It is debatable whether mandatory plebiscites correspond with the realm of MDDs "from above"; this is why there is a dashed line around the categories "required by the constitution" and "top-down." On the one hand, they could be considered "from above" because, after all, they depend on the wishes of an institution of the state (usually the legislature), which is formed by individuals who are well aware that if they maintain a certain course of action, this proposal will eventually be decided at the ballot box. For example, since the early 1990s, Uruguayan legislators had been debating about the reform of the almost century-old electoral system. They knew perfectly well that if a significant majority was reached, the reform would have to be approved directly by the citizens in a popular vote, which was the case in 1996. Did this come from above? Many would argue "yes" because the MDD was, after all, triggered by the majority of legislators. On the other hand, these are not sudden MDDs that come from nowhere because one day someone "from above" wakes up and says, "Let's have a popular vote on X issue."

Moving to the right in Figure 1.1, we then find the cluster of facultative (or unregulated) top-down MDDs. This category is composed of two major and different proactive MDDs, facultative and consultative plebiscites, and a reactive one, legislative counterproposals. A facultative plebiscite is, by far, the most frequently used MDD in several regions of the world, especially Latin America, Africa, and the Commonwealth of Independent States. These facultative plebiscites occur when the political establishment (executive, legislative, or both) submits a proposal to the citizenry, and whatever is decided then becomes law (either regular or constitutional – it does not matter at this level of aggregation). Frequently, these mechanisms are used as legitimizing tools for a tough policy, to avoid the political price of adopting such a policy (Setälä 2006a; 2006b), or as a means to bypass other state institutions (in presidential regimes, the legislature is usually the bypassed institution).[17]

---

[16] For example, most (but not all) presidential regimes in Latin America force mandatory plebiscites facing a constitutional reform.

[17] The term *plebiscite* encapsulates a plethora of different types of the phenomenon: legislators' minority initiative; legislative initiative, or executive order. There is not enough room to argue whether it is a wise decision to subsume under the concept of plebiscite those that are initiated

A consultative plebiscite occurs when the executive or legislative branch of government consults the opinion of the citizens regarding a matter with no legal consequence; that is, it is not legally binding. Sometimes governments submit combined questionnaires regarding diverse topics to the citizenship (as was the case in Ecuador in 1995, 1994, and 1986) and ask simple questions regarding ratification of peace treaties (as in Argentina in 1984 regarding the Beagle Treaty with Chile), the partitioning of territories, such as the Schleswig Plebiscites of 1920 (see Laponce 2004), or pose miscellaneous unique questions, such as the obligatory conscription military service question posed in Canada in 1942.

Finally, within the sphere of those coming from above, we encounter legislative counterproposals. The very name of these MDDs indicates that they are reactive because they respond to an alteration of the status quo by another agent that is usually the citizenry (through a popular initiative or another plebiscite of the establishment itself). These are top-down binding-reactive measures. Facing a popular initiative, some countries (e.g., Switzerland, Liechtenstein, and Uruguay) allow their legislatures to make counterproposals to be voted on simultaneously against the citizen-initiated measure. This vote is held concurrently with the original initiative and implies multiple (at least three) choices for citizens (Measure A [citizens'], Measure $\neq$A [legislature], and the status quo). Perhaps one of the most vivid examples of legislative counterproposal comes from Uruguay in 1966, when a jointly sponsored proposal by the major parties of the country faced two simultaneous counterproposals. Yet if the vote under examination does not react to another MDD and if it is binding, it should be characterized as a facultative plebiscite and, if nonbinding, a consultative plebiscite.[18]

Lately, a wave of popular votes has blossomed in several European countries with regard to accession, integration, and enlargement of the European Union (EU) (Auer 2007; Hug and Schulz 2007), yet important differences exist among them, serving as an example of different measures coming from above. In some countries, these votes were mandated plebiscites (Ireland, Switzerland), whereas in other countries, consultative plebiscites (France, Norway) or facultative plebiscites (Denmark, Lithuania) were the norm. The difference between

by the legislative branch and thus potentially by the opposition. It is, instead, reasonable to claim that these are two different types of plebiscites that follow different causal logics. In other words, the conditions explaining plebiscites initiated by the government narrowly defined are likely to look different from those that explain plebiscites initiated by the opposition. In this research, however, these differences are tackled more profoundly from Chapter 5 forward (Latin America and Uruguay, respectively).

[18] Given that legislative counterproposals were sometimes used to derail popular initiatives in Switzerland, in the latest reform of the Swiss Constitution (1999), Art. 139 (6) stipulates that citizens may vote simultaneously for the popular initiative as well for the counterproposal made by the legislature, against the status quo. In a separate question, citizens also may indicate which drafts they prefer (in case they voted for two of the proposals against the status quo). If one of the drafts obtains the majority of the people's vote and the other the majority of the cantons, neither of them shall come into force, and the status quo prevails.

the last two concerns how authorities relate to the measure, despite that in practice, both may have the same political consequences. In other words, if a vast
majority of the citizenry rejects a certain measure in two democratic countries,
it matters relatively little if it is a consultative or a facultative plebiscite, despite
the first being nonbinding and the second binding. Instead of emphasizing the
content of the proposals dealt with in an MDD, the key aspect is who was in
charge of triggering the MDD and how the process takes place.

I now turn to CI-MDDs. As operationalized, two types of MDDs compose this particular subgroup: binding and nonbinding MDDs from "below."
Within the first subgroup there are two types: popular initiatives and referendums. Although the two types have different objectives, the mechanisms to
trigger a CI-MDD are basically the same: Organizers of the measure have to
gather a minimum number of signatures from the electoral body (each country has a different threshold) and propose a specific measure to the electoral
authority. If the number of signatures passes the legal thresholds and they are
subsequently validated, the electoral authority authorizes and implements the
mechanism. The vote for the CI-MDD, also dependent on the country, must
be held either during a delimited amount of time from the approval of the
signatures or in the following general election.

A popular initiative is a proposed law, statute, or constitutional amendment
supported by a group of citizens that offers an alternative to the status quo.
It is the classic proactive power in the hands of the citizens and for some is
the most democratic institution within the scope of direct democracy (Hautala,
Kaufmann, and Wallis 2002). Unlike a popular initiative, a facultative referendum allows citizens to reject (veto) an adopted law.[19] In the Americas, Uruguay
continues to be the only country in which referendums have been used systematically at the national level, with varied degrees of success. Although the
referendum aimed at abrogating a law of 1986 on amnesty for those involved
in human rights violations during the military dictatorship (1973–1985) failed
in 1989, the withdrawal of the privatization law in 1992 was a success. This
success was extremely visible in Latin America (and beyond) because it was
one of the first democratic responses that sought to halt the then-fashionable

---

[19] The concept of *referendum* has a Latin-origin meaning: "something to be referred." *Plebiscite*,
on the other hand, is defined by the *Oxford English Dictionary* as "the direct vote of all the
members of an electorate on an important public question." The concept of plebiscite comes
from ancient Rome, referring to a law enacted by the plebeians' assembly in approximately
the fifth century A.D. (from Latin *plebs*, "the common people" and *scitum*, "decree") (Suksi
1993). This concept was used not only since 1793 in France for the popular consultations on
the Montagnarde Constitution and the formation of the National Assembly of two-thirds of
the Constitutional Council (twice each) but also to describe the resolution votes of boundary
conflicts in the League of Nations and to categorize the popular votes of legitimization of the
Nazi regime in Germany (Kobach 1993: 4; Suksi 1993: 97–103). The concept of referendum
was used for the first time in Switzerland in the constitutional vote on the legitimization of the
new regime of the Helvetic Republic, which was imposed by the French conquerors in 1798
(Kobach 1993: 4).

Washington Consensus in the region. For other examples of referendums we must look to Europe, particularly Switzerland, Liechtenstein, and Italy.[20]

Also, within the realm of binding, proactive CI-MDDs, there is a subtype that deserves some attention: the recall – an institution that allows citizens to dismiss and replace an elected authority. Despite the fact that some scholars are reluctant to include these actions within the direct democracy realm – because they are aimed at persons and not issues (Kaufmann, Büchi, and Braun 2008: 91) – the recall fulfills the definition of an MDD provided at the beginning of this section. It is not widely used internationally, and this institution characterizes a more locally driven rather than a national-scale MDD. So far, this mechanism has been used only once at the national level, in Venezuela in 2004 against President Hugo Chávez. In fact, discussions about its use brought Venezuela to the brink of a civil war during 2002 and 2003. Perhaps the soundest use of the recall in recent years was in California in 2003, which paradoxically resulted in the recall of Governor Joseph Graham Davis Jr. (Democrat) and the simultaneous election of the protagonist of the 1990 film *Total Recall*, Arnold Schwarzenegger (Republican).

Recalls are notably stressful situations for party systems, particularly for the party to which the recalled representative belongs. Given that recalls are motivated by political reasons, the party of the incumbent is most likely to shield the politician in question, but it also needs to present an alternative candidate in case the recall succeeds.[21] Thus, a party could easily find itself defending one incumbent while simultaneously promoting a different candidate for the same, and indivisible, post.

In this type of election, two simultaneous votes are held: one for the recall itself and one for electing the substitute in case the first vote wins. These situations may produce seemingly illegitimate results (even undemocratic for some) because the elected candidate can easily receive far fewer votes than the recalled incumbent. For example, if 45 percent of citizens vote against the recall and 55 percent in favor of it, the incumbent needs to leave office. However, if, in the simultaneous election for filling the vacant post, three candidates receive barely one-third of the votes each, the winner has received far fewer votes than the removed incumbent.[22]

---

[20] With regard to the Italian experience, Uleri has fine-tuned the typology of referendums (1996; 2002), differentiating between whether a referendum goes against an already enacted law (abrogative) or against laws that are not yet in force (rejective). Given that for a worldwide study of direct democracy, the amount and quality of information required for this classification are almost impossible to gather, I will simply use the category of facultative referendum.

[21] No crime has to be committed by an incumbent in order to be recalled. If an elected official commits an illegal act, that person could be impeached and then sent to regular justice. On impeachments, see Pérez-Liñán (2007).

[22] Although this procedure is not uncommon in the United States, it has been successful only twice. The first successful recall was in North Dakota in 1921 when Governor Lynn Frazier was censured by citizens. See Cronin (1999: chap. 6). On the particular case of the 2003 California recall, see Alvarez, Goodrich, Hall, Kiewiet, and Sled (2004); Bowler and Cain (2004); and Stone and Datta (2004).

Strictly speaking, both popular initiatives and facultative referendums promote an alteration of status quo through rejecting an approved law and proposing a new legislative (or constitutional) measure. Yet in a country where the facultative referendum exists, one can only talk about the status quo when the time limit for a referendum has expired. Only at that point does the considered law or statute become the *new* status quo. When time prescribes, even if the MDD tries to abolish a law, this has to be considered a popular initiative.

Finally, at the extreme bottom right of Figure 1.1, there are the consultative initiatives and the consultative referendums, which are a seldom-used prerogative in the hands of citizens. These are odd in that significant efforts have been made to force a vote, yet the measures do not make the results binding. Why is this so? The answer is generally found in the constitutional texts of some countries. Indeed, the only recorded evidence I have found of a consultative initiative occurred in Colombia in 1990, when a rather amorphous social movement, led by the student unions of the country, succeeded in including an informal ballot calling for a constituent assembly to reform the Colombian Constitution. Massive support for the measure in the form of opinion polls and a push to include the ballot in the vote led the establishment to count the votes of the initiative. Then, in a legally questionable measure, the Supreme Court of Justice retrospectively declared it binding.

As noted, of the twelve theoretically possible combinations, five do not have correlates in real life. For example, consultative mandatory plebiscites (in either proactive or reactive subtypes) appear at the far-left side of the figure. Although theoretically possible, I am not aware of the existence of such an alternative. In the proactive subtype, we could imagine the constitution of a country stating that before carrying out "X," a consultative plebiscite would have to be held. This is an odd case of a constitutional mandate requiring a nonbinding vote on a certain issue, and the question is what the constituents would have had in their mind when creating such a nonstandard institution.

It is important to note what is not included in the typology offered here. By definition, this typology does not include what are usually called legislative popular initiatives (LPIs). An LPI exists when the citizenry forces the legislature to consider a proposed action or a bill (though the legislature will not necessarily accept it), which represents control over the agenda rather than a tool for political change. Given that there is no popular vote whatsoever, LPIs are not considered in this research. Moreover, it is important to differentiate between MDDs and other institutions of deliberation or political leverage. Thus, I also leave aside all the institutional products of the newly fashionable decentralization wave, even when citizens have the right to directly influence politics, as in the Bolivian Organizaciones Territoriales de Base or the new experiments at the Colombian municipalities. None of the mechanisms of participatory budgeting used in several cities in Latin America (e.g., Porto Alegre, Rosario, and Montevideo) counts as an MDD in this typology.[23] In these cases, despite the fact

---

[23] For participatory budgeting, see Goldfrank (2002; 2006).

that citizens might participate in public deliberations, there is not necessarily a universal and secret vote on such agreements, if a vote even occurs. Needless to say, no informal mobilizations of people (e.g., the Piqueteros in Argentina or the Movimento dos Trabalhadores Rurais Sem Terra in Brazil) are considered here. I am not stating that these forms of civic participation are not important enough to be studied. On the contrary, I am stating simply that they do not fulfill the operationalization of the concept offered here and therefore are not included in this research.

As we see, there is a plethora of MDDs; some of them are used quite frequently, whereas others, though theoretically possible, remain unused. The importance of spending time to deal with each of the categories of MDDs is further justified by the fact that, for instance, the recently so-called presidential recall in Bolivia (2008) was no more than a facultative plebiscite called by President Morales as a confidence vote (see Chapter 5). Along the same lines, despite being officially called a referendum, the October 2007 Costa Rican vote on the Central America Free Trade Agreement with the United States must be considered a facultative plebiscite because it was triggered by the President Arias with the legislature to deactivate a potential popular initiative.[24] In other words, there were no referendums or recalls whatsoever in Latin America in 2007 or 2008, but there were critical presidential plebiscites in two countries in the region.

Finally, it is important to point out that this typology is not sensitive to the administrative or political level where MDDs take place, whether local, regional, or national. Because my research agenda is primarily focused at the macro level, local or subnational MDDs are not taken into consideration.

2. The Devil Is in the Details: Institutional Requirements and Constraints on Mechanisms of Direct Democracy

As the popular phrase states, the devil is in the details. Even within a single type of MDD, there exist important differences at the procedural level as well as among the available possibilities for their deployment. These differences are crucial for assessing the degree of potential penetration and an eventual operationalization of direct democracy. Almost any binding procedure in the hands of citizens must fulfill some requirement of support, and this foundation is universally achieved through signatures.[25] Promoters of an MDD must show the authorities a predetermined portion of citizens endorsing their objectives; once checked, the measure is triggered.[26] This proportion of the electorate oscillates between 2 and 3 percent of the electorate for popular initiatives

---

[24] For a meticulous concatenation of events regarding this popular vote, see Breuer (2009a) and Feoli (2009).

[25] In some countries, signatures have to be accompanied by fingerprints.

[26] The procedures for checking the signatures vary significantly from place to place, even within the very same country, such as in the United States. These procedures could be as varied as a manual check of each and every signature (as in Idaho, Massachusetts, and Maine); a check

(e.g., in Hungary, Slovenia, or Switzerland) to 25 percent for a referendum as in Uruguay. Of course, in countries such as Uruguay, which encompasses a massive diaspora, this 25 percent of the electorate in real terms could be close to 30 percent of the citizens living in its territory. This phenomenon can be classified as an *entry hurdle*. But there are other critical aspects to take into account: participation quorums, approval quorums, time limits (or circulation time for triggering an MDD), decisiveness of the MDD (whether binding or not), and qualifiers (exclusion of potential issues to consider). I deal with these aspects related to any MDD in due time, but first I offer a brief introduction.

The approval of an MDD differs from country to country and even within the same country with regard to the particular variety (e.g., popular initiatives and referendums). Also, approval quorums must be studied alongside participation quorums given that in some countries, the decision at the polls is contingent on a minimum number of citizens participating in the procedure, which is concomitant with the existence of compulsory voting for certain measures. For example, in some countries, MDDs are approved by simple majorities, yet differences persist in whether the simple majority relates to all votes or only to all valid votes. In other countries, an MDD is approved if a majority of all citizens endorse the MDD.

The required majorities for approval must consider whether the final decision lies uniquely in the citizens' desires for other types of majorities. Some federal countries (e.g., Switzerland and Australia) require double majorities (i.e., they must win both a majority of citizens' votes *and* a majority of states in the country) for the MDD to be approved. Ceteris paribus, double majorities are more difficult to obtain because there are other institutional veto players to overcome along the way. Double majorities constitute safeguards in relation to what James Madison once called the *tyranny of the majority*. In other countries, super-majorities rather than double majorities are required. For instance, it is quite common to require the absolute majority of all enrolled citizens, regardless of whether they vote. However, super-majorities do not constitute another veto point; they have exactly the same objective as double majorities.

The debate on the necessary requirements for approval of an MDD opens the door for other discussions. One is related to the imputed preferences of passive citizens (those who do not vote). Assume, for example, that there is a participation quorum of 35 percent (as with obligatory referendums in Uruguay) and 70 percent of the electorate is willing to vote. Among those willing to vote, a significant majority, about 70 percent, support "A" (the objectives of the MDD) and about 30 percent support "B," opposing its objectives. A superficial perception of the situation is that the "B" option is likely to be overwhelmed by "A," but a more cautious view provides an alternative interpretation. If "B"

on signatures until the minimum number needed is met (as in Alaska and South Dakota); a random sampling (as in Arizona, California, and Oregon); and even, as in Oklahoma, where signatures are not checked and presumed valid, unless challenged (Silva 2003: 22–24).

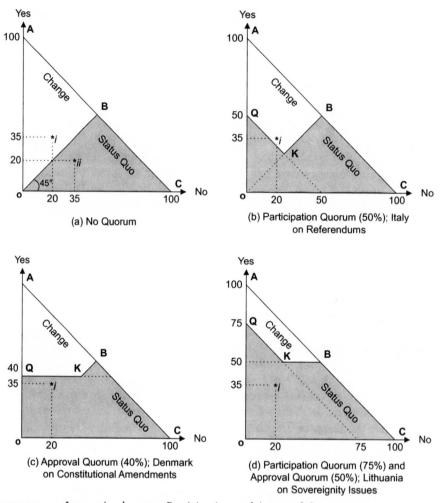

FIGURE 1.2. Interaction between Participation and Approval Quorums.
Source: Adapted from Aguiar-Conraria y Magalhães (2009; 2010) and Hug (2004).

voters stay at home on the decision day, their opinion will prevail because the 35 percent quorum will not be obtained.

As the study of Aguiar-Conraria and Magalhães demonstrates, all possible results of an MDD could be represented in the surface delimited by two orthogonal axes (yeas and nays), taking into consideration their interaction with participation and approval quorums (Aguiar-Conraria and Magalhães 2009; 2010). In Figure 1.2(a), no required quorums are needed for the measure to be approved. In other words, it does not matter how many people vote or how much of the electorate those people represent. In this figure, there is a 45-degree line that divides in two equal sizes all possible results of a typical two-choice MDD, the segment $\overline{OB}$. The vertical axis represents the "yea" votes and the horizontal, the "nays." Thus, point B represents a situation in which *all* citizens voted, with a perfect fifty–fifty distribution. For instance, if the results fall in point i, then 35 percent of the citizenry voted for and 20 percent against, and if the results fall in ii, then otherwise. For any i point closer to O than to B, this signifies a higher rate of abstention.

In Figure 1.2(b), however, there is a participation quorum of 50 percent of the citizenry. In other words, if fewer than half of the citizens participate, the result is not binding regardless of the relative strength of each camp; even if 100 percent of voters vote affirmatively, results are not legally binding. Indeed, any result falling below $\overline{QKB}$ would be nonbinding. As seen, the status quo's region increases drastically from a surface of 50 percent in Figure 1.2(a) to 62.5 percent in Figure 1.2(b). In this situation, if the results fall in point i, the decision is still binding. This requirement of 50 percent participation is widely used, most evidently in Italy, as seen in the next section of the chapter.

In Figure 1.2(c), there in no participation quorum but rather an approval quorum, which is why the segment $\overline{QK}$ is horizontal instead of parallel with segment $\overline{AB}$. In this case, the votes in favor must gather at least 40 percent of all citizens, but there is no explicit required participation quorum. Of course, there is no possibility of reaching the 40 percent of necessary affirmative votes if less than a minimum of 40 percent participates. Thus, there is an implicit participation threshold of 40 percent. This type of approval quorum is used in Denmark for constitutional amendments. In this case, point i produces nonbinding results.

Finally, Figure 1.2(d) illustrates a situation that combines both participation and approval quorums. This double requirement is rare and greatly reduces the size of the potential "change" field. This is the case of Lithuania on MDDs on sovereignty issues. For this type of vote, there is a participation quorum of 75 percent and an approval quorum of 50 percent. The area of change is reduced to less than 20 percent of the triangle $\triangle OAB$ (exactly 18.75 percent).

One could think that the former scenarios were created for the sake of the explanation, but they were not. Some political actors (e.g., nongovernmental organizations and parties) frequently get involved in boycott campaigns to support a side of the discussion when they perceive that they would be defeated at the ballot box. A prime example of where this type of campaign is rather recurrent is Italy, which has a participation quorum of 50 percent for its citizens on both abrogative and rejective referendums (Uleri 2002).

On February 19, 2004, the Italian Parliament passed Law 40, *Norme in materia di procreazione medicalmente assistita*, introduced by Berlusconi's coalition government, which also succeeded in gaining support from a significant sector of the opposition.[27] For its supporters, this was the first attempt to regulate an arena that hitherto had been out of their control. To its detractors, it was a law that extended the Catholic Church's conservative

---

[27] The full text of the bill is available at http://www.camera.it/parlam/leggi/04040L.htm.

FIGURE 1.3. "Every One of Us Is a Former Embryo" (Posters in Rome against Referendum on "Procreazione Medicalmente Assistita").

preferences to the detriment of the health of women seeking medically assisted procreation.

The Radical Party campaigned to cancel in a referendum the law as a whole, but the Constitutional Court ruled that it was not acceptable to scrap the new legislation altogether.[28] Despite the fact that the required number of signatures to override the law had been collected, the court only allowed the possibility of removing four of the most controversial articles.[29] The referendum was finally on the way. The Radical Party gathered the support of the Democratici di Sinistra, Socialisti Democratici Italiani, Rifondazione Comunista, and other liberal and progressive civic associations. The church and conservative sectors of Italian politics and society actively called for a boycott of the referendum aimed to loosen restrictive fertility laws for women. As shown in Figure 1.3,

---

[28] A very similar decision was made by the Oregon Supreme Court of Justice in 1998 in a case known as *Armatta v. Kitzhaber*. On this occasion, the court invalidated an initiative on the grounds that it involved multiple changes to the state's constitution, which should have been considered separately by voters (Miller 2003: 461).

[29] In substance, these clauses limit the number of embryos that may be created during a cycle of medically assisted conception, ban the storing of embryos, control which tests may be carried out on the embryo, ban the use of gametes from outside of the couple, and limit the availability of medically assisted conception to couples according to certain criteria.

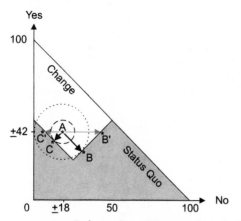

FIGURE 1.4. Italy 2004 on *"Procreazione Assitita."*
Source: Adapted from Aguiar-Conraria y Magalhães (2009; 2010) and Hug (2004).

members of the conservative Alleanza Nazionale integrated the so-called Committee for an Active Abstention. The question is why they called for abstention and not for a negative vote.

The clergy, with the support of the then–brand-new pope, reasoned as follows: If someone votes "no," that person will be strengthening the "yes" camp simply by helping that camp reach the 50 percent participation quorum. Given that the "yes" was a clear majority of those who cared about the vote, abstention became the most rational way to fulfill their political preferences (for those who opposed the "yes" camp). Even the words of Pope Benedict XVI were illustrative: *"What is the principle of wisdom, if not to abstain from all that is odious to God?"*[30]

Given the distribution of preferences regarding the legislation targeted by the referendum and opinion polls, which indicated that only 60 percent of citizens were considering turning out to vote, it was much more rational to demobilize the citizenry than to mobilize it against the referendum.[31] Graphically speaking, in Figure 1.4, it was easier (i.e., shorter) to go from *A* to *C* than from *A* to *B*. In this case, it is assumed that the demobilization efforts would affect all individuals evenly (regardless of whether they are in favor of or against the referendum). Even in the case of a highly emotional topic, where the demobilization efforts would impact mostly the "no" camp, it is more rational to demobilize than to mobilize against the referendum (i.e., to go from *A* to *C′* than from *A* to *B′*) when turnout is expected to be close to the requisite quorum.

The church's strategy was eventually a success. Despite the vote in favor of the measures being more than 80 percent (Table 1.1) of the votes counted, it

---

[30] Pope Benedict XVI, in a speech made in June 8, 2005, four days before a referendum on in vitro fertilization in Italy, cited by Aguiar-Conraria and Magalhães (2009).
[31] For a rather complete series of opinion polls, see Angus Reid Public Opinion at Angus Reid Global Monitor, http://www.angus-reid.com/.

TABLE 1.1. *Results of the Italian Referendums on Assisted Procreation*
(Procreazione Assistita), June 2005

Question	For (Votes)	Against (Votes)	Invalid (Votes)	For (%)	Against (%)	Approved
1 – Limit to the clinical research and experiences on the embryos	10,743,710	1,461,217	870,740	88.0	12.0	NO
2 – Norms on the limits of access	10,819,909	1,367,288	910,500	88.8	11.2	NO
3 – Norms on the finality, subject rights, and access limits	10,663,125	1,492,042	960,855	87.7	12.3	NO
4 – Prohibition of in vitro fertilization	9,391,161	2,744,895	979,679	77.4	22.6	NO

Electorate: 49,648,425; abstention: 36,910,807; participation: 25.90 percent.
Source: Italian Ministry of Interior, http://www.referendum.interno.it/.

never attained the 50 percent quorum. In a way, this case supports the idea that the maximization of the vote is not always rational, as McCubbins and Rosenbluth neatly explain in their theoretical view of Japanese party politics (1995). A basic question that arises is why participation quorums exist in the direct democracy realm but not in the representative one. As Verhulst and Nijeboer state, participation quorums "give unequal weighting to the votes of supporters and opponents of an initiative, provoke calls for boycotts, and negate the role of the mandate in direct decision-making" (2007: 21).

The existence of a quorum has one perverse effect and one ironic potential outcome. In the words of Aguiar-Conraria and Magalhães,

The perverse effect is that, in some situations it gives incentives to people to mask their true preferences and to abstain, acting as if they were indifferent. The ironic potential outcome is known in the literature as the "No-Show paradox": it is possible that the quorum is not reached precisely because of its existence or, in other words, turnout exceeds the quorum only if this requirement does not exist. (Aguiar-Conraria and Magalhães 2009)

Moreover, there is one potential, and even more basic, consequence of a demobilization campaign: the violation of the secrecy of the vote, particularly in rural or small urban areas where close social ties exist. The historical record of MDDs shows several occurrences of threats to, and abuses of, people in order to compel them to abstain from voting.[32] As Suksi remarks, "[I]n a case where

[32] After World War I, landed aristocrats of Germany demanded that the state compensate for the expropriations they were subject to during the war. The only way the Weimar Republic

it is possible to influence the outcome by abstention, the act of voting itself might become a statement on the policies an individual was supporting" (Suksi 1993: 211).

A second typical discussion about MDDs relates to how to delimit the demos. This topic is particularly acute in questions concerning women's rights, sovereignty, or international settlements of disputes (Rourke, Hiskes, and Zirakzadeh 1992). With regard to women's rights, in both Switzerland and Liechtenstein, the struggle for them was agonizingly long because of the quite stubborn and conservative popular vote of men. Women had only an indirect influence, if they had any at all. Indeed, male decisions at the polls pushed these two countries to be the latest comers in the Western Hemisphere regarding the extension of such rights (Switzerland in 1971 and Liechtenstein in 1984).

Also, the delimitation of the demos is critical in terms of sovereignty. For example, some Canadians have voted twice (in 1980 and 1995) regarding the possible independence of their largest province, Quebec. An important debate took place regarding who should compose the demos in such instances (see, e.g., LeDuc 1993; 2003; Nadeau, Martin, and Blais 1999). Was this a matter for all Canadians or just for the Quebecois? In Canada, the answer was in both instances, only for the Quebecois. Yet a provocative question can be asked: Is Spain ready to allow the Catalans or the Basques to vote for independence on their own? What about the minorities within those independence-leaning regions – are they to be "protected" or not? This problem is especially acute when there is an evident unevenness of power between minorities (e.g., the French in Algeria) and the rest of the population.[33]

There are other "details" that must be taken into account to complete the picture of MDDs and their procedures. For example, it seems evident that it would be harder to gather the required signatures if only three months were available to do so instead of, say, one year – which is related to the size of the country in consideration. For instance, gathering 10 percent of citizens' signatures in Peru is presumably much harder than gathering the same 10 percent in Liechtenstein, where the required number of signatures almost could be gathered in the main piazza in a couple of days. Certainly, it could be claimed that everything is proportional, even the resources to gather signatures.

could cover those costs was by drastically increasing taxation. In 1926, both the Communist and Socialist Parties launched an initiative that sought to "confiscate without compensation, in the interest of general welfare" the property of members of the nobility. Supporters of the aristocracy, the German Nationalist and the German People's Parties, the press, and other conservative forces joined what Verhulst and Nijeboer call "the mother of all boycott campaigns" (2007: 82). They ordered their followers to stay away from the polls on election day and publicized false announcements that the election had been postponed. Furthermore, "Threats were made by the Nationalists that those who went to the polls would be noted as Communists or Socialists" (Gosnell 1927: 121). This strategy was a success for the nobility, as 39.1 percent of citizens voted and, therefore, the participation quorum (50 percent) was not attained. The results were, however, eloquent: 96.1 percent in favor and just 3.9 percent against.

[33] See Margalit and Raz (1990).

Yet, even assuming that this is so, urbanization and distance are likely to make a huge difference.

Finally, and just as an introductory note, the qualifiers seem unmistakably significant, and the Hungarian case fits like a glove in making this point. In Hungary, despite CI-MDDs that can be triggered more easily than in other Central and Eastern European countries, the constitution explicitly forbids the realization of CI-MDDs for seventeen topics (and another one in the electoral law). CI-MDDs may not be held on the following subjects: a) laws regarding the central budget, the execution of the central budget, taxes to the central government and duties, customs tariffs, and the central government's conditions for local taxes; b) obligations set forth in valid international treaties and on the contents of laws prescribing such obligations; c) the provisions of the constitution on national referendums and popular initiatives; d) personnel and restructuring (e.g., reorganization and termination) matters falling under Parliamentary jurisdiction; e) dissolution of the Parliament; f) the government's program; g) the declaration of a state of war, a state of emergency, or a state of national crisis; h) the use of the armed forces abroad or within the country; i) dissolution of the representative body of local governments; and j) amnesty (Hungarian Constitution 2003, Art. 28c). The question then is: What remains?

This section is intended to introduce the reader to little nuances that might make big differences. Indeed, the list of "details" could be extended almost to infinity. For example, who pays for the campaigns, who is in charge of wording the question to be answered, and so on. Most of these details, however, are discussed throughout the course of this research.

3. Organization of the Research

Although our knowledge of direct democracy has grown rapidly in recent years, there are still many unanswered questions concerning the use of direct democracy in the context of representative democracies. Unlike other aspects of contemporary political life, such as electoral or government regimes, which are mainly centered on technical discussions, the world of MDDs is deeply related to the very (normative) idea we have regarding democracy, its citizens, and more important, their capabilities as reasonable beings able to make responsible decisions. The general question addressed in this book is: Under what conditions does direct democracy supplement or undermine representative democracy?

This research is approached both theoretically and empirically (from a variety of perspectives and methodological points of view). Theoretically, the aim of this book is to analyze the potentialities and the problems inherent in the use of direct democratic institutions within representative democracies. Empirically, the aim is to outline the role of MDDs in different political systems and regimes. The research is organized as follows:

Chapter 2 lays out the basis for the theoretical dimension of the book. There is no doubt that democracy constitutes a key component of the current debate in political science. Most of the comparative literature analyzes elections (a sine qua non component of any democratic regime) and the associated rights and preconditions for them to be fair and free. However, less attention has been devoted in the literature to what happens between elections. Although some key institutions and processes have been examined (i.e., rule of law, human, social, and economic rights) a central dimension of democracy – popular sovereignty – has been surprisingly absent in mainstream comparative political-science debates. Popular sovereignty is critical because, even assuming a reasonably well-functioning state, representative institutions alone generate incentives for narrow and selfish interests that must be controlled by citizens. This chapter demonstrates that CI-MDDs are the institutions that allow popular sovereignty to flourish within contemporary representative democracies.

Nonetheless, this is not an easily made theoretical claim. On the one hand, diehard opponents of direct democracy argue that representative democracies are inherently inimical to one or another aspect of direct democracy based on arguments such as the risks of the tyranny of the majority. It also has been argued, from a social-choice perspective, that there is not one universal and fair system of aggregation of interests; thus, the use of majority rule could lead us down a road of cycling and alternating decisions and, consequently, instability. On the other hand, supporters of direct democracy claim that it is simply a strong medicine against most pathologies of representative democracy and, therefore, more direct democracy is advisable. I argue that most of the debates regarding direct democracy are approached in the wrong manner. They ask the wrong questions, and most of their critiques are based on incorrect assumptions about not only direct democracy in general but also about representative democracy itself.

Chapter 3 asks why some countries use MDDs exceptionally frequently, others rarely, and still others not at all. No theory thus far has comprehensively offered an answer to this question, and most conjectures are usually based on anecdotal evidence from a few selected cases. Most analyses of direct democracy select on the dependent variable, which, as a rule, we learn not to do in graduate school. Thus, this chapter contributes to filling this lacuna by analyzing an original database examining the use of MDDs (either top-down or citizen-initiated) on an annual basis in *all* countries in the world from 1985 to 2009.

This unique database presents a year-by-year picture of every country, providing almost five thousand observations and including information about the use of different types of MDDs in each and every country (we may call them "events"), plus several independent variables. The foci of study at this stage are the tools of direct democracy used at the national level only; I do not consider nonofficial or subnational MDDs. Also, this chapter studies the actual use of MDDs, not the legal possibility for their realization, as do Hug and Tsebelis (2002). The prevalence of zeros and the tiny values and discrete nature of the dependent variable (non-negative and integer valued) make the ordinary least-squares technique unsuitable for this research. Therefore, given that the dependent variable is a non-negative count (events of MDDs per country per year), a negative binomial cross-sectional time series regression is the most appropriate tool for statistical inference.

This statistical analysis undermines many of the assumptions in the literature while confirming a few others. Contrary to much of the conventional wisdom, evidence supports the claim that direct democracy is strongly associated with higher levels of democracy. Therefore, the idea that MDDs are not part of the truly democratic world seems to be disconfirmed. Consequently, many of the arguments about the nondemocratic nature of MDDs are weakened. Moreover, the findings also help to redirect some of the hypotheses advanced directly or indirectly by previous researchers.

Chapter 4 goes down one step in the ladder of generality (Collier 1991; Sartori 1970), examining MDDs from a lower perspective: the political regime. Given that this manuscript deals with the relationship between direct and representative democracy, this chapter takes the opportunity to deal with the flip side of the coin: the use of MDDs in nondemocratic regimes. The dynamics of the political game are different when played within an authoritarian regime (not to mention totalitarian regimes) than in a democracy. On the one hand, some authoritarian leaders have never resorted to top-down MDDs (e.g., Somoza and Pol Pot). On the other hand, some nondemocratic leaders (e.g., Lukashenko and Jean-Claude "Baby Doc" Duvalier) frequently did so to advance their political interests. This chapter asserts that the use of plebiscites under non-democratic regimes is typically motivated by the maintenance of an illusion of an existing democratic process (to observers both within and outside the country), to cement a psychological and emotional bond between the regime and the population through its mobilization and excitement, and to show the strength of the regime (also for both those within and outside the country).

In this chapter, I also try to answer a frequently forgotten question: Having approximately all the tools necessary to rig a plebiscite, why do some authoritarian regimes accept defeat when they have held an MDD? According to my historical records, in only three nondemocratic regimes did officials recognize their defeat at the ballots (i.e., Uruguay 1980, Chile 1988, and Zimbabwe 2000). What factors determined the acceptance of these results? I assert that a surprise factor, the international leverage and institutional design, provides – in differing degrees – the answer for this question.

Chapter 5 returns to the democratic framework and expands the theoretical discussion from Chapter 2, which assumes that certain levels of horizontal and vertical accountability are present within the environment where MDDs are practiced. In Latin America, unregulated plebiscites are blamed for triggering delegative democracies, but this shows that delegative democrats use MDDs, not the other way around. Despite the use of MDDs by questionable leaders to foster their particular interests, sometimes MDDs open a window of opportunity in the context of minimum democratic guarantees. The question thus is whether MDDs have helped to further undermine the already-weak institutions that several of these countries exhibit. I claim that there is a reasonable amount of skepticism regarding this argument.

If Venezuela had had a constitutional arrangement wherein constitutional amendments were approved only by the sitting Congress without consultation with any other actor, Chávez's 2007 constitution would have been adopted without major issue because of the absolute majority he enjoys in Congress; however, this was not the case. Undeniably, the history of the continent is plagued by a long list of regimes altering the rules of the game without any scrutiny by their respective citizens and within an environment of poor democratic performance. A few examples include the Dominican Republic (1994), Honduras (1982), El Salvador (1983), and Nicaragua (1987, 1995).

Chapter 6 shifts our perspective from the general to a single case study: Uruguay. Four facts make Uruguay a particularly interesting case study for this research. First, it presents wide variation in the dependent variable (it employs referendums, mandated plebiscites, popular initiatives, and legislative counterproposals). Second, the institutional design of Uruguayan presidentialism has varied substantially since it became a democratic regime, so we will be able to assess the impact of different institutional designs on uses of direct democracy while holding other variables constant. Third, Uruguay has a peculiar party system that makes it relatively easy to observe what is happening inside parties because the internal divisions are in the open. Finally, Uruguay is the most prodigious user of CI-MDDs in the global south (i.e., it does not belong to the "developed" north and is not a member of the Organisation for Economic Co-operation and Development [OECD] or Europe). All of these factors make Uruguay a manageable case for understanding direct democracy.

Chapter 6 is divided into two major sections. The first accounts for the historical and legal context of direct democracy; the second examines how the use of CI-MDDs challenges existing theories of voting behavior in Uruguay. It is possible to trace direct democracy in Uruguay to the constitutional discussions of the early twentieth century. Although the mandatory plebiscite was included in the constitution of 1934, along with popular initiatives, it was already being used in 1917. Since 1934, obligatory referendums (also known as "constitutional plebiscites") and popular initiatives were employed several times, but it was not until the constitution of 1967 that facultative referendums were included (through an obligatory referendum, of course).

The second section of Chapter 6 deals with the "first cut" usually made in studies of direct democracy: results and voting behavior. The literature on direct democracy tends to suggest that economic interests or social groups could easily use direct democracy for their own particular benefit, making it, in the end, harmful to representative democracy. Nonetheless, this chapter will show that, at least in the Uruguayan case, this argument does not hold equally and consistently for all uses of MDDs. Using a "linear" logic, I examine how the use of CI-MDDs in Uruguay challenges existing theories of voting behavior. I find that when Uruguayans go to the polls to vote on a popular initiative, their vote choice is primarily the result of their party loyalty rather than a direct reaction to economic conditions. In testing my hypotheses, I rely on the following statistical methods: King's ecological inference, multivariate regression, and path analysis.

Chapter 7 continues with the case of Uruguay, but the question and the methodological approach differ from that of Chapter 6. I analyze the possible combinations of institutional and political factors under which MDDs manage to limit the action and political desires of the government, thus becoming a weapon of political control in the hands of the citizenry. With this objective, this analysis selects from all MDD occurrences in Uruguay in which the government and the promoters of the initiative held contrasting positions. Simply stated, using the Uruguayan experience, Chapter 7 explains which combination of factors is necessary and/or sufficient conditions to approve a CI-MDD, a subset of MDDs when governments lose (and organized citizens win). In so doing, I rely on a qualitative comparative analysis (QCA), an analytic technique that uses organized and logical case comparisons anchored in the rules of Boolean algebra, to distinguish the mixture of explanatory variables that are exclusive to a particular result.

Substantively, Chapter 7 shows that when the executive opposes the objectives of the promoters of a measure, governments lose at the polls under specific configurations. This occurs when: a) economic issues are at stake, the MDD attempts to maintain the status quo, there is a negative evolution of real wages, and there is a strong lobby or union behind the MDD; or b) economic issues are at stake, the MDD is concurrent with elections, there is a positive evolution of real wages, and there is a strong lobby or union behind the MDD.

The results of the QCA are notably solid in terms of theory confirmation. However, the flip side of the coin also deserves analysis. Thus, the second section of this chapter deals with how political elites approach direct democracy. I had the opportunity to meet with the last three presidents of Uruguay – whose programs were derailed on several occasions by CI-MDDs – and talk extensively with each regarding direct democracy. I also successfully conducted structured interviews with deputies at the national Parliament. Indeed, I can safely say that based on these interviews, ninety-one of ninety-nine deputies confirmed (contrary to conventional wisdom) that most power holders think rather highly of the use of MDDs.

Chapter 8 concludes with the argument that an overall normative evaluation of MDDs as either inherently *good* or *bad* for representative democracy must take into account the very different institutional contexts in which these mechanisms are used. Furthermore, it must consider the strength of the political actors involved as well as the type and purpose of the MDD used. Indeed, the discussion of "direct democracy" as a homogeneous category is not conducive to any serious theoretical or empirical learning because it constitutes different and sometimes opposing institutions.

This book claims that the existing debates on direct democracy tend to be mired in theoretical stereotypes of how direct and representative democracy work; however, these debates could be illuminating insofar as they offer fertile ground for interesting research enquiries. Nonetheless, the question is how realistic these theories are. How often do we see this circulation of votes in the direct-democratic game, and how often do we witness a blooming of populists' policies? Even in countries where CI-MDDs are comparatively easy to trigger, we have not witnessed any circulation of votes regarding a certain issue. This is because CI-MDDs are not simply about a blind use of majority rule. Those understanding CI-MDDs as mere votes on certain issues are ignoring possibly the most crucial part of the direct-democratic game: the process itself. The evidence does not suggest that Switzerland or Uruguay seems more vulnerable to populist policies than other purely representative democracies in their respective regions, neither do they seem to be performing poorly in terms of democratic processes, even with regard to political outcomes.

In Uruguay, MDDs in general, and CI-MDDs in particular, do not undermine representative democracy because their passage depends largely on the mobilization efforts of organized partisan groups operating outside the conventional legislative arena while still accepting and playing the political game within the formal representative institutions. The central actors working for the approval of MDDs are political parties' factions and the basic institutions of electoral, legislative, and political representation.

MDDs are reasonable barometers for society, even in a context of weak democratic institutions. They force a finer tuning between party elites and citizens and serve as institutionalized intermittent safety valves for political pressure. In a way, MDDs can be understood as the calcium against potential party-system osteoporosis. MDDs help ground the political system in reality.

Terms of the Debate Surrounding Direct Democracy

There is no doubt that democracy constitutes a key component of the current debate in political science. Most of the comparative literature analyzes elections (a sine qua non component of any democratic regime) and the surrounding rights or preconditions for them to be fair and free. However, less attention has been devoted in the literature to what happens between elections. Although some key institutions and processes have been examined (e.g., rule of law; human, social, and economic rights), a central dimension of democracy – popular sovereignty – has been surprisingly absent in mainstream comparative political science debate. Popular sovereignty is critical because representative institutions generate incentives for narrow and selfish interests that must be controlled by citizens. Despite MDDs being either loved or hated institutions, this chapter shows that many of the critical arguments within the discussion about direct democracy are based, to an important degree, on stigmatization of how both direct and representative democracy work.

This chapter has two sections. The first section shows how free and fair elections are a necessary but not sufficient condition for democracy to flourish. For democracy to re-enchant citizens, serious consideration must be given to the popular sovereignty dimension of democracy. I claim that this can be done by returning sovereign power to the citizens. Of course, this sovereign power has its risks; thus, in the following section I tackle the most important apprehensions associated with the direct-democratic game.

1. Democracy Is More than Simply Free and Fair Elections

The importance of direct democracy in current debate in the discipline is enhanced by the fact that "normal" electoral politics are problematic. Today, this debate is even more intense because we face two contradictory scenarios.

On the one hand, never more than before have so many people around the globe been free to elect their leaders in a democratic manner. On the other hand, more often than not, democratic performance seems to be challenged by the emergence of public disaffection, weak rule of law, the corruption (both real and assumed) of elected officials, an increasing gap between the rich and the poor, a lack of accountability and transparency, and the continuous marginalization of important groups in society, among other factors. It is clear that unless something changes, the aforementioned problems will continue their course in eroding democracy, its representation, and its normative hegemony.

Some students of democracy claim that free and fair elections are sufficient conditions for the existence of democracy. This is true insofar as we agree to overcome the ultraminimalist procedural definition of democracy. It is crucial because the way we think about representation is correlated with the way we think about democracy, and the way we think about democracy has its correlates in the way we approach direct democracy.

Representation itself constitutes the common denominator of contemporary democracies, no matter whether this is considered a *necessarily evil*, a *technical necessity*, or a *positive good*. Whatever (implicit or explicit) stance the researcher adopts regarding representation, it is usually described as a principal-agent relationship in which "we can conceive of the citizens as principals represented by agents to whom the citizens temporarily delegate the power to make public policies" (Powell 2004: 274). This definition opens the door for what Pitkin calls the "mandate-independence controversy" (Pitkin 1967:145), in which the tension centers on whether representatives should behave as *delegates* (with a significant quantity of independent judgment) or as *trustees* (simply as transmission belts) for their voters. After all, the expectation is that whatever shape representation takes, representatives – sooner or later, individually or collectively – are obligated to explain and justify their actions to their constituents. In other words, representatives are accountable to their voters through regular elections, in which they may be sanctioned or rewarded on the basis of their proceedings (Kiewiet and McCubbins 1991; Mayhew 1974; Setälä 2006b: 703).

If someone believes in the delegative view of representation, direct democracy may be seen as a device that gives a more precise depiction of the will of the majority without the deformation caused by representation. In terms of the principal-agent model, direct democracy may be a corrective institution when agents fail to represent their principals' views on some issues (Setälä 1999a). However, the classic principal-agent problem eclipses representation and democratic accountability in several ways. Particularly in the context of weak, inchoate, or poorly institutionalized party systems, such as many in the Latin American milieu, personalistic electoral movements manage to be elected, according to a successful mobilization of the discontented, and once in office, their leaders often betray the programmatic principles articulated during their campaigns (Stokes 1996; 2001; Weyland 1998; 2002).[1] Of course, these betrayals are not the exclusive capital of Latin American presidential regimes, as Maravall illustrates. In his study of the Spanish case, the Socialist Party used misleading campaign methods to cling to power from 1982 to 1996 (Maravall 1999). Clearly, these phenomena back the status quo and generate strong challenges not only to representation but also to democratic legitimacy, performance, and stability.

Free and fair elections are a necessary but not sufficient condition for democracy to flourish. Determining the other conditions of democracy has been a major focus of the comparative politics "quality of democracy" research agenda. The major lines of research can be divided into two broad categories: those that underline the outcomes democracies ought to produce and those based on the procedures for making decisions. Those in the second group have asked who participates and what the scope of their participation is. This includes Gerber, for whom "all democracies face a fundamental problem in deciding how much political participation to allow and by whom" (1999: 3). By the turn of the twentieth century, a broad consensus had been reached with regard to who has the right to participate (usually, all adults in society who possess a reasonable degree of mental health and who are not imprisoned, generally absenting any other considerations) – a consensus shared by most liberal democracies on earth. Yet the scope and type of this participation still is a topic for debate; for some, the basic role of the citizenry is selecting ruling elites, whereas at the other extreme, the citizenry must be a consistently active player whenever political decisions are taken.

a. Democratic Preconditions for Direct Democracy

Schumpeter (1950) offered perhaps the first attempt to provide a working definition that challenged the classical, more normative doctrine of democracy. In his view, democracy was not an end in itself but rather a "political method. That is to say, a certain institutional arrangement for arriving at political – legislative and administrative – decisions [. . .] in which individuals acquire the power to decide by means of a competitive struggle for the people's vote" (1950: 269). He was severely criticized for the elitist character of his definition. In his view, the elite had a paramount role in politics, and the only role of citizens was to elect governments. Furthermore, given that the extension of suffrage was something to be decided by each society, it was perfectly plausible that elites in a given society reduced the suffrage to such a minimum that "they could fully exclude popular preferences from the process of competition" (Munck 2007: 28). An even more negative twist of this Schumpeterian electoralist definition is given by George Bernard Shaw, for whom democracy is "the substitution of

---

[1] These infidelities follow a similar direction "from 'welfare oriented' campaigns to 'efficiency-oriented' policies" (Stokes 1999: 100). Moreover, Stokes shows that the excuses advanced by these presidents who, once in office, discovered information they previously did not have about the fiscal health of the state could not be sustained.

election by the incompetent many for appointment by the corrupt few" (Shaw quoted in Danziger 1998: 155).

Other authors attempted to go beyond purely electoralist definitions of democracy by taking into consideration the institutional requirements needed for a democracy to transpire. In this vein, Dahl (1956; 1971; 1989) coined the concept of *polyarchy* in an attempt to distinguish it from the notion of democracy, which he viewed as an ideal rather than a real possibility. The concept of polyarchy was originally developed to refer to extant democracies. In this view, polyarchies were characterized by the ability of the government to continuously address the demands of the citizens without any form of political discrimination against them. To reach this goal, there were two requirements: Citizens should be able to publicly voice their preferences, and participation in the political system should be as inclusive as possible. Thus, polyarchy could be reduced to participation and opposition (or competition), assuring a required minimum threshold of individual rights.

Dahl defines a polyarchy as a regime that elects its leaders through free and fair elections as well as one in which most of the adult population has the right to vote and run for public office. He conceived this as a multifaceted concept composed of eight different institutional requirements: freedom of organization and expression, the right to vote, eligibility for public office, the right of political leaders to compete for support, the presence of alternative sources of information, free and fair elections, and institutions linking public preferences to policy outcomes (Dahl 1971: 3). Dahl's definition constitutes the classic procedural minimum characterization of democracy par excellence.

Defining democracy as a procedural minimum – a set of necessary conditions – has several advantages. First, it is broad enough to acknowledge a common denominator of democracy that travels far in comparative research. Most students of democracy would probably agree with this basic definition, if only because it is broad enough to accommodate several perspectives. More important, "[I]t is thin enough *to omit* mention of many qualities that are commonly associated with democracy, such as majority rule, judicial independence, separation of powers, local autonomy, [...], not to mention socioeconomic equality, *direct democracy*, small population, and public-spirited harmony" (Coppedge, *Approaching Democracy*: chap. 2; italics are mine).

Dahl's definition of polyarchy hinges on a set of institutional conditions allowing mass participation and free opposition to the ruling elite. The lack of such conditions determines the absence of polyarchy. However, even if all conditions are present to some extent (making the country a member of the polyarchic collection of regimes), limited violations of civil and political rights may hinder the quality of democracy. Countries in which some specific regions or social groups are affected by political violence or electoral manipulation are clearly worse off than democracies in which the whole population effectively exercises its rights – of course, no country has a *perfect* record. Dahl's polyarchy is a good starting point, but this does not mean that a polyarchical setup will necessarily turn itself into a democracy, even if we witness free and fair elections.

Dahl's dimensions of participation and competition reflected the *right* to participate and compete, not the actual rate of participation or competition. Indeed, Dahl was rather ambiguous regarding whether he was talking about rights or effective conduct. Dahl is not alone in this ambiguity in terms of his definitions and thresholds. For Bobbio, democracy is "first and foremost a set of procedural rules for arriving at collective decisions in a way which accommodates and facilitates the fullest possible participation of interested parties" (Bobbio 1987: 19). Yet he never spells out what "fullest possible" really implies in terms of a threshold. Despite the ambiguities pointed out herein, the literature shows that very few scholars would challenge the idea that one essential characteristic of contemporary democracies, a sine qua non element, is free and fair elections, and that for elections to be free and fair, certain preconditions are to be met. Moreover, those who are elected are to continuously address citizens' demands expressed in an orderly and legal way.

Modern democracy is mainly based on the hypothesis that voting in elections of representative bodies fulfils the ideal of popular co-determination: the people leave their decision-making rights for a certain period of time to an assembly, which in principle, ought to be a cross-section of the people and which therefore ought to reflect the opinions of the people (Suksi 1993: 1).

Delving deeper into the participation dimension of Dahl's work, most scholars contend that voter turnout (effective participation) should not be part of a definition of democracy. But many others have argued that turnout is an important measure of the *quality* of democratic life (Altman and Pérez-Liñán 2002; Brasil De Lima 1983; Hill 1994; Lijphart 1997; Miller 1988; Moon, Harvey, Ceisluk, Garlett, Hermias, Mendenhall, Schmid, and Hong Wong 2006; Schattschneider 1960; Teixeira 1987). Greater participation – whether voluntary or encouraged by "compulsory vote" – makes democratic governments responsive to a larger share of the population. The health of a democratic regime is particularly poor when some citizens are effectively disenfranchised as a consequence of poverty, lack of basic education, or sheer apathy. Some analysts contend that low participation may reflect high satisfaction with the political regime, but I dispute this because most studies have shown that the less educated (i.e., those with fewer opportunities in the system) people are, the less inclined they are to vote, and vice versa (Almond and Verba 1963; Lijphart 1997; Powell 1986; Rosenstone and Hansen 1993; Wolfinger and Rosenstone 1980).

With regard to Dahl's second dimension of polyarchy, students of democracy and elections have developed different measures of *competition*.[2] All recognize

[2] Competition is understood as the struggle between two or more agents to capture scarce, limited, and valued resources within a defined system or context. It is often assumed that competition is a zero-sum game in which one participant's gain or loss is exactly matched by the loss or gain of

the theoretical leverage of this dimension; however, an agreement on how to operationalize this variable still remains elusive.[3] What is clear is that competition fosters uncertainty and, for many, it is this uncertainty that differentiates democracies from non-democracies: "Democracy is a form of institutionalization of continual conflicts [...] of uncertainty, of subjecting all interests to uncertainty" (Przeworski 1986: 58).

Despite all the possible theoretical shortcomings of the procedural minimum definition of democracy, there is no doubt that this approach is sensible for distinguishing between polyarchies and non-polyarchies. Nonetheless, the Dahlian approach to democracy does not lend much assistance in the differentiation between polyarchic regimes. In other words, although Dahl's contributions make it possible to distinguish a democratic from a nondemocratic regime, after we cluster the universe of democracies, we can say very little about the nuances, main characteristics, and even the asymmetries of power coexisting within those regimes. This limitation has become particularly obvious in light of the third wave of democratization (Huntington 1991).

In the context of the latest wave of democratization, students of comparative politics have noticed, not without satisfaction, a decreasing range of variance in their favorite dependent variable: the political regime. Explaining the conditions for the emergence, breakdown, or survival of different types of political regimes has been the bread and butter of comparative studies.[4] Political regimes have tended to remain democratic in many countries, which means that the dependent variable no longer shows significant variance. This situation has led scholars to new and subtler questions about the preconditions for democratic consolidation and to more detailed analysis of the institutional features of new democracies. Moreover, it has sparked a growing interest in the prospects of consolidation and the quality of democratic life – factors that clearly vary from country to country and even within the same country.

another. Political competition involves the struggle for power, for example, through elections in a democratic regime. It is a concept employed in virtually all subdisciplines of political science because it is a universal aspect of human life. Although everyone is affected by it in one way or another, a clear definition of the concept remains elusive.

[3] For example, Ranney (1965) built a multidimensional index of competition in the American states over several decades, and Powell (1986) measured competition as the frequency of alternation in power over a nineteen-year period. For some, such as Przeworski, Alvarez, Cheibub, and Limongi (2000), alternation in office constitutes prima facie evidence of contestation. See also Hill and Leighler (1993) and Hill (1994). This long-term perspective is not very useful for new democracies in which just a few elections may have taken place. Other students have measured competition as the winner's percentage of the votes (Patterson and Caldeira 1983), the percent margin of victory (Cox and Munger 1989), and the raw vote margin of victory in elections (Cox 1998). In a way, the already-classic effective number of parties developed by Laakso and Taagepera (1979) is a widely used measure of political party fragmentation that is highly correlated with any of the measures of political competition expressed here.

[4] Among those who maintain the classic quantitative cross-national analysis, we can emphasize Cutright (1963), Huntington (1968), Bollen (1979), Bollen and Jackman (1985; 1995), and Muller (1988; 1989; 1995).

Knowing that democracy entails more than free and fair elections has prompted scholars to pursue two main goals: to develop a differentiated conceptualization of democracy that captures the diverse experiences of these countries and to extend the analysis to a broader range of countries without stretching the concept of democracy, as Collier and Levitsky (1997) have shown. These goals resulted in a series of conceptual innovations that led to the "adjectivization" of democracy. In other words, the main way that scholars could reflect the empirical diversity within the universe of democracies was to attach an adjective to the concept (e.g., neopatrimonial-, authoritarian-, or delegative-democracy). Although several types of definitions for democracy are found, a substantial consensus emerged around a procedural minimum or expanded procedural minimum definition of democracy, such as that elaborated by Dahl.[5]

Often from case-oriented research (also known as small-N or qualitative analysis), some scholars recognize substantive defects that negatively affect democratic life in a given country or set of countries (Karl 1995; O'Donnell 1993, 1994; Valenzuela 1992). To deal with these cases of "reserved domains," lack of "horizontal accountability," or "electoralism," to mention just a few, scholars have developed a whole array of diminished subtypes of democracy (Collier and Levitsky 1997; Diamond 1999). This perspective has been extremely lucid in identifying challenges for (and flaws of) new polyarchies, but it has usually avoided a comprehensive definition of democracy and tended to ignore problems of cross-national measurement (these last issues, however, fall beyond the scope of this research).

Because of the immense variety of countries and societies, one of the consequences of previous research agendas was the acknowledgment of a rather simple conclusion: It is virtually impossible to find a magical formula for obtaining and maximizing democracy and each of its oft-debatable components (e.g., rule of law; civic participation; civil, political, and social rights). All of these aspects and dimensions can hardly be tackled in a comprehensive way in a limited work such as this one. What is clear, though, is that "there is no one answer, and there are no shortcuts. In most countries that lack stable and effective governance today, we must be prepared to work on a number of fronts over a prolonged period of time" (Diamond 2003).

From my perspective, most of the rights underlined by Dahl are sine qua non conditions for democracy. But the checklist of freedoms and rights is fairly elastic, and it would be almost impossible to spell out what O'Donnell calls the *minimal sufficient set* of freedoms (O'Donnell 2004b: 18). Those who are concerned mainly with the preconditions of democracy tend to focus on those

---

[5] These five definitions are: 1) Electoralist – reasonably competitive elections, devoid of massive fraud, and having broad suffrage; 2) Procedural Minimum – basic civil rights are present; 3) Expanded Procedural Minimum – elected governments have effective power to govern; 4) Prototypical Conception of Established Industrialized Democracies; and 5) Maximalist Definition (Collier and Levitsky 1997).

rights that enable citizens to be agents. To be citizens, individuals must be free of deprivation: If they do not eat and if they cannot feed their children, they will not be able to choose what type of life they want. In other words, they will be driven only to fulfill these basic needs and, as such, will remain prisoners of their own deprivation. If this is the case, citizens will be unable to fulfill their *agency* potential as responsible and reasonable beings. One of the critical debates in the literature of democracy acknowledges that most definitions of democracy have their purpose in free and fair elections, yet they differ in the necessary and sufficient conditions for achieving this. Citizens need either a "decent social minimum" (Nussbaum 2000), a minimum degree of "social integration" (Munck 2007: 31), or "human development" (Sen 1999). Of course, the meaning and content of these preconditions vary both spatially and temporally and are outside the scope of this book.[6]

Democracy "is not just a matter of the preferences of each citizen being treated equally in the process of forming a government" (Munck 2007: 31), and "fair elections are not sufficient for characterizing a democratic regime" (O'Donnell 2004b: 15). The question is how we should proceed with our empirical and theoretical aims of grounding democracy. The debate has diverged into looking at either the preconditions for democracy to flourish or the outputs democracy should produce. At this point, I enter the murky "quality of democracy" theoretical and conceptual space.

There is a substantial difference between addressing the quality of democratization and the level of democratization of a political regime. Every analysis of the quality of democracy must assume a minimum degree of democratization (i.e., Dahl's procedural minimum). Yet questions arise, and Dahl's work deserves a closer look – must citizens have the right to participate, or must they participate? What happens if they do not participate? Furthermore, most definitions of democracy observe that most of the adult population must be able to play the political game and, in the Western world, the standard of eighteen years is set as the minimum age for citizenship.[7] However, if a regime includes those older than sixteen years (as in Austria, Brazil, and Nicaragua), is this country – ceteris paribus – more democratic than one that allows only those older than twenty-one (as in Gabon, Central African Republic, and Fiji)

[handwritten margin note: right to participate w/ participate]

[6] These other rights, those belonging to the so-called second or third generation, must be evaluated (Méndez 2004). However, this book is not intended to discuss how and which rights or freedoms must be considered new constitutive parts of democracy or whether they should be isolated from the democratic definition (e.g., habeas data). Moreover, rights per se are problematic as well; "for instance, the freedom of speech can become the freedom to slander or the freedom to incite via hate speech. The freedom of the press can become the freedom to libel and defame one's political opponent. The freedom of religion can become the freedom to create hatred and significant social cleavages. And, the freedom to associate can become the freedom to revolt or even overthrow the democratic government itself" (Marcus, Mease, and Ottemoeller 2004: 115).

[7] Clearly I am speaking here of the type of inclusion that incorporates people within reasonable limits of age, mental health, and so forth.

to participate? Also, if by democracy, we understand a political regime to be one that makes electorally binding political decisions from time to time, which is more democratic – the country that votes for the executive every four years (e.g., Chile) or that in which citizens vote every six years (e.g., Mexico)? It is difficult to gauge the quality of democracy based on these characteristics alone.

As an example of the dimension of quality versus quantity of democracy, *The Federalist Papers* opens an interesting line of reasoning with regard to the discussion of the frequency of elections. Elections are not to be held just once in a while, they state; they should be as frequent as possible for electoral accountability, and a finer tuning between voters and the elected should take place:

As it is essential to liberty that the government in general should have a common interest with the people, so it is particularly essential that the branch of it under consideration should have an immediate dependence on, and an intimate sympathy with, the people. Frequent elections are unquestionably the only policy by which this dependence and sympathy can be effectually secured. But what particular degree of frequency may be absolutely necessary for the purpose, does not appear to be susceptible of any precise calculation, and must depend on a variety of circumstances with which it may be connected (Madison in Hamilton, Madison, and Jay 1961: 295).

Despite Madison being supported by data showing that "the longer the period between elections the less responsible or the more independent representatives will behave relative to the desires of their polity" (Amacher and Boyes 1978), he does not represent a uniform consensus on this topic. For some elitists, the frequency of elections is rather problematic:

The kind of democracy that thus survives is not, however, popular rule, but rather an intermittent, sometimes random, even perverse, popular veto. Social choice theory forces us to recognize that the people cannot rule as a corporate body in the way populists suppose. Instead, officials rule, and they do not represent some indefinable popular will. Hence that can easily be tyrants, either in their names or in the name of some putative imaginary majority. Liberal democracy is simply the veto which it is sometimes possible to restrain official tyranny (Riker 1982: 244).

This concern is unfounded. In modern and complex societies, elections are not to be held every day, and representatives are thought to be as professional as possible. Yet, as mentioned in Chapter 1, no matter how well intentioned our leaders are, the infamous "corridors of power" generate incentives for perverse interests and behaviors (Pettit 2003). Therefore, contemporary democracies must be able to provide tools for controlling these behaviors both horizontally (by other institutions) and vertically (by citizens).

When we compare the quality of democracy across countries, we are not comparing which countries are more democratic. Rather, we are analyzing in which countries democracy performs better given some normative standards. Indeed, much of the debate about the quality of democracy is about the identification of these normative standards (Altman and Pérez-Liñán 2002). According to Coppedge, "[W]e should seek the path of finding out what constitute 'more' and 'better' democracy and what implies 'less' or 'worse' democracy. To do so, we need not formulate any absolute right or list of absolute rights; we only need to know how much of each good corresponds to what degree of democracy" (Coppedge 2004: 246). This is especially important because "there cannot exist a theory that establishes a firm and clear line that would determine [. . .] *a minimal sufficient set* [of political rights]" (O'Donnell 2004b: 18).

I claim that a country that allows its citizens to activate MDDs, either in its proactive or reactive forms, is more democratic than one that does not. This claim does not constitute "just another" voluntaristic inclusion in the *set of rights* we have discussed so far, and this statement is not coming from nowhere. Rather, it is linked directly to democracy and even to the first predemocratic ancestors of contemporary democracy and deals with the first polyarchy transformation. We may or may not like it, but there are very few institutions as embedded in the democratic tradition as the citizenry deciding whether its political concerns are just – concerns that are concomitantly defined by the citizens themselves. Moreover, "the institutions and mechanisms of representative democracies are the main objects of the analysis of the quality of a democracy. *This is not to ignore direct democracy as the highest expression of democratic quality*, but to acknowledge the secular experience of representative democracies and their real potential for improvement" (Morlino 2004: 13; italics are mine).

2. Do Mechanisms of Direct Democracy Represent *More* and *Better* Democracy?

Direct democracy does not constitute a panacea for solving problems of current democracies, nor is it something intrinsically wrong to be avoided at any price. Indeed, discussions about "direct democracy" as such will not reach a safe harbor simply because they involve consequentially different nuances and institutions, as discussed in Chapter 1. As is evident, the appraisal of direct democracy in general will depend on how, why, where, when, and which institutions of direct democracy are used. As Suksi remarks, "[W]hen speaking about the institution of the referendum, it is often forgotten that it is not an indivisible monolith, but a multidimensional phenomenon, consisting of diverse forms all of which have their special features" (1993: 3).

Despite having been excluded from most definitions of democracy with which comparative political scientists work (including even those maximalist definitions of high quality of democracy), direct democracy is intimately related to democratic theory and some aspects of direct democracy; that is, CI-MDDs are the true descendants of the purest democratic ideal. Within the realm of democratic regimes, the debate between supporters and detractors of direct democracy has been extensive. Even though this has not traditionally been a major topic of democratic theory, the debate is of increasing political theoretical relevance. This section addresses the most prominent concerns with regard to the use of CI-MDDs. Before I continue, I emphasize that the bottom line of this debate can be reduced to the following: Opponents of direct democracy usually tend to accuse it of using stereotypes of direct and representative democracy. Indeed, most (if not all) of the concerns raised by those who tend to be reluctant about the possibilities of CI-MDDs can be turned around and eventually expressed as legitimate concerns regarding representative democracy itself. Yet, despite the fact that this comparison is not extremely lucid in its attempt to undermine the assessment of direct democracy, it helps us to be more careful in our own assessment.

Direct democracy has become increasingly relevant during the last few decades. On the one hand, the rise of single-issue interest groups drive measures onto the ballot, and popular distrust of government and politics leads citizens to go over leaders' heads by voting on policies directly.[8] Additionally, as technical advances in communication and media provide citizens with better access to information, their ability to vote on more political issues is increased. Because of these factors, many argue that citizens should be expected to employ MDDs more frequently. The assumption behind this claim is that citizens should be given the opportunity to decide directly on policy matters.

On the other hand, some scholars argue that political, economic, or social groups could easily use direct democracy for their own particular benefit, making it, in the end, harmful to representative democracy. As Bell mentions, "[T]here is ample reason today to give serious consideration to the founding fathers' cautious approach to direct democracy. They were closer than we to those basic structural arrangements by which individual rights in a free society must be protected against the tyranny of the majority" (1978: 28–29). In the same vein, scholars claim that citizens lack all the information needed to make decisions about complex political issues.[9]

A group of outstanding political scientists have indirectly explored the tensions between representative democracy and such decision-making forms.[10] In general, these social scientists have not been comfortable with MDDs because of their "uncontrollable and unforeseeable" character (Suksi 1993). Moreover, some scholars, such as Gamble (1997), go beyond this uncertainty and claim that MDDs are essentially reactionary. The central arguments against MDDs maintain that a) they weaken the power of the representatives elected by the citizens; b) the ordinary citizen is unable to make informed (or rational) decisions about extremely complex problems; c) the MDD actor behaves as the electoral actor – alone, by him- or herself, and without debate or participation, so there is no chance to measure the intensity of beliefs; d) it establishes a zero-sum game, in which the majority wins everything and the minority loses all,

---

[8] In this sense, the Italian experience could be considered the clearest example of bypassing the representative structures of the country by referendums. They are also "symptomatic of a more general crisis of representative democracy and the resurgent ideas of direct democracy" (Uleri 1996: 120).

[9] For a good treatment of the effect of information on voting behavior regarding direct legislation, see Gerber and Lupia (1995), Gerber (1999), Lupia (1994), and Lupia and McCubbins (1998).

[10] Cunningham (2002), Dahl (1989), Phillips (1991), Sartori (1987), and Held (1993).

leaving no possibility for compensation or concessions regarding the problems presented; furthermore, there is a risk of the tyranny of the majority over the minority; and e) there are extra costs in terms of time and money. Finally, as Parkinson observes, "[I]n complex societies deliberative participation by all those affected by collective decision-making is extremely implausible" (2003) or even manipulated by political elites (Higley and McAllister 2002).[11]

In Uruguay, which has used CI-MDDs far more frequently than any other country in Latin America, the negative implications of this popular decision-making tool have been highly debated. Professor Romeo Pérez Antón considers that "since 1967 [the Uruguayan] governmental regime involves at the same time presidentialist, parliamentarist, and direct democracy institutions, which consequently results in a system of mutual paralyzations" (Interview, September 1995). Before the two popular initiatives of 1994, the influential Uruguayan weekly report *Búsqueda* argued:

(...) It is a new kind of corporativist behavior, which is without doubt a worrisome fact because it produces distortions, threatens the actions of the next government, and tries to incorporate into the Constitution the specific interests of particular groups in society. Nobody could affirm that the history of plebiscites is the history of democracy. Moreover, what history teaches us is that usually corporativism and plebiscites go together, never for the people's welfare (Author's translation; *Búsqueda*, Nov. 1994: 2).

Yet those who support MDDs argue that "if enthusiasm for democracy is to be sustained, ways may have to be found to make individuals feel more involved" (*The Economist*, June 17, 1995: 21). One of the most outstanding premises of the supporters of MDDs is that the citizen feels more concerned with democracy because a) all of the issues can be contemplated and thus avoid the passage through intermediate organizations; as *The Economist* asserts, "more referendums might be an antidote to more lobbyists"; b) public decisions are achieved publicly; c) the popular will is more accurately expressed: "The popular will is the sum of the citizens' individual wills. When the will is expressed directly, without intermediation of any kind, it is bound to be expressed accurately" (Butler and Ranney 1978: 31); d) such public involvement combats apathy and alienation; the citizen will feel more concerned when issues relevant to the public are considered;[12] e) human potentiality is maximized (this premise is distrusted by the feminist critique of representative democracy); and f) as a pedagogical tool, increased opportunities for participation in the legislative process

---

[11] Kriesi gives another twist on the negative impact of direct democracy. He says: "The bad news is that uncertainty about how to vote is, in part at least, cognitively determined. That is, those who do not have a sufficient amount of cognitive resources at their disposal are more likely to be uncertain about how to vote, and, therefore, less likely to participate in the vote" (2002: 185).

[12] In a study carried out in Switzerland, Frey, Kucher, and Stutzer (2001: 271) show that the "reported subjective well-being of the population is much higher in jurisdictions with stronger direct democratic rights. This is not only the case because people value political outcomes higher but also because they derive utility from the political process itself." A similar argument was sustained by Olken (2008).

will make citizens more civilly aware and virtuous and, in some sense, freer (see Qvortrup 1999). In short, MDDs (especially from below) have been considered as the prescription for the current democratic disaffection that distresses most democracies. In the words of scholars who have studied this phenomenon:

According to numerous recent cross-national studies of public support for democracy, citizens of both well-established and newer democracies continue to share a strong commitment to the ideals and principles of representative democracy. Paradoxically, however, these same citizens are increasingly "critical" of and "dissatisfied" with the performance of their national democratic institutions. One response has been to call for the "re-invention of government" through the use of referendums and ballot initiatives (Freire and Baum 2003: 135).[13]

There is a recurrent group of challenges advanced by the literature against direct democracy. Of course, these concerns do not constitute a unified theory against direct democracy. Indeed, many of these fears contradict each other. On the one hand, one of the strongest concerns has been the risk of a tyranny of the majority over the minority. On the other hand, another recurrent apprehension is exactly the opposite: the impossibility of finding majorities at all; in other words, the impossibility of majority rule.[14] There exists a certain tension between these arguments: Although MDDs play in favor of narrow (perhaps economic) interests, they also turn out populist policies. As we see, these arguments contradict each other. The evident contradictions in these positions do not imply that either is without merit.

a. Tyranny of the Majority and Cycling Decisions

The debate on the tyranny of the majority is not new. Aristotle was concerned with the fact that a democracy could easily lend itself to demagoguery – a concern shared by Tocqueville. However, the ideas of the Founding Fathers of the American Revolution provide the context for the extreme caution with which the subject matter is considered in modern times. Their utmost desire was the prevention of all forms of tyranny – including that of the government or the majority – through a system of checks and balances. They were rather sophisticated electoral engineers and were conscious of nearly every crucial trade-off that institutional design encounters. For instance, with regard to vertical accountability, they were aware that the social heterogeneity of a district, which is closely related to the number of people within it, affects the treatment of minorities.

In article 9 of *The Federalist Papers*, Hamilton argued that the tyrannical capacity of a majority would be constrained by the "enlargement of the orbit" (Hamilton, Madison, and Jay 1961: 41) and, in article 10, Madison advocated

---

[13] See also Frey and Stutzer (2000).

[14] Although those scholars fearing tyranny could be called, in this regard, the "liberals" because of their concerns regarding the protection of human independence, those in the second group could be called the "conservatives" because of their obsession with the order and stability of political outcomes.

that the area of a democracy be extended because, in small jurisdictions, "more frequently will a majority be found of the same party" and "more easily will they concert and execute their plans of oppression" (Hamilton, Madison, and Jay 1961: 51). This idea appears several times but is best spelled out in article 51: "[S]ociety itself will be broken into so many parts, interests, and classes of citizens that the rights of individuals, or of the minority, will be in little danger from interested combinations of the majority" (Madison in Hamilton, Madison, and Jay 1961: 292).

Still, there is no consensus on how the shape and size of districts might encapsulate the risks of a majority tyranny, and no more than anecdotal evidence has been traditionally presented from a theoretical perspective. Without a doubt, most of the statements with regard to this issue are theoretical conclusions, such as Svensson's assertion that popular initiatives and referendums are "better suited for small and homogeneous societies than large societies with many conflicting interests" because the larger the community, "the more interests and opinions exist, and the more difficult it is to achieve complete or just approximate agreement and correspondence between popular opinions and policies" (2007) – exactly the opposite of Hamilton's concerns.

In the last ten years, however, an especially noteworthy debate emerged on this subject, triggered by a controversial article by Gamble (1997). Gamble's hypothesis claimed that "without the filtering mechanisms of the representative system, direct democracy promotes the tyranny of the majority as the scope of civil rights conflicts expands and citizens vote on civil rights laws" (1997: 245). Studying seventy-four MDDs in five areas of civil rights in California, she claimed that "anti civil rights initiatives have an extraordinary record of success: voters have approved over three-quarters of these" (1997: 261). Not only was this position directly challenged by Frey and Goette, who claimed that in Switzerland, only 23 percent of MDDs had a conservative character (1998),[15] demonstrating that direct democracy protects civil rights, but more interestingly, Donovan and Bowler, using the same type of initiatives in the same jurisdictions, showed results that contrasted with Gamble's. They found that only 18 percent of MDDs could be said to have produced decidedly antiminority policy outcomes (Donovan and Bowler 1998: 1022). They went a step further, controlling for the jurisdiction's population to test whether MDDs treated minorities better in larger jurisdictions, as could be inferred from Publius.

---

[15] Of course, they claim this despite controversial measures having been put forward in Switzerland, such as the popular initiative in November 2009 for a constitutional amendment banning the construction of new minarets. This popular initiative was approved by 57.5 percent of the participating voters (turnout was 53 percent). The initiative was triggered by a conservative alliance of the Swiss People's Party and the Federal Democratic Union. The Federal Council and the Federal Assembly, along with many social organizations (e.g., the Amnesty International's Swiss office, Swiss Federation of Jewish Communities, and Federation of Swiss Protestant Churches, among many others), recommended that the proposed amendment be rejected as inconsistent with basic principles of the constitution. As expected, the ban provoked reactions from within Switzerland and the rest of the world.

They showed strong evidence that the larger the constituency, the more supportive of gay rights the legislation outcomes were.

The Donovan and Bowler study shows that minorities are less protected
by direct democracy in "smaller communities – places that we assume have
a greater homogeneity of interests." But they are also careful not to make
theoretical derivations from this information: "[T]his evidence should not be
used to imply that direct democracy per se is abusive of minorities" (Donovan
and Bowler 1998: 1023). Indeed, they open the question of whether there is a
substantial difference in how minorities are protected in *any* small community
under *any* form of democracy (representative or direct). Thus far, evidence
suggests that the smaller the community – in terms of population – the lower
the level of protection that minorities receive (Wald, Button, and Rienzo 1996).

Perhaps there is no better place than the Alps (Switzerland and Liechtenstein) to illustrate how, through these types of mechanisms, other rights may be
considerably delayed. In 1968, there was a consultative vote in Liechtenstein
triggered by Parliament when the question arose of whether the right to vote
should be granted to women. On this occasion, women and men voted separately, and electoral records indicate that the female vote was barely positive
(50.5 percent in favor) and the male was negative (60.1 percent against). Three
years later, in 1971, men voted in a binding legislative plebiscite to confer these
rights on women, and the vote again was negative (51.1% against), although
closer to an even fifty–fifty than before. This happened again in 1973, but the
negative vote was larger this time (55.9 percent against). Women had to wait
another eleven years, until 1984, before their national voting rights were finally
accepted by men. Equal rights for women and men were later introduced in
the constitution by the decision of the *Landtag* (Liechtenstein's Parliament)
without a popular vote in 1992, and a law on equal rights for women and men
followed in 1999.[16]

In Switzerland, the historical record shows a less linear development than
in Liechtenstein. After World War II, with the incorporation of the Social
Democrats into government, an expansion of the social security system
occurred with a concomitant invigoration of women's movements. After all,
women were the backbone of the Swiss economy during the war (men were
mobilized in the army for long periods of time). Although the political environment seemed to be fertile for the extension of citizens' rights to women,
a complete wave of cantonal popular votes thwarted any aspiration in this
regard. It was only in 1957 that the executive sent a bill to the Federal Assembly, and by late 1958, a referendum campaign was already in progress. On
February 1, 1959, a majority of men rejected women's right to vote – 654,939
(66.9 percent) versus 323,727 (33.1 percent) for. In 1971, the Federal Council

---

[16] It is worth noting that the Princely House law is the only area left without gender equality.
Only men have the right to vote within the House of Liechtenstein and only men can become
ruling prince of Liechtenstein, an office that retains important political power (he can veto and
even refuse to sign a law).

pushed again for the extension of rights, and this time an obligatory referendum was also held on February 7. The women's vote was accepted by a majority of 621,109 (65.7 percent) versus 323,882 (34.3 percent). Although Switzerland conferred electoral rights to women in 1971 at the federal level, some cantons maintained their traditional exclusion of women into the late 1980s. Actually, it was not until 1990 that the Federal Supreme Court forced the last canton – Appenzell Innerrhoden – to abide by the federal law and grant women the vote on local issues at the Landsgemeinde.

Most agree that democracy is simply the government of the majority while respecting the rights of minorities, but others warn about the risks of majorities bypassing minorities' rights and behaving as steamrollers in society, as one might infer from social-choice theorists. This is especially problematic when we take into consideration some elements of the very same social-choice theory, such as the Arrow's paradox or, going further back, Condorcet's paradox of voting (Arrow 1963 [1st ed., 1951]).[17]

It has been argued from social and rational choice perspectives that there is not one universal and fair system of aggregation of interests; thus, the use of majority rule can lead us down the road toward cycling decisions and, consequently, a road of instability. The basic tenet is that

a vote by members of the same population among several options can yield different results depending upon whether a series of pair-wise votes is taken or voters assign weights to each of the options, called, respectively, a "Condorcet" vote and a "Borda" count (. . . .) This is because an option could be knocked out of the running in an early vote in a Condorcet series even though it had more points on a Borda count than one that survived the pair-wise voting (Cunningham 2002: 66).

The literature on the problems of preference aggregation is amazingly large and too diverse for the scope of this book; however, this literature has made us think in a cleaner, more parsimonious, and more ordered manner.[18] Nonetheless, the question is how useful these theories are in understanding real-world politics – how often is this circulation of votes in the direct democracy game seen (and why not in representative democracy as well)?[19] Mechanisms of direct democracy are majoritarian institutions par excellence. If there is any place where we ought to find cycling, it is within the realm of direct democracy, yet we have not. Even in countries where CI-MDDs are comparatively easy to trigger, such as in Switzerland, we have not witnessed any indication of cycling. One of the plausible reasons is that a decision taken through a direct democratic procedure enjoys a large legitimacy that hardly anyone wants to immediately

No cycling [handwritten margin note]

---

[17] See also Downs (1957) and Riker (1982).
[18] For examples of uses of formal modeling in regard to direct democracy, see Ingberman (1985) and Hug (2004).
[19] Setälä does a great treatment of theoretical dilemmas of social choice applied to direct democracy (1999a: chap. 2).

erode.[20] The closest example we have seen is the reiterated use of direct democracy procedures for decades to decide certain issues such as alcohol prohibition in New Zealand, which has been voted on dozens of times since the late nineteenth century. However, this does not imply a circulation of majorities at all; rather, it highlights the impossibility of finding any.

b. Erosion of the Power of Elected Officials

It has been also argued that CI-MDDs abate the power of the representatives elected by the citizens (Butler and Ranney 1978) and temper the role of political parties in the policy-making process. This opens the potential for the production of inconsistencies and incoherence because the legislature pushes for one aim while the citizenry pulls in the opposite direction. However, if this is the case, we should not be questioning direct democracy per se but rather the political parties in a given democracy. I am not claiming, however, that political parties must be perfectly reflective of citizens' preferences at all times and in all policy spaces. I simply mean that without somewhat stable (i.e., institutionalized) political parties with a reasonable degree of established, programmatic commitments to the electorate, it is impossible to articulate the cycles of accountability that characterize representative democratic governance (Kitschelt, Hawkins, Luna, Rosas, and Zechmeister 2010).[21]

In a democratic context, CI-MDDs can be used to threaten the government and ultimately to force a change in the status quo. In this case, evidence of the success of a potential CI-MDD is provided by a change in the government's political actions. Logically, the lack of a CI-MDD could mean a positive reaction by the government in the direction of the issue sought by the CI-MDD organizers. Therefore, the potential for use of a CI-MDD alone can make it unnecessary to follow through. Paradoxically, in this scenario, evidence of

---

[20] Anthony Downs (1957) delivered a model of political competition of candidates with respect to their ideological position in a single-issue dimension. Along a single-issue dimension, a two-party competition is expected. Parties will experience strong pressures to converge upon the position of the median voter if they wish to avoid electoral defeat. Important works have been devoted to showing that this predicted convergence is only partial in real life given that Downs's theory relies on highly restrictive assumptions; for example, much of this literature has been centered on direct democracy or voting in committees, where very few players are involved. The median-voter theorem produces a Nash equilibrium, in which no player has anything to gain by changing strategies unilaterally. The literature that emanated from Downs's seminal work was strongly influenced by Duncan Black's median-voter model (1958), probably one of the founding texts of social-choice theory, and by Kenneth Arrow's discussion of the dilemmas of aggregating single-peaked individual preferences into a collective choice (1963 [1st ed., 1951]). All of them were predated by Harold Hotelling's model of spatial competition – the location of different sellers in a market with respect to one another, probably the pioneering paper in public choice (1929). When a policy space has three or more dimensions, no Condorcet winner will exist under majority rule. Even in a two-party contest or a two-sided debate, competition is enormously unstable, as McKelvey-Schofield shows (1986).

[21] See also Aldrich (1995); Cain, Ferejohn, and Fiorina (1987); Cox (1987); Mayhew (1974); and Freidenberg (2003).

failure is provided by the CI-MDD's presence. If a CI-MDD is deployed, it means that, as a mechanism of threat, it did not work. Yet do legislators really take into consideration potential MDDs when they legislate? Empirical research supports this tenet: More than 70 percent of Uruguayan legislators consider that the presence of a potential referendum is a sufficient reason to look for a broad consensus within the political parties (for further discussion, see Chapter 8 and Appendix 2). Evidence suggests that this potential influence is also robust in other latitudes, for example in the Swiss experience. "In Switzerland, when a deliberative consultation is effectively requested, it is already a sign of failure of 'Konkordanz'" (Papadopoulos 1995: 430). Indeed, "ironically, the blunt majoritarianism of the referendum has done much to foster the politics of consensus" (Kobach 1994: 151). For this reason, a proper study of CI-MDDs ideally should not only analyze the CI-MDDs held but also take into account the successful attempts at holding CI-MDDs without their actual occurrence (see also Gerber 1999).

The presence of this type of mechanism usually opens the door for cooperation between branches of government and more fine-tuned legislation with regard to citizens' preferences (closeness with median voter [Hug 2004] or even "inducing sitting legislatures to govern more effectively" [Lupia and Matsusaka 2004: 463]). Regardless, Ladner and Brändle (1999) advance a series of arguments about why we may see some negative impacts on the relationship between political parties and direct democracy – some of them already found in work by Kobach (1993). It is clear that even in Switzerland, by far the world champion of direct democracy, most legislation and governmental activity is run as in the purist representative democracy (Serdült 2007). Thus, the evidence demonstrates that we should not infer any downgrading in the crucial role played by political parties or any other representative institution should they coexist with direct democracy.

Although there is no universal pattern of relationship between parties and MDDs, evidence does not suggest that direct democracy necessarily undermines parties' power more than it normally would in its absence. Indeed, Altman shows that when Uruguayans go to the polls to vote on a CI-MDD, their vote choice is motivated primarily by party loyalty rather than by their reaction to economic conditions (2002b). In Switzerland, political parties are also crucial players in the direct democratic game (Kriesi 2006) and elsewhere (Hobolt 2006b). This gives parties a greater role in mediation in parliaments (Lutz 2006). In Italy, "parties were the main actors in referendums as far as the mobilization of voters was concerned. Indeed, the parties gave birth to a variety of alignments, some supporting mobilization and competition, while others encouraged abstention and effective demobilization" (Uleri 2002). In Ireland, although voting behavior at referendums has been heavily conditioned by the positions taken by the political parties, parties' advice on voting at referendums carries less weight than it did in the past (Gallagher 1996b: 94), while "the Austrian experiences make clear how the instrument of the initiative has an in-built advantage for the party employing it" (Müller 1999: 303).[22]

These examples of the role of political parties regarding MDDs contrast to a considerable extent with their roles in other realms. In California, because party labels and incumbency are lacking, "the general willingness of the electorate to adopt new policies varies with economic conditions" (Bowler and Donovan 1998: 69). For that matter, across the United States, parties play a much less relevant role than in other democracies because of their "ideological unprincipledness, weak and undisciplined parties, and locality centered politics" (Sartori 1997: 89).

It is important to emphasize that there is an argument against the uses of MDDs that is closely related to the erosion of the power of elected officials, albeit in an indirect manner. I am referring to the claim that opening the lawmaking process to other actors, such as the citizenry, through MDDs makes the lawmaking process more complicated, longer, and more uncertain. Let me provide a graphic display of this argument.

Figure 2.1(a) represents a decision-making tree in a typical presidential regime without any form of direct democracy, and Figure 2.1(b) the same but in a presidential regime with the most commonly seen MDDs. Because 60 percent of all national MDDs between 1985 and 2005 transpired in presidential democracies (28 percent in parliamentary and 12 percent in semipresidential regimes), my examples are based on presidential regimes. In both figures (a and b), the first move is made by the legislature. To simplify, I decided to start with the legislative because, despite the fact that the executive is a major proactive player in the lawmaking process, the executive's bills have to be approved, modified, or rejected by Parliament.[23] This occurs even in cases when presidential decrees' control the legislative process (on this topic, see Negretto 2004).

In simple terms, in a typical presidential regime without any potential formal involvement of the citizenry in the process (Figure 2.1[a]), the legislature approves a bill, which may be accepted or partially/totally rejected by the executive. If the bill is rejected by the executive (partially or totally), the legislature either accepts the executive's observations or it overrides the presidential veto. Alternately, if the bill is accepted by the executive, it becomes a law. If the legislature overrides the veto, the executive usually has no recourse other than

---

[22] See also Kriesi (2006); Donovan and Karp (2006); de Vreese (2006); Scarrow (1999); and Ladner and Brändle (1999). It is possible to relate MDDs with almost any aspect of the political life, so the list presented here could be endless. Nonetheless, another issue that gained much attention, and deserves at least to be mentioned, is the relationship among the will of political elites, the media, and MDD outcomes. On this relationship, see Trechsel and Kriesi (1996), Kriesi and Trechsel (2008), and Trechsel and Sciarini (1998).

[23] It would be perfectly reasonable to suggest starting the figures with the executive sending a bill to Congress and continuing the game from that point. After all, even in cases where legislatures are supposed to play a much more significant role than is the continental average, such as in Chile, Costa Rica, and Uruguay, the executive constitutes a crucial player, impacting the legislative agenda by sending bills to the parliamentarian floor or vetoing laws.

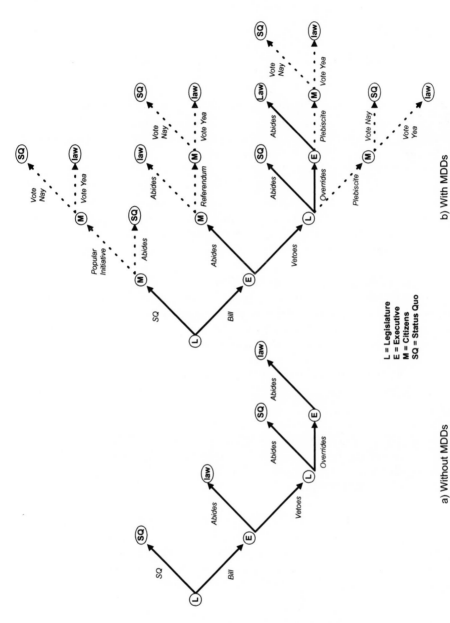

L = Legislature
E = Executive
M = Citizens
SQ = Status Quo

a) Without MDDs

b) With MDDs

FIGURE 2.1. Decision-Making Process in a Typical Presidential Regime with and without Mechanisms of Direct Democracy.

promulgating the law. Note that in these figures, I am not referring to all of the movements (back and forth) that a bill usually makes between legislative commissions or the lower or upper chambers of Congress.[24]

In a presidential regime with MDDs, the lawmaking process is evidently more complex than in the previous scenario. All of the players move basically in the same way as before. However, if the bill is accepted by the executive, it becomes a law or, if the president is not satisfied with the enacted law, he may call the citizenry to make the final decision on the matter with an executive facultative plebiscite, if such a prerogative exists. If the president is satisfied with the enacted law, the citizenry still has the opportunity to have the final word, calling a facultative referendum opposing the new law. If the referendum is approved, the law is derogated by the citizenry; otherwise, it is sustained.

In the case that the legislature is reluctant to change the status quo on certain topics, the citizenry can bypass Parliament by gathering enough signatures to force a vote on the issue via popular initiative. If the popular initiative is approved, no matter how unattractive the law or constitutional reform is in the eyes of the executive or legislative, it becomes law. Otherwise, the status quo prevails. Note that in these figures, I avoid making any assessment of players' potential payoffs in adopting a particular strategy because the costs and benefits associated with each move, for each player, for each particular case, would have to be taken into account.[25]

The elongation of the decision-making process with MDDs is a powerful argument because there are very few counterarguments. One simple question remains: Is a longer and more uncertain lawmaking process necessarily worse than a short and executive process? It could be argued that in the contemporary world, where some decisions need to be taken in matters of minutes at times, it is. Yet, overall, the entire discussion about whether MDDs attenuate the powers of elected representatives could be viewed as a consequence rather than a disadvantage – actually, having a second chamber weakens the power of the first chamber, but that is not necessarily a disadvantage.

c. Populist Policies and the Role of Money

California's Proposition 13 of 1978 constitutes a landmark in the study of direct democracy. In the proposition, Californians voted for drastically cutting property and other taxes in an act that, for many, appears to have been an act of selfishness by the homeowners.[26] This measure concomitantly spilled

---

[24] Starting with the legislature does not mean that the legislature is not reacting to a popular initiative campaign that could change the SQ. In other words, L is reacting in order to deactivate a measure that presumably is farther away from the L ideal point than the SQ or a bill that would pass presidential veto.

[25] For example, the number of legislators needed to override a presidential veto varies from country to country. Also, the popular support for certain decisions varies concomitantly with the issue at stake. Obviously, this is not a viable option in a large-N account such as the one presented.

[26] This proposition was officially titled the "People's Initiative to Limit Property Taxation," and popularly known as the "Jarvis-Gann Amendment."

over into several other states. The effect of this vote was enormous in the American literature dealing with direct democracy, important sections of which claim that direct democracy produces populist and irresponsible policies. "Who would be as insane as voting against her own interests?" it questions. Yet what this portion of literature does not emphasize enough is that California's Propositions 99 (1988) and 108 (1990) increased taxes and public spending.

Generally, the literature on the policy effects of direct democracy highlights two broad conclusions. First, "states with the initiative spent and taxed less than states without the initiative, they decentralized spending from state to local government, and they raised more money from user fees and less from taxes" (Matsusaka 2004:3). In that sense, these institutions exert leverage on policies toward a fiscally conservative direction. Second, "opinion surveys throughout the period show that a majority of people supported each of these policy changes" (Matsusaka 2004:3). Thus, policies adopted more closely reflect the policy preferences of the median voter (Hug 2004).

Both Swiss and American literatures on the policy effects of direct democracy have shown no patent evidence of an irresponsible use of direct democracy to reduce taxes; neither is there any vestige of a suicidal policy of reducing revenues with a simultaneous increasing of expenditures (Matsusaka 2004). In other words, the citizenry is capable of balancing (short-term) costs against (longer-term) benefits with regard to public finances (Kaufmann, Büchi, and Braun 2007: 82). Indeed, "policy outcomes are more efficient in direct than in representative democracies" (Feld and Kirchgässner 2001: 362). For example, in Swiss cantons where citizens have an impact on budgetary policy in direct legislation, they also have lower tax evasion levels than in cantons where they do not have such institutional prerogatives (Pommerehne and Weck-Hannemann 1996), and gross domestic product is, ceteris paribus, higher in more directly democratic cantons (Feld and Savioz 1997).

At the same time, some scholars argue that powerful groups could easily use direct democracy for their own particular benefit. According to Broder, "the experience with the initiative process at the state level in the last two decades is that wealthy individuals and special interests – the targets of the Populist and Progressives who brought us the initiative a century ago – have learned all too well how to subvert the process to their own purposes" (2000: 243).[27] Because "large sums of money can be used to shape and confuse voters' attitudes on specific ballot measures... those who can afford access to the mass media can unduly influence the outcome of direct ballot lawmaking"

---

[27] There is a consensus that the origins of direct democracy in the United States are strongly related to the Populist and the Progressive eras (late nineteenth century and beginning of the twentieth century, respectively). But the push toward greater involvement in direct legislation during these two eras had different motivations (Cronin 1999). The Populists sought to increase the power of the people as a way of returning to a simpler (less industrialized) way of life. In turn, the Progressives sought greater popular involvement as a way to minimize corruption, to counteract the concentration of wealth and the manipulation of the political apparatus by narrow economic interests (Gerber 1999), and to foster an "enlightened citizenship" (Smith and Tolbert 2004).

(Cronin 1999: 90). The concern regarding "the alleged transformation of direct legislation from a tool of regular citizens to a tool of special interests" has been called the *populist paradox* by Gerber (1999: 5) and is repeatedly raised in the U.S. literature on direct democracy (see, e.g., Magleby 1984). This is unsurprising.

Unlike presidential and legislative campaigns in the United States, where strict legislation in regard to contributions and expenditures exists, there is no limitation on contributions to and expenditures on direct legislation campaigns. The reasons for such uncontrolled campaigns come from a series of decisions by the U.S. Supreme Court: *Buckley v. Valeo* [424 U.S. 1 (1976)],[28] *First National Bank of Boston v. Bellotti* [435 U.S. 765 (1978)],[29] and *Citizens Against Rent Control v. City of Berkeley* [454 U.S. 290 (1981)].[30] Thus, critics of direct democracy should throw their darts in a reliable and valid manner: Popular votes are not to be avoided because money plays a role; rather, legislation controlling such influences should be reformed. Examples of the "big money" involved in the game include a record-setting $154 million that was spent on a single proposition (California's Proposition 87 in 2006 that would have placed a bonus profits tax on oil corporations), and $55 million that is likely to set the record for spending on a social issue (California's Proposition 8 in 2008 on same-sex marriage) (Initiative & Referendum Institute 2008).

Although it is reasonable to expect corporations and powerful citizens to try to maximize their benefits using all of the legal tools they have available, the inconsistency with which the U.S. legal system treats spending in national elections on the one hand and direct democratic elections on the other is non-sensical. However, even considering the legal inconsistencies on contributions and expenditures in both types of electoral campaigns extant in the United States, empirical research indicates that money definitely plays a role in the game of direct democracy, but a rather nuanced one. The literature also suggests that money matters if spent by opponents – but not proponents – of the political outcome (Gerber 1999).

In many states of the union, signatures are collected in what Magleby calls the "initiative industry," which buys – literally – citizens' signatures (at the time he wrote his book, each valid signature earned the collector one dollar; today, it may reach ten dollars per signature). This industry was stimulated in 1988 when, in *Meyer v. Grant* [486 U.S. 414 (1988)],[31] the U.S. Supreme Court struck down Colorado's law that made it a felony to pay petition circulators based on the argument that the Colorado ban violated the First Amendment.[32]

---

[28] See the full text of the case at http://supreme.justia.com/us/424/1/case.html (for greater detail on these judicial decisions, see Gerber 1999: 43–44).

[29] See the full text of the case at http://supreme.justia.com/us/435/765/case.html.

[30] See the full text of the case at http://supreme.justia.com/us/454/290/case.html.

[31] See the full text of the case at http://supreme.justia.com/us/486/414/case.html.

[32] According to the U.S. Supreme Court, circulating petitions involves "core political speech," and prohibiting the payment of petition circulators by sponsors severely burdens this speech – that is, violates their First Amendment rights – in two ways: "First, it limits the number of voices

"Without preexisting public support, the financial resources of business groups are ineffective in changing the status quo, and the financial resources of most citizen groups are too scarce to bring about much change" (Lupia and Matsusaka 2004: 472).

In 2006, the situation became worse when Governor Arnold Schwarzenegger vetoed a bill that would have banned paying petition circulators according to the number of signatures they collected. For the promoters of this law, paying on a per-signature basis was a strong incentive to dupe potential supporters of a cause. Also in 2005, he rejected a bill that would have forced the initiators of a petition to declare whether the signatures had been obtained by volunteers or paid workers and account for the five largest contributors to the campaign's account. The governor justified his stand on the basis that both measures have made it tougher to meet the requirements for petitions (Lawrence 2008).

Still, in terms of the "initiative industry," the American experience differs substantially from evidence gathered in other countries, such as Switzerland and Uruguay. In these two countries, there are no signs of a signature-gathering industry; however, in other nations, such as Colombia, this is not the case. During the winter of 2008, a campaign to allow the president a second consecutive reelection was carried out by the movement Primero Colombia ("Colombia First"). One of its officials, Luis Guillermo Giraldo, stated that the cost of the signature-gathering campaign for the constitutional reform was about $180 million (without considering nonmonetary contributions). The well-known Colombian weekly magazine *Semana* reports that at least one company received as a minimum $400 million for about 1,200,000 signatures (*La Semana*, November 8, 2008). Considering that more than 5 million signatures were gathered, the whole campaign would have cost at least 2 billion Colombian pesos.[33]

In short, the literature has offered important nuances about both the role that money plays in direct democracy and the potential populist syndrome affecting these mechanisms. Evidently, these arguments contradict each other: Either the few rich/wealthy/powerful advance their interests using these tools, or the many impose their will through voting on their preferred (majoritarian) desires. Contradictory arguments do not mean that both are similarly weak or empirically unjustified. They simply cast a shadow of doubt on those arguments by using both simultaneously. The problem of the involvement of money in direct democracy can be minimized by legislation and judicial acts, as it has been in many countries in regard to general elections. The question that persists

---

who will convey [the petition sponsors'] message and the hours they can speak and, therefore, limits the size of the audience they can reach. Second, it makes it less likely that [the petition sponsors] will garner the number of signatures necessary to place the matter on the ballot, thus limiting their ability to make the matter the focus of state-wide discussion" (Gloger 2006: 1–2). For the full text of the case, see http://supreme.justia.com/us/486/414/case.html.

[33] Controlling for the American versus the Colombian purchasing power parity in 2008, it would be approximately U.S. $3.50 per signature.

concerns citizens' competence in making wise decisions when faced with a choice at the fork in the road.

d. Competence and Alienation of Citizens

Some scholars argue that to avoid potential CI-MDDs, populist policies will flourish in an environment of direct democracy. This conjecture has led to concerns about rampant populism or instability. The basic principle of this idea is that correspondence between popular preferences and political outcomes does not mean necessarily that wise decisions have been made. The crucial point raised here is whether simple, normal, and mortal citizens are sufficiently able or competent to decide wisely on the matter of a given subject.

The incompetence argument has been a classic in the literature against direct democracy and, until recently, against representative democracy (e.g., regarding the extension of enfranchisement to certain groups in society). Assuming for the moment that citizens are incompetent, how can we explain, from a macro perspective, the survival of Switzerland after one hundred and fifty years of systematic use of direct democracy? One can easily argue that Switzerland's survival is due to the nation's extreme wealth, but this argument does not hold. When Switzerland began to develop MDDs, it was one of the poorest countries in Europe, and currently it performs quite well in GDP per capita, unemployment, competitiveness, human development, and many other aspects of social life. I am not claiming that such outstanding performance is a result of direct democracy but rather maintaining that direct democracy has not been as disruptive as some scholars would argue.

Yet it may be the case that a citizen, alone in the secrecy of the ballot, feels fear and incompetence in deciding particular issues. The incompetence argument was elegantly advanced by Montesquieu and revitalized by Schumpeter, Sartori, and other scholars. They claimed that "ordinary" citizens have only the capability to select people to decide on their behalf, not more. According to Sartori's prediction, direct democracy should be self-destructive and should have come to a rapid and catastrophic end on the reefs of cognitive incapacity (Sartori 1987). Nonetheless, it remains to be clearly demonstrated why a misguided choice about policy should be more destructive than a misguided vote for a party or president every four or five years.

Theoretically, the question on voter competence is crucial, but evidence – gathered thanks to advances in methodological instruments designed to answer it – seems to suggest that the people are capable of finding information and remaining consistent with their beliefs when faced with complicated issues in an MDD.[34] People behave differently and think differently; thus, "stereotypes about voter incompetence rely on shaky theoretical and empirical foundations"

---

[34] For a good treatment of the effect of information on voting behavior regarding direct legislation, see Gerber and Lupia (1995); Gerber (1999); Lupia and McCubbins (1998); Nadeau, Martin, and Blais (1999); and Clarke, Kornberg, and Stewart (2004). See also Christin, Hug, and Sciarini (2002) and LeDuc (2002).

(Lupia and Matsusaka 2004: 470). As a matter of fact, if there is an empirically oriented literature that has clearly evolved from a rather pessimistic view of citizens' abilities to decide (see the classic work of Campbell, Converse, Miller, and Stokes 1960), a much more positive view of our capabilities also exists (see, e.g., Lupia and McCubbins 1998).[35]

Current research suggests that citizens use simple pieces of information – heuristics – to make decisions on complicated matters (Lupia 1994). For Bowler and Donovan, citizens "vote in predictable ways, in ways that respond to information demands, and in ways that often are consistent with their ideology and... their interests. At a basic level, then, direct-democracy voters appear sufficiently competent to make informed choices" (1998: 41–42). They add that voters "appear able to figure out what they are for and against in ways that make sense in terms of their underlying values and interests. Failing that, others appear to use a strategy of voting *no* when information is lacking or when worries about general state conditions are greatest. Just as legislators do, these voters make choices purposefully, using available information" (Bowler and Donovan 1998: 168).

The fact that citizens use several types of information and do not necessarily respond uniquely to the question of the MDD, but that their votes are a mixed bag of reasoning, has been a topic for discussion as well, particularly with regard to votes that go beyond national borders, such as those related to the EU. It is interesting to note that it was the wave of national rejections on further European integration that triggered these concerns rather than the previous wave of support for Europe.[36] There is sufficient evidence that a citizen's vote is a complex combination of the voter's beliefs regarding the question addressed, the environment of the economy where that person lives, and political parties' advice, among other factors. According to Franklin and colleagues, the bottom line is whether citizens' votes represent "second order" elections or not (Franklin, Eijk, and Marsh 1995). If they are right, as Svensson (2002) argues, there may be negative implications for the use of popular votes at the transnational level.[37] As expected, they are only partially correct, as the work of Hobolt (2008) shows.

---

[35] See also Benz and Stutzer (2004).

[36] Danish citizens in 1992, already a part of the Common Market of Europe, rejected the Maastrich Treaty and rejected Euro accession in 2000. In 2001, the Irish rejected the Treaty of Nice, but authorities succeeded in passing the same issue a year later. In 2003, the Swedish followed their southern neighbors, rejecting the Euro accession, and in 2005, both the French and the Dutch rejected the European Constitution (Schuck and Vreese 2008). The last and soundest rejection occurred in the June 2008 referendum when the Irish rejected the Lisbon Treaty, which caused many to express their concern about how it was possible for 4 million Irish men and women to halt a process that affected 400 million EU inhabitants. The Lisbon Treaty was once more submitted to a direct popular vote on October 2009, but this time was approved by two-thirds of the vote.

[37] For the use of national MDDs in the process of European interaction, see also Kaufmann, Wallis, Leinen, Berg, and Carline (2006). On the potentially (ir)responsible uses of these MDDs, see Auer (2005, 2007).

The competence argument is emphasized by most critics of direct democracy, but it is usually accompanied by another argument: the potential alienation of citizens. Some scholars would claim that an excess of CI-MDDs may generate voter fatigue and alienate citizens (Hill 2003: 505–6). Certainly, this has been a recurrent argument for explaining the very low turnout in Swiss national elections (Bühlmann, Nicolet, and Selb 2006). Yet so far, the evidence only partially supports this claim. On the one hand, it is argued that a culture of active CI-MDDs stimulates citizens' political interest (Hajnal and Lewis 2003), knowledge (Mendelsohn and Cutler 2000; Smith 2002), and participation (Tolbert and Bowen 2008; Tolbert and Smith 2005; Wernli 1998). According to Tolbert and Smith, "turnout effects of ballot propositions are well established both in the US and cross-nationally" (Tolbert and Smith 2006: 33). Tolbert and Smith find that there is a positive association between the number of state ballots and electoral participation in both midterm and presidential elections.[38]

On the other hand, this positive view of the side effects of MDDs is challenged by other studies on direct democracy. For example, revising how different degrees of the use of MDDs at the cantonal level in Switzerland impact electoral participation, Freitag and Stadelmann-Steffen (2008) show a negative relationship between direct and representative democracy due to voters' fatigue and explain this by arguing that intensive direct democracy use makes regular national elections less significant than they would be without direct democracy. This argument on significance was first used by Jackman and Miller (1995) and constitutes a "classic" explanation for the extremely low rate of electoral participation in Switzerland; see also Bühlmann and Freitag (2006). In short, the literature has been rather eclectic on this topic.

3. Summary

Political institutions not only interact among themselves, they also influence and shape the attitudes, behaviors, identities, and preferences of individuals (Mainwaring 1993: 198). They also frame the choices available to individuals through incentive mechanisms (Hall and Taylor 1996; Schofer and Fourcade-Gourinchas 2001). Yet political representative institutions are far from perfect. In the typical representative democratic process, candidates may manipulate citizens to get elected (Maravall 1999) and leaders may cheat once in office (Stokes 2001) or advance their narrow, selfish interests (Pettit 2003). There is no vaccine against these risks.

---

[38] They assess an increase of one percentage point in turnout for the presidential race per initiative appearing on a state's ballot and two percentage points of turnout increase in midterm elections (Tolbert and Bowen 2008). See also Tolbert and Smith (2005). However, Schlozman and Yohai (2008), on the one hand (2008), and Cebula (2008), on the other, claim that voter initiatives in American states have restricted effects on turnout. Grummel (2008), conversely, finds that ethical policy ballot measures generate higher turnout in midterm elections but not in presidential elections.

From a neo-institutionalist point of view, CI-MDDs act as an "opportunity structure" (Freitag and Stadelmann-Steffen 2008). The bottom line of this chapter and, indeed, of the book is that CI-MDDs serve as an intermittent safety valve against the perverse or unresponsive behavior of representative institutions and politicians. On the flip side of the coin, with the coexistence of direct and representative democracy, politicians are subject to an additional, strongly binding external constraint on their behavior (Frey, Kucher, and Stutzer 2001).

Nobody can ensure that CI-MDDs are not risky insofar as they can embrace irresponsible results. However, this also can be claimed with regard to representative democracy itself. As we have seen, some crucial points within the discussion about direct democracy are based on stereotypes of how it is used, as well as on how representative democracy works. Thankfully, as scientific research progresses, many questions intimately related to CI-MDDs are starting to acquire evidence, fill in the blanks, or at the very least, provide partial answers.

About one hundred years ago, democracies were embroiled in ferocious discourses about the extension of suffrage. That discussion partially resembles the current debate on CI-MDDs. At that time, the debate took many diverse shapes, sizes, and degrees in different latitudes across the globe and usually turned focus to the levels of education and property ownership of those to be enfranchised. Those arguments employed ideas such as the following: "[I]ncluding those without property is going to produce irresponsible policies" (because, they claimed, *responsibility* was something that only those with property and wealth acquired). Other arguments touched on gender, race, and education. Currently, some would say that CI-MDDs would also produce irresponsible policies.

However, the irresponsible results of direct democracy, in the context of a liberal democracy, can be minimized, as with any other institution within a legal context that limits its potential scope of action. In other words, any CI-MDD should be constrained by the rule of law reigning in a given polity, which, of course, also includes the international conventions and agreements each polity has signed.

Democracy is, at least theoretically, the definitive distribution of political power, political authority, or "sovereign authority," in the words of Rousseau. Nevertheless, as we know, "this ultimate dispersal of power has never been realized" (Walzer 2004: 22) and may well never be.

3

Myths and Facts behind the Use of Mechanisms of Direct Democracy

A Worldwide Analysis

Why do some countries use mechanisms of direct democracy (MDDs) exceptionally frequently, others seldom, and still others never? No theory, so far, has comprehensively offered an answer to the previous question, and most conjectures are usually based on anecdotal or impressionistic evidence from a few selected cases. This chapter contributes to filling this lacuna by statistically analyzing the use of MDDs (either top-down or citizen-initiated) on an annual basis for every country worldwide.

Using a series of multivariate statistical analyses specially designed for "rare" events – such as negative binomial – and ordinary least squares (OLS), this study undermines many of the assumptions in the literature while confirming others. The findings suggest that both families of MDDs (citizen-initiated and top-down) are positively associated with the level of democracy, the age of the regime, the type of colonial heritage, and the number of MDDs used in neighboring countries in the immediate past. Contrary to commonly made theoretical assumptions, neither the size nor the social diversity of the population has any effect on the use of MDDs.

A great consensus exists on the contemporary challenges of representative democracies in several corners of the world. Some argue that a possible improvement for this state of affairs would be "to give back" to the citizens the capacity of control (reestablishing accountability), turning them into veto players through the activation of MDDs wherein specific policies could be proposed or vetoed and elected officials removed from their offices. But how MDDs or experiences with direct democracy serve to strengthen representative democracy is still an open question for two reasons.

First, unlike other aspects of contemporary political life, such as electoral or government regimes, which are mainly centered in technical discussions, the world of MDDs is, as noted in Chapter 1, profoundly related to the views we have about democracy, its citizens, and their capabilities as beings able to make accountable choices. The point is that "theoretical debates about direct and representative democracy tend to be based on unrealistic assumptions about how direct democracy – and sometimes how representative democracy – works" (Lutz 2006: 45).

Second, the bulk of the literature on MDDs focuses on a few countries in the "north" – particularly Switzerland (the world champion of MDDs) and, at the state level, the United States. These two cases are sometimes accompanied by other countries (usually European) and notably are influenced by those MDDs related to very particular issues, such as the progress of the European Union. The consequences of these research projects are evident: We now know a great deal about differences in the uses of MDDs, but if we continue to focus only on cases using MDDs in a certain part of the world, we will be unable to understand the different degrees of the use of direct democracy around the world. Thus far, no theory has comprehensively offered an answer to the previous question, and most conjectures are usually based on anecdotal evidence from a few selected cases.

This chapter contributes to filling this gap by analyzing an original database covering the use of MDDs on a yearly basis in the entire population of countries in the world in the last quarter of a century (from 1985 to 2009). The question that guides this chapter refers to the factors that shape the extent and manner of use of MDDs worldwide. A very preliminary answer relates to the basic constitutional setting within each country. For instance, some countries require that any constitutional change be approved directly by the citizenry at the ballot box (e.g., Switzerland and Uruguay), whereas other countries (most notably Germany) explicitly forbid any direct consultation of the citizenry at the federal level. This explains some differences in the use of MDDs, yet a logical concomitant question would be why some countries maintain their constitutional prohibition of the use of MDDs (either explicitly or implicitly). In this study, I refute the constitutional determinism that would have voters and governments forever fettered by constitutional provisions. Many of the constitutions of a rather large group of countries in the world provide for some sort of direct democracy, but MDDs are also carried out without explicit constitutional support (Suksi 1993).[1]

The hypotheses in this chapter originate in an increasingly complex literature, which so far has not raised this query and, to a much lesser degree, obviously has not answered it. Nevertheless, very feasible hypotheses and potentially interesting questions emanate from this literature: Are authoritarian regimes more disposed to employ MDDs than democratic ones (given that authoritarian regimes would be enchanted by the "democratic legitimization"

---

[1] Constitutions can be reformed to allow MDDs. It might be that the costs associated with reforms are too high to merit altering the constitution (super-majorities, etc.). Yet evidence shows that most countries with high records of MDD uses did not have these prerogatives in their first charters; they were changed. In the context of nondemocratic regimes, this problem is less relevant because a plethora of autocracies have resorted to MDDs regardless whether it was constitutionally allowed.

that a [rigged] popular vote would give them)? Do different government regimes (presidential, parliamentarian, mixed) or different degrees of democracy affect the use (and type) of MDDs? Do richer countries use more MDDs than poorer ones? Do countries facing tough economic times use MDDs more often than stable economies? Is there any diffusion effect in the use of MDDs worldwide?

The questions most closely related to the present study are found in Butler and Ranney (1978; 1994), Scarrow (2001), Qvortrup (2002), Altman (2002a), LeDuc (2003), Anckar (2004), Lutz and Hug (2006), Fiorino and Ricciuti (2006; 2007), and Breuer (2007). Indisputably, these works, among several others, shed light on the multifaceted use of MDDs in democracies. Yet these studies are based on a few select cases, comprising few countries with a certain commonality (e.g., region or size) or even subnational geopolitical units (see, e.g., Freire and Baum 2003; Frey and Stutzer 2000; Gerber, Lupia, and McCubbins 2004; Tolbert and Smith 2006; Tranter 2003; Uleri 2002).

If the question is which factors explain the use of MDDs, it makes no sense to select only cases with occurrences of MDDs. If the research agenda on direct democracy does not broaden its focus, it will never illuminate the question that motivates this piece. In other words, we should let our independent variables oscillate as much as possible rather than select on the dependent variable (King, Keohane, and Verba 1994). Consequently, we must study all countries regardless of their use of MDDs. We must consider different countries at different levels of development, on different continents, with different institutions, and with diverse uses of MDDs. In short, this chapter claims that we must move beyond the arena of established democracies. A different type of analysis is necessary if we are to reach a more solid conclusion about MDDs in the contemporary world.

This chapter proceeds as follows. First, I define the dependent variables of this study and describe how we operationalize them. Second, to estimate the causes behind the use of MDDs, several factors must be taken into account; therefore, I tackle the variables that the literature has put forth either directly or indirectly. Third, I present the statistical analysis and provide interpretations of the evidence. Finally, I discuss the conclusions that can be drawn from the study.

1. Global Trends in the Use of Mechanisms of Direct Democracy since 1900[2]

As discussed in Chapter 2, there is an overwhelming amount of discourse between those supportive to the use of MDDs and those who tend to be more than skeptical about these mechanisms. Each group tends to support its argument based on "assumptions" that, more often than not, lack rigorous analysis. For example, sympathizers of MDDs tend to affirm that the use of

---

[2] A previous version of this section was presented at the 2007 Joint Sessions of the European Consortium for Political Research (ECPR), Helsinki.

direct democratic devices is constantly increasing over time and that this is desirable. Alternately, those who are less enamored of the use of MDDs tend to assume that these mechanisms are strongly correlated with nondemocratic regimes (despite the obvious examples of Switzerland and others) and therefore should be normatively repudiated and their use halted. Thus, are MDDs more intimately related to autocracies than to democracies? Is there such an increase in their use, or are we simply paying more attention to a previously ignored phenomenon? Which side is correct?

Current literature on direct democracy tends to assume that the use of MDDs is on the rise worldwide. This assessment is usually based on a simple count of MDDs in a given series of years (e.g., by year, by decade), but it does not necessarily mean that countries are using more MDDs than before. Evidently, an increase in MDDs does not tell us anything regarding the spread of MDDs cross-nationally because the number of polities in the world has increased almost exponentially; thus, it is urgent to control for the number of countries before making any informed assessment.

Two evident problems arise before we are able to answer the former question: how to code MDDs and how to count countries. Coding and counting MDDs might seem a simple task, but it becomes much more complicated as soon as we dig deeper into the complex world of direct democracy. For instance, if in country *A* there was a direct vote on subject *Y* on a specific day, we would have no problem – there would be a unique MDD. But what happens if there were two unrelated votes on the same day? Still, this does not present a major concern: There simply *were* two MDDs. Italy is a good illustration of this example. On June 11, 1995, twelve unrelated MDDs were held simultaneously.[3] Indeed, fifty-seven MDDs transpired from 1985 to 2009. But these fifty-seven MDDs occurred on fifteen different dates. Therefore, for the period under consideration, Italians voted, on average, simultaneously on four different MDDs each time they arrived at the ballot box. Obviously, organizing a vote costs a significant amount of money, time, and resources; therefore, there is no sense in allowing simultaneous voting to artificially decrease the number of MDDs counted.

In a typical MDD, the vote usually takes the form of a "yes" or "no," but sometimes the list of choices is longer. For example, voters might have to opt among proposals "A," "B," and "C." In this case, the question is considered a unique MDD, regardless of the number of possible options it offers.[4] This type of MDD constitutes a marginal number of the MDDs within the universe of direct democracy (less than 3 percent). Moreover, in the country that has

[3] On June 11, 1995, Italians had to vote simultaneously on issues as varied as abolition of municipal powers regarding liquor licenses; revoking the law limiting the possession of TV stations to three; abolition of elections in two rounds from municipalities of 15,000-plus inhabitants; ending direct deduction of contributions to labor unions from salaries and pensions; restricting house arrest for Mafiosi to their proper residence; and so forth.

[4] On multiple alternatives referendums, see Lagerspetz (2006).

consistently used multiple choices most, New Zealand (i.e., the issue of alco-
holic prohibition has been considered more than thirty times since 1894),
citizens had to select from three possible alternatives.

The situation is simpler when a given MDD faces a counterproposal. For
instance, in a case where a group of citizens may force a vote on subject "A"
with solution "W," it could very well be that the legislature simultaneously
proposes a solution "Y" to subject "A." Thus, citizens would have to decide
whether to vote for "W" or "Y." If this is the case, we are faced with an
either/or situation, and I codify this as two MDDs. Counterproposals have
been widely used in Switzerland, Liechtenstein, and Uruguay.

In cases when citizens had to vote on a series of questions, each question was
coded as a unique MDD unless the choices were mutually exclusive. However,
there is an exception to this rule when the origin of the initiative differs (by
origin, I mean those individuals or institutions who trigger the MDD). For
example, if the executive branch of government fosters the approval of reform
"X" but the opposition legislative forces option "Z," the two alternatives have
been treated as independent observations, despite the fact that the alternatives
occur in the same event and are mutually exclusive. This exception does not
hold if the law stipulates the occurrence of an alternative choice.

Problems arise when we deal with "omnibus" questionnaires in which the
questions are not as unrelated as in the Italian case described previously. An
executive may send a complete set of questions to the citizenry – in this case:
Should we count the whole questionnaire as a unique MDD or each question
as an MDD? This question acquires more importance when we realize that the
responses also tend to be "omnibus" responses. Azerbaijan, Ecuador, Colombia, and Belarus are global leaders in this area because of their high frequency
of use of these type of questionnaires. In such a case, I consider each unrelated
question as a unique MDD despite being perfectly aware that sometimes by
knowing the answer to just one of these questions, the answer for the rest of
them can be estimated within a reasonable confidence interval.

If we want to control for the number of countries, it might seem logical to
simply count them. Yet counting countries, despite being a relatively easy task,
could easily become quite complex. One proxy usually used in the literature is
considering the member states of the United Nations (UN). This might be fine
if we include only countries that have existed since the mid-1940s, but even in
this case, not all countries wish to belong to the UN (e.g., Vatican City) and
some countries that are partially recognized by the international community
cannot belong to the UN because of the veto of some member of the Security
Council (e.g., Taiwan).

One possible way to count countries (at least since 1900) is to find some
resource explicitly acknowledging the number of countries in a given year. I
was unable to find any. Given the lack of a clear starting point in which to
know exactly how many countries are in the world, I use backward induction
to estimate the number of countries since 1900. We know all countries in the
world in 2010 and can easily go backward until a given country's official date

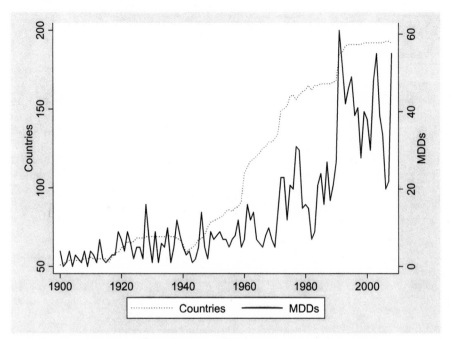

FIGURE 3.1. Countries and Mechanisms of Direct Democracy since 1900.

of independence, thus accounting for events such as the breakup of the Soviet Union or Yugoslavia, as well as the unification of Germany or Vietnam. There are, indeed, very few instances in which this number decreases (Figure 3.1).[5] Today, we can safely estimate that there are approximately two hundred countries in the world.

Figure 3.1 plots the evolution of the number of countries and the national uses of MDDs since 1900. It is evident that both measures tend to increase as time goes by, yet by using this figure alone, it is impossible to assess whether MDDs use grows faster than the number of countries. Figure 3.2, however, shows the change in the use of MDDs by country by year. MDDs are used almost twice as frequently today (about 0.2 MDDs per country per year) compared with fifty years ago and almost four times more than at the turn of the twentieth century.

2. Uses of Mechanisms of Direct Democracy within Different Regimes

Presumably, a regime, whether democratic or not, should have an enormous influence on the use of MDDs. Some scholars tend to assume that MDDs are

---

[5] The number decreases the most with the creation of the Soviet Union and its annexations immediately after World War II. Since then, we have seen at least two major waves of independence: the 1960s, mainly in Africa, and the 1990s after the collapse of the Soviet Union.

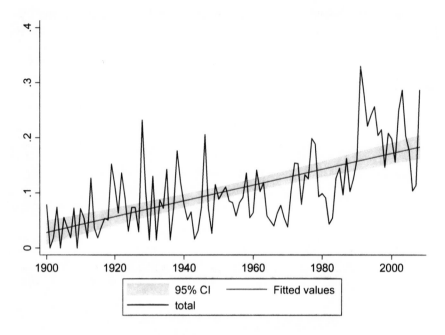

FIGURE 3.2. National Uses of Mechanisms of Direct Democracy per Country per Year since 1900.

a characteristic of nondemocratic regimes, whereas "real" democracies do not abuse such instruments (this contention is addressed profoundly in Chapter 4). Is this necessarily so? In this section, I attempt to distinguish the differences in nature of democracies and non-democracies.

It is not the intention of this research to contribute to the debate of what a democracy is or how to measure it. I simply use the debate to clarify – with all the limitations and shortcomings of the literature – the relationship between direct democracy and democracy. For the sake of parsimony, I simply use a procedural minimum definition of democracy. In this chapter, I use polyarchy (à la Dahl) as the minimum level of democracy; that is, a competitive and inclusive regime wherein basic freedoms are respected. Despite working with a minimal definition of democracy, there is an enormous amount of debate on how to code democracy.

What is the nature of the variable for democracy itself? Is democracy an either/or phenomenon, or we can conceptualize it as a continuum of different degrees? For some authors, democracy must be understood through a dichotomy (Huntington 1991; Przeworski, Alvarez, Cheibub, and Limongi 1996; Przeworski, Alvarez, Cheibub, and Limongi 2000; Przeworski and Limongi 1997); other scholars, however, prefer studying democracy from a trichotomous perspective (Mainwaring, Brinks, and Pérez-Liñán 2001). Still, most prefer the gray-shaded continuum. Elkins's (2000) study suggests that indices of democracy based on a continuum have a higher degree of validity and confidence than either dichotomized or even categorical measures.

Unfortunately, there are few instruments for coding democracy, and fewer still if we expand our universe of analysis and time frame. Generally, there are two available databases that travel well in terms of inclusion of cases and temporal domain:[6] Polity IV and Freedom House.[7] There are other indices that the literature tends to consider more solid, but they do not travel as far as the Polity IV and Freedom House databases in temporal or geographical terms.[8] Unfortunately, most indices in the first group provide basically the same information, so they are highly correlated. Ward writes, "It is truly remarkable that we have nine recognizable databases that contain comparative data about the regime characteristics among contemporary and historical polities and truly lamentable that they are correlated highly with one another. Instead of congratulating ourselves about their convergence, we should instead be worried about their independence" (2002: 46).

Hadenius and Teorell (2005) have found that the evidently robust combined-level correlations among different indices are noticeably weakened when computed at unlike levels of the democracy scale or within a critical zone proximate to the dichotomous separating line between democracy and autocracy. Moreover, it has been shown that Freedom House has political and geographical

---

[6] We could include Vanhanen's (2000) work because of the universe and the time span covered; however, despite Vanhanen's simplicity, his index is not considered because it is not sensible in the context of the fundamental characteristics of democracy as posed by Dahl.

[7] The Polity variable oscillates from −10 (high autocracy) to 10 (high democracy). This variable is computed by subtracting AUTOC from DEMOC (Marshall and Jaggers 2001). DEMOC ranges from 0–10, where 0 = low; 10 = high. The democracy score is based on the general openness of political institutions. This 11-point democracy score is constructed additively. AUTOC ranges from 0–10, where 0 = low; 10 = high. Autocracy Score is based on the general closeness of political institutions. The 11-point autocracy scale is constructed additively. This is available at http://www.cidcm.umd.edu/inscr/polity/index.htm. Since 1972, Freedom House has ranked all independent countries from 1 (the best score – highest level of democracy) to 7 based on measures of both civil liberties and political rights. These scores "provide a reasonably differentiated measure of democracy and offer comprehensive scope over nearly three decades" (Mainwaring, Brinks, and Pérez-Liñán 2001: 53). The formula utilized to normalize Freedom House scores is the following:

$$FH(Normalized)_{it} = \frac{(14 - (PR_{it} + CL_{it}))}{12}.$$

where PR_{it} is score of Political Rights of country i-*th* at year t, and CL is the score of Civil Liberties of country i-*th* at year t.

[8] To the best of my knowledge, there are few relative large-N indices that agree on the minimal and complete definition of polyarchy and that simultaneously pass the exam of conceptualization, measurement, and aggregation. These are the Latin American Democracies (Mainwaring, Brinks, and Pérez-Liñán 2001; 2007) and the Electoral Democracy Index ["EDI"] (Munck 2009; PNUD 2004). Other examples could be found in the indices developed by Bollen (1993) or Hadenius (1992), to mention only two. For the concept's conceptualization, measurement, and aggregation, see Munck and Verkuilen (2002) and Goertz (2005).

predispositions to the advantage of conservative regimes and Latin America, contrary to the leftist regimes in Central and Eastern Europe (Bollen 1993; Bollen and Paxton 2000; Mainwaring, Brinks, and Pérez-Liñán 2001). Also, Hadenius and Teorell demonstrate that Polity IV is more "dichotomous" in character, concentrating countries in general terms on either the far low or far high extremes of the scale, with relatively few in the gray zone.

Hadenius and Teorell, comparing Freedom House and Polity IV, concluded that "with the two indices deviating in different ways, it is reasonable to assume that the divergences should be evened out when we compute their mean score. [...] The *combined index has a better fit than both of its individual components* in terms of mean difference and spread. This holds for the entire time-period and for both sub-periods individually" (Hadenius and Teorell 2005: 37, italics are mine). Therefore, following their advice, I combine both normalized Freedom House scores and the polity measure from Polity IV as proxies of democracies for the entire period analyzed.[9]

Despite our tendency to colloquially categorize most regimes in an either/or manner with regard to the presence of democracy, a trichotomy achieves greater differentiation and forestalls several of the problems associated with gathering data that the fine-grained continuous measure of democracy would require. Of course, someone could ask why we should move from a continuous variable to a trichotomous one if that move will cause us to lose information. To this concern, I respond that, just for this section of the analysis, a trichotomy (democracy, hybrid, and autocracy) best illuminates the relationship I am trying to clarify: direct democracy in different types of regimes.[10]

Given the lack of precise cut points among democracies, hybrid regimes, and autocracies, I am forced to establish them. Indeed, the selection of the cut points must ultimately be arbitrary; I follow Epstein and colleagues, who base their research on Polity IV. They write, "Using the Polity IV scaling of regimes from −10 to +10, we categorize regimes as Autocracies (Polity value −10 to 0), Partial Democracies (+1 to +7), or (Full) Democracies (+8 to +10)" (Epstein, Bates, Goldstone, Kristensen, and O'Halloran 2006: 555).[11]

Figure 3.3 includes not only the number of countries but also their distribution in terms of this threefold category of regimes (democracies, hybrid, and authoritarian). Using Epstein's criteria for differentiating democracies from

---

[9] Of course, the combination is done basically for all countries of the world from 1972 to 2004 (the last year for which polity is available). For 2005 and 2006, the new measure is based uniquely in Freedom House. Before 1972, the variable FREEPOL comes only from polity of Polity IV.

[10] Of course, I am aware that "instruments designed to grade regimes in a wide range between full authoritarianism and full democracy might lack the sensitivity to discriminate within the pool of polyarchies clustered at one extreme of the range" (Altman and Pérez-Liñán 2002: 86).

[11] This procedure is also followed even by well-known and widely used databases that collapse their respective continuums into categorical measures (Freedom House into democracies, partial democracies, dictatorship; Bertelsmann Transformation Index into democracies, defective democracies, highly defective democracies; UN Development Programme [UNDP] into high, medium, and low human development; and so forth).

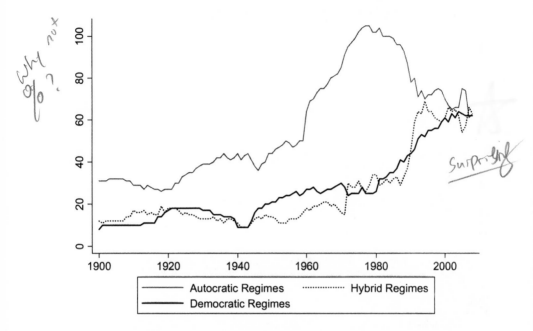

FIGURE 3.3. Number and Type of Countries since 1900.

autocracies and hybrid regimes and combining it with Freedom House, it can be seen that despite the growth of democracies, they are far from being the most common regime worldwide. Indeed, democracies make up only one-third of all countries.[12]

Figure 3.4 summarizes the answer as to which regime type tends to use more MDDs. This figure does not, of course, give any consideration to controls (e.g., the number of countries belonging to a certain regime type). As shown in the figure, almost forty national-level MDDs are predicted per year, worldwide, during the first years of the twenty-first century. This graph also sheds light on how different regimes use direct democracy. It notes that the use of MDDs is concentrated heavily in the democratic world, followed by hybrid regimes, and finally by autocracies. Since the 1950s, democracies have pulled away from other regime types in terms of the number of MDDs used. This demonstrates a significant increase in the levels of MDD use compared with the final decades of the previous century.

Nonetheless, once we control for the number of countries belonging to different categories (democracy, hybrid, and autocracy), the picture changes drastically. The predicted number of MDDs per country-year within the three types of regimes is conspicuously superior in democracies versus other regime

---

[12] Freedom House uses a much more relaxed cutting point among these three types of regimes, arguing that 64 percent of the countries today are "electoral democracies." See http://www .freedomhouse.org/template.cfm?page=368&year=2007.

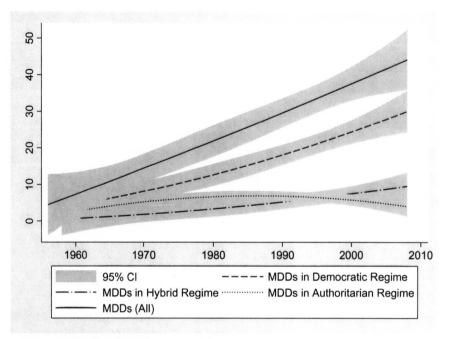

FIGURE 3.4. Predicted Mechanisms of Direct Democracy over Regime Type (1955–2009).

types. In Figure 3.5, (unlike in Figure 3.4), democracies are not mixed with other types of regimes (as seen by the lack of an overlap in the confidence intervals, the gray bands).

However, caution is required when analyzing these figures. Given that these figures are based on aggregated data, they do not tell us anything about how many countries in each category use MDDs. This is important because it may be the case that a unique democracy held a great number of MDDs, whereas in the other regime types, the use of MDDs was spread more evenly across several countries. Indeed, by assuming an even distribution of MDDs within each of the regime types, we would be committing a gross error whereby inferences about the nature of individuals are based solely on aggregate statistics collected for the group to which those individuals belong (type of regime/country). These figures, however, can tell us that in general terms, MDDs do not belong only to nondemocratic regimes. Quite to the contrary, as far as the evidence has shown, MDDs belong much more to the democratic world than to any other (hybrid or authoritarian) regime.

3. Explaining the Reasons behind the Use of Mechanisms of Direct Democracy

This section contains a cross-national, longitudinal analysis of the uses of MDDs from a global perspective. The universe of the analysis consists of all

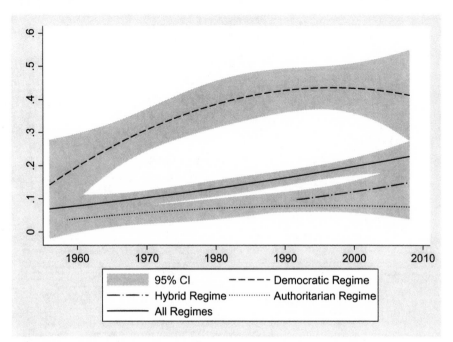

FIGURE 3.5. Ratio of Mechanisms of Direct Democracy by Country-Year by Type of Regime (1955–2009).

countries in the world but, given research limitations, I have opted to limit the longitudinal analysis to the last twenty-five years (from 1985 through 2009). Basically, this database provides a yearly picture of each country, totaling almost five thousand observations, and includes information about the use of different types of MDDs in each country, plus the independent variables. The objects of study at this stage are the tools of direct democracy used at the *national* level only; I am not considering nonofficial or subnational MDDs. Also, I must emphasize that in this chapter, I am studying the actual use of MDDs and not the legal possibility for their realization, as do Hug and Tsebelis (2002). Therefore, I am not dealing with legal and constitutional details.[13]

After subtypes of MDDs are taken into consideration, a first snapshot of the past twenty-five years suggests a rather ambiguous picture. No obvious tendency regarding the use of MDDs is visible, as demonstrated in Figure 3.6. Given that a potential finding of a tendency toward more (or less) use of different types of MDDs worldwide is, after all, an important point of

---

[13] Some works emphasize that more than 70 percent of countries in the world have some provisions for holding MDDs. These provisions are "not mere relics of long-forgotten commitments to ideals of participatory democracy known in Athens" (Qvortrup 2002: 1). As a matter of fact, more than 90 percent of the countries in the world today have experienced at least some MDDs (Kaufmann, Büchi, and Braun 2007).

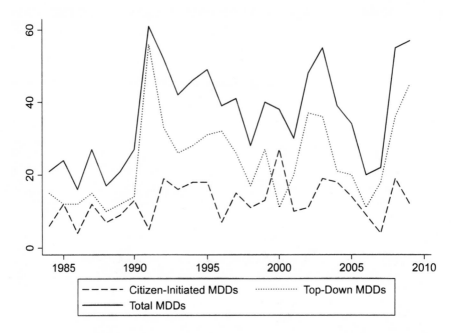

FIGURE 3.6. Worldwide Trends in the Use of Mechanisms of Direct Democracy.

this analysis, I smooth the data with the LOWESS function (Figure 3.7).[14] Figure 3.7 is more readable because it allows the general tendencies of the parameters to be understood. It can be seen from the figure that although there is a drastic increase in use of MDDs from the mid-1980s to the mid-1990s, from the mid-1990s to 2009 their use seems to have mostly stagnated.

Overall, I have registered 949 MDDs, of which 328 have been initiated "from below" and 621 "from above." The database constructed relies heavily on the C2D Database,[15] *Suchmaschine für direkte Demokratie,*[16] and on other sources of information (e.g., Keesing's Worldwide, international press).[17] The database includes 4,734 observations. Each observation corresponds to a country-year and the number of times MDDs occurred that year. The maximum value acquired by an observation is twenty-nine (by Azerbaijan in 2009). I have also determined whether the MDD was top-down (in which case the maximum value corresponds also to Azerbaijan's plebiscite of March 2009)

---

[14] LOWESS acronym comes from "locally weighted scatter plot smoothing." See Cleveland (1979).
[15] See http://www.c2d.ch/.
[16] "Search Engine for Direct Democracy," http://www.sudd.ch/index.php?lang=en.
[17] See Mittendorf (2007) for a discussion about the pros and cons of different databases on direct democracy.

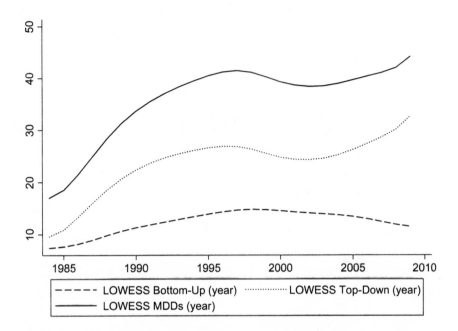

FIGURE 3.7. Worldwide Trends in the Use of Mechanisms of Direct Democracy (LOWESS Smooth).

or citizen-initiated (again, Switzerland ranks first, with thirteen in 1992 and 2000, and Italy is second, with twelve in 1995). Though the overall mean of MDDs per country-year indicates that they still constitute a relatively "rare event" in contemporary politics worldwide, it is worthy of note that MDDs occur much more frequently than other well-documented political phenomena, such as coups-d-état or revolutions.[18]

The distribution of events of MDDs according to country is interesting. CI-MDDs are mainly used in as few as seven countries: 90 percent of these events occurred in Switzerland, Italy, Liechtenstein, Uruguay, Lithuania, Latvia, and Hungary (Figure 3.8). To reach this percentage for top-down MDDs (TD-MDDs), we would need to aggregate the counts of more than fifty countries (Figure 3.9). This simply means that TD-MDDs are much more evenly distributed worldwide than CI-MDDs.

Every year, Swiss citizens see an average of 6.42 CI-MDDs and 2.69 TD-MDDs for a combined 9.12 instances of MDDs (Table 3.1). A table including all countries that have had at least one experience with any kind of MDD is presented in Appendix 1; there are 127 countries (of 195). Switzerland indisputably excels with regard to relevance and the use of MDDs among nations.

---

[18] In this regard, see also Setälä (2006a).   TD-MDDS are more evenly dispersed worldwide

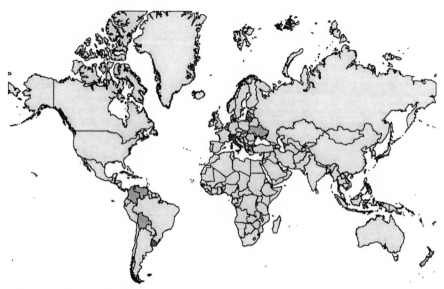

FIGURE 3.8. Worldwide Uses of Citizen-Initiated Mechanisms of Direct Democracy (1985–2009).

As a matter of fact, it uses 3.2 times more CI-MDDs than the next country in the table, Italy. The fact that Switzerland accounts for about 50 percent of all CI-MDDs used raises some issues for the analysis. These are discussed in Section 3.b of this chapter.

FIGURE 3.9. Worldwide Uses of Top-Down Mechanisms of Direct Democracy (1985–2009).

TABLE 3.1. *Yearly Average of Mechanisms of Direct Democracy (1984–2009)*

		Yearly Average of Events of CI-MDDs	Yearly Average of Events of TD-MDDs	Yearly Average of Events of All MDDs
1	Switzerland	6.42	2.69	9.12
2	Italy	2.00	0.19	2.19
3	Liechtenstein	1.27	0.42	1.69
4	Uruguay	0.46	0.19	0.65
5	Lithuania	0.42	0.31	0.73

a. Hypotheses and Independent Variables

In this section, I put forth the independent variables of my research and their corresponding hypotheses. Given that there is no unified theory of MDD use, my hypotheses have different theoretical inspirations. Also, because alternative theoretical implications could exist for the same variable, I advance competing hypotheses where they correspond.

Basically, I cluster the determinants of MDDs into three large groups: political, economic, and social. The independent variables belonging to the political realm are related to the level of democracy, type of regime, and administrative architecture of the state. Those in the cluster of economic causes are the degree of development and economic performance. The social group is arranged by size and degree of heterogeneity of each country's society. Finally, I include as a series of controls the colonial heritage of each country, the age of its regime, and, more important, the uses of MDDs in its neighborhood (international diffusion).

It is well known that MDDs do not fall exclusively in the domain of established or even mediocre democracies. Butler and Ranney assert that "a few admirable democratic societies have never tried the device, while some authoritarian ones have grotesquely abused it" (1994: 3). We could then ask: Are authoritarian regimes more prone to use MDDs than democracies? The former statement has profoundly marked the predisposition of analysts in the study of MDDs – for instance, the simple remembrance of Hitler's consults produces shudders for obvious reasons. We do not have to go back in history to study how deplorable regimes have abused and manipulated these MDDs (I do this to some extent in Chapter 4). Nonetheless, the observation that abominable regimes have used and abused MDDs does not necessarily make MDDs "abominable" in and of themselves. If we think in those terms, we might arrive at the conclusion that taxes, for instance, are abominable because some abominable regimes have abused taxes. Evidently, there is fallacy in this reasoning.

Undeniably, we could infer from the previous statement of Butler and Ranney that direct democracy is inversely related to the quality of the regime. Is this so, or is such thinking the result of a biased focus on a few MDDs? Evidence shows that they have been used by many regimes, regardless of whether they satisfy the criteria to be considered democratic. Yet the previous section of this chapter pushes us to think otherwise. Thus, I expect that despite the use of MDDs by notably undemocratic governments, in general terms, the more democratic a regime, the higher the occurrence of MDDs, regardless of whether they are top-down or bottom-up.

Direct democracy relates to the distribution of political power in a given society. The higher the number of veto players within a political system (i.e., the greater the diffusion of power), the more common the use of MDDs. Larger numbers of veto players in terms of executive and legislative relations usually bring out more conflicts (because more actors are involved) and, consequently, it will be more difficult to achieve a consensus. In this scenario, I imagine that MDDs constitute a tool for overriding stalemates.

Within the realm of democracies, different regime structures account for different amounts of veto players. Ceteris paribus, presidential regimes have more veto players involved in the decision-making process than parliamentarian regimes, and mixed regimes fall somewhere between the two. Evidently, the possibility of a stalemate between the executive and the legislature is much less frequent in parliamentarian regimes simply by definition (the survival of the executive depends on the desires of the legislature). However, there is a second reason why I expect to see fewer MDDs in parliamentarian regimes than in any other within the realm of democracies. In a parliamentary regime, sovereignty lies with the parliament, not in citizens' hands. Parliament is the depository of the will of the people (Linton 2001).[19] Of course, the logic of power distribution also affects nondemocratic regimes.[20]

The classification of regimes is not as straightforward as it seems. Some countries show important deviations from standard criteria, yet these situations require a consistent methodological approach. As a matter of fact, there is an important debate about the sine qua non characteristics that a government regime needs to fulfill to be clearly included in a typology. For this classification, I use Cheibub and Gandhi's categorical codification of regimes in six types (2004; 2005).[21] These categories are divided into two broad groups: democracies and non-democracies, each divided into three subcategories. Within the arena of democracies are the following: presidentialism, mixed regimes, and parliamentarism. The nondemocratic regimes are composed of military, civic, and royal dictatorships. With each observation (country-year), I have included a dummy variable for these six categories, using parliamentarian regimes as the baseline for comparison in my statistical analysis.

Again, I expect that the more veto players there are, the more common the use of MDDs will be. The number of veto players depends on the arena

---

[19] See Schmidt (2002).

[20] Not all dictatorships are alike in terms of the number of veto players (see Castiglioni 2005 for a treatment of this point in which he compares the number and type of veto players during the military governments of Chile and Uruguay). See also Barros (2002).

[21] See also Gandhi (2008) and Wintrobe (1998).

Sine qua non = an essential condition

we are analyzing. In terms of national organization of the state, I speculate that countries with multilayer (federal) governments are more used to power-sharing structures than unitarian polities and, therefore, more likely to make use of direct democratic institutions. As Vatter maintains, "[P]lebiscites and mandatory referendums without quorums of consent are shown to correspond to majoritarian forms of democracy, whilst optional referendums and initiatives with quorums of consent are shown to share similarities with power-sharing forms" (2000: 171).

I have created a dummy variable (federal) that notes the federal character of a country (0 = unitary, 1 = federal). Again, given the notorious conceptual problems delimiting what federalism is, I rely on previous research (Cameron and Faletti 2005) that defines a federal state as one that presents courts and legislatures at subnational levels of political organization (e.g., states or governorates). Using Cameron and Faletti's (2005) criteria, it is possible to count twenty-seven countries worldwide that should be classified as federal. These include Argentina, Australia, Austria, Belgium, Bosnia and Herzegovina, Brazil, Canada, Comoros, Ethiopia, Germany, India, Malaysia, Mexico, Micronesia, Nigeria, Pakistan, Russian Federation, Saint Kitts and Nevis, Serbia and Montenegro, South Africa, Spain, Sri Lanka, Switzerland, United Arab Emirates, United Kingdom, United States, and Venezuela.

Perhaps one of the most recurrent discussions in the literature of MDDs is the role played by economic variables in the results of MDDs. In the most simplistic terms, two general schools, or models, of voting behavior have been developed: the party-identification model and the economic model. According to those endorsing the economic model, economic variables, along with political factors, significantly influence the results of MDDs (see also Key 1966; Kramer 1971; Lewis-Beck 1988; Szczerbiak and Taggart 2004). Precisely, these studies assume that voters withdraw support from incumbents (or their parties) when economic conditions worsen (Bowler and Donovan 1998: 71). MDDs thus could be understood as votes of confidence for or against the government, regardless of the issues at stake (Hobolt 2006a).[22]

The evident problem is determining which variable best corresponds to, or captures, the "economic atmosphere" that reigns in a country given that all of the classic variables of macroeconomics are generally highly correlated (e.g., GDP per capita, inflation, unemployment, and salaries). It may be useful to examine growth, but this variable does not necessarily affect citizens' perceptions. Inflation, however, is a much more pervasive variable because it directly affects citizens' well-being. It is, however, possible to imagine a situation in which inflation does not negatively impact citizens' perceptions; additionally,

---

[22] Common knowledge suggests that the outcomes of electoral decisions depend very much on the environment in which they are held. The discussion on whether MDDs tend to be "first" or "second" order elections has been one of the most seminal in this literature. In this regard, see Reif and Schmitt (1980); Reif (1984); Franklin, Eijk, and Marsh (1995); LeDuc (2002); Svensson (2002); and Franklin (2002).

personal income generally will be found to co-vary with inflation. Hence, real wages seem to be the best indicator (because most citizens are workers) and, despite the fact that this measure may conceal important differences between sectors of employees (i.e., public versus private), it seems a reasonably good indicator of the economic atmosphere. Unfortunately, the available data on these variables for the majority of countries are, at best, extremely poor. The unavailability of data forced me to remain in the mainstream for this type of study, including only data available across nations. Such data include GDP growth, GDP purchasing power parity (PPP), and inflation. These data come from the World Development Indicators of the World Bank and the financial database of the International Monetary Fund.[23]

Common sense would dictate that the smaller the polity (citizenry), the easier it would be to trigger and use MDDs. I recognize that this idea might be an "Athenian bias" that we carry along with us, but it nevertheless is raised frequently. Evidently, there are differences among the civic relationships in San Marino, Liechtenstein, Andorra, Kiribati, and Tonga (each has fewer than one hundred thousand inhabitants) in terms of potential deliberations, discussions, and meetings, versus countries such as China, India, Indonesia, and Brazil, which easily surpass the hundreds of millions of inhabitants. Most studies tend to assume that direct democracy will flourish more so in small polities than in large ones. Consequently, it seems reasonable to control for population size. Nonetheless, given the obtuse differences in population size, I have reasons to believe that having passed a certain threshold, it does not matter whether a country has 60 million or 600 million inhabitants. Thus, I have opted to calculate and include in the models the natural log of population.

Despite that in a divided society MDDs could easily become a weapon in the hands of the powerful or the largest group in order to advance their interests (Bell 1978), some authors argue that in a more heterogeneous country, direct democracy can build consensus on sensitive issues by uniting different groups (Kaufmann 2004). Thus, paradoxically, MDDs could foster politics of consensus, as previously shown for the Swiss case (Kobach 1993). Evidently, we are facing a manifest tension between both perspectives and should let the data speak for themselves regarding this empirical question.[24] Again, the problem is that no index captures the multidimensional diversity of contemporary societies, and it is clear that the operationalization of this variable is not straightforward (Fiorino and Ricciuti 2006). Nonetheless, there are several proxies for capturing some of the aspects of diversity.[25] In any case, these indices are calculated for different numbers of countries and for different periods of time. Trying to match these to my universe of analysis, I find that the indices of fractionalization of Alesina and colleagues (2003) (based on linguistic, ethnic, and religious differences within countries) are the best fit for my

---

[23] See http://devdata.worldbank.org.
[24] For a somewhat related question, see Elkins and Sides (2007).
[25] Montalvo and Reynal-Querol (2005), Rummel (1997), Vanhanen (1999), Reynal-Querol (2002), and Fearon and Laitin (2003).

purposes, and I use the maximum value of the three measures as a proxy for social diversity.

It could reasonably be argued that there are other several critical aspects that indisputably play a significant role in the adoption and use of direct democracy worldwide: history, experience, and, quite possibly, political culture. Some aspects of these dimensions must be included. Nonetheless, as they stand, they are hardly operationalizable; therefore, we must use proxies to capture some of their effects.

Institutional traditions or cultural aspects of political life have been poorly operationalized in large-N comparative research. Nonetheless, there are instances, though imperfect, where we can control for "culture." For instance, the inclusion of a variable accounting for a British colonial past has been recurrent in the literature on democratization, given its presumed positive impact on fostering accountability and democracy in general (Bollen and Jackman 1995; Lipset, Seong, and Torres 1993; Muller 1995; Rustow 1970). Additionally, the socialist past of the former Soviet Union and its allies suggests that these countries will use plebiscitary MDDs more systematically than countries in other regions. I account for these influences by including dummy variables for British colonial and Soviet historical ties where applicable.

Currently, there is a revival of the domino theories with regard to different aspects of political phenomena. Perhaps one of the most prolific subfields has been the so-called diffusion effect and the study of its impact on democratization (Brinks and Coppedge 2006; Doorenspleet 2004; Maor 1998; Starr 1991), economic policies (Li and Reuveny 2003; Weyland 2005), and populism (Rydgren 2005), among other topics. Based on this body of literature, I expect countries to replicate experiences with MDDs if such events have occurred in neighboring countries.[26]

Evidently, there are several criteria to assess whether a country neighbors another, but physical contiguity has been the predominant criterion (Brinks and Coppedge 2006). Again, I rely on previous research; this time I use Brinks and Coppedge (2006) and their criteria for accounting for vicinity. Three different variables were constructed and will be checked: 1) a weighted average of neighbors (in terms of population) and their use of MDDs at time t and its impact on each country at time $t + 1$;[27] 2) a nonweighted average of all neighbors and their use of MDDs in time t on each country at time $t + 1$; and 3) the simple sum of MDDs in neighboring countries at time t and its impact on a country at time $t + 1$.[28]

---

[26] Note that no implicit directionality of the diffusion effect is assumed here. For a compelling argument that reverses the common directionality of institutional diffusion – that is, from the center to the periphery – see Markoff (1999).

[27] Of course, other types of weightening factors could be used, but I leave them for future research.

[28] Hug (2004) suggests that a major use of these institutions occurs in countries with provisions allowing an opposition group to propose policies to be adopted by referendum and, consequently, that such provisions should lead to more popular votes. In a way, he proposes a self-reinforcing dynamic, as Auer (2007) does. Auer claims that direct democracy can only be

A forgotten and usually assumed variable has to be time itself (Marenco 2006; Pierson 2004), and its relevance for explaining social phenomena is based, essentially, on political learning. Presumably, the older a regime is, the more acquainted governing elites and citizens are with the decision-making process and, consequently, the less are the perceived risks of advancing MDDs. Particularly in older democracies, citizens may try other types of participation besides those offered by representative institutions as the old politics extenuate.

b. Empirical Findings

The prevalence of zeros and the tiny values and the discrete nature of the dependent variable (non-negative and integer-valued) make OLS unsuitable for this analysis. Therefore, given that the dependent variable is a non-negative count (events of MDDs per country per year), a negative binomial time-series cross-sectional (TSCS) regression is the most appropriate tool for statistical inference. At first glance, it might seem that the data fit better within the Poisson distribution; however, this distribution assumes that the variance is equidistant from the mean (a rather restrictive assumption). If attention is paid to Table 3.2 for summary statistics of the core variables, it is evident that this condition would be violated if I employed Poisson. Thus, we should use negative binomial, which simply assumes that the variance is proportional to the mean (King 1989; Milner 2006).

This type of regression assumes that events are independent in the sense that the occurrence of an MDD will not make another more or less likely. Also, given that the negative binomial distribution is a discrete probability distribution, it communicates the likelihood of a number of events happening in an unchanging period of time if these events take place with a known average rate and are independent of time since the last event. I am aware that different interpretations of independence may be raised because it is possible to argue that the mere realization of an MDD could lead to more occurrences of MDDs. Furthermore, it could be argued that the presence of an MDD could fatigue voters and leaders, so the probability of holding one MDD after another diminishes. Consequently, given the strong contradictions about the manner in which the independence assumption might be violated, I maintain the assumption of independence.

After the robustness checks are done, and if no major problems are found, we are ready to run the models. This stage of the research is divided into two parts. First, I make a distinction between the two major categories analyzed thus far: bottom-up and TD-MDDs. For each of these types of MDDs, I run two models (one with a lagged dependent variable and one without). Also, given the huge fraction of all bottom-up MDDs that are contributed by Switzerland (50 percent), it makes sense to study the impact of dropping

reformed by direct democratic means and, consequently, although it possibly could be stopped or discontinued, direct democracy can rarely be eliminated.

TABLE 3.2. *Summary Statistics of Core Variables*

Variable	Obs.	Mean	Std. Dev.	Min.	Max.
All MDDs	4,964	0.191	1.172	0	29
CI-MDDs	4,964	0.066	0.624	0	13
TD-MDDs	4,964	0.125	0.888	0	29
FREEPOL	4,734	0.593	0.340	0	1
Durable	4,716	24.590	30.138	0	200
Mixed Regime	4,747	0.103	0.304	0	1
Presidential Regime	4,747	0.169	0.375	0	1
Civil Dictatorship	4,747	0.242	0.429	0	1
Military Dictatorship	4,747	0.154	0.361	0	1
Royal Dictatorship	4,747	0.073	0.261	0	1
Federal State	4,938	0.137	0.344	0	1
Population (Natural Logarithm)	4,871	1.605	2.097	−4.61	7.19
Purchasing Power Parity	4,723	8,684.7	10,644.3	8.11	87,716.73
GDP (Growth)	4,733	3.223	6.654	−67.94	106.28
Former Colony of GBR	4,943	0.343	0.475	0	1
Former Communist State	4,943	0.136	0.343	0	1
MDDs around (ALL)	4,961	0.773	2.520	0	29
MDDs around (CI)	4,961	0.303	1.548	0	22
Social Diversity	4,863	0.583	0.208	0.01	0.93

the Alpine federation from the data set on the estimated association between the independent variables and bottom-up MDDs. Thus, the last two models replicate the previous ones but without considering the Swiss experience.

Model 1 in Table 3.3 considers all TD-MDDs (those that are triggered not by citizens but by formal institutions, either because the constitution demands it or the executives and/or legislatures will it). Model 2 is exactly the same as Model 1 except that it includes a lagged measure of the dependent-variable on the independent-variable side of the equation.[29] This is a critical step, given that this term usually absorbs a lot of the statistical significance of the other independent variables, which concomitantly lose their significance and occasionally even take the wrong sign (Achen 2000). In this case, despite its impact being nondiscernible from zero, the lagged variable did not siphon significance from its contenders at all because they retained their slopes.

Both models (1 and 2) are highly statistically significant and consistent with each other. Interestingly, they simultaneously support and undermine some of the hypotheses advanced in the previous section. First, democracy, as measured by FREEPOL, has a positive impact on the use of TD-MDDs, proving that the more democratic a regime is, the more likely it is to use them. Interestingly,

[29] On the inclusion of a lagged dependent variable in this type of model, see Rasler (1996).

TABLE 3.3. *Economic, Political, and Social Determinants of Top-Down and Citizen-Initiated Mechanisms of Direct Democracy*

	TD-MDDs		CI-MDDs		CI-MDDs (without Switzerland)	
	Model 1	Model 2	Model 3	Model 4	Model 5	Model 6
Lagged Dependent Variable		-0.004		0.148*		-0.163
		0.116		0.079		0.218
FREEPOL	1.426**	1.427*	13.351***	12.881***	13.059***	13.239***
	0.634	0.634	3.257	3.161	3.286	3.411
Durable	0.010***	0.010***	0.025***	0.022***	0.012**	0.012**
	0.004	0.004	0.005	0.005	0.005	0.006
Mixed Regime	0.094	0.094	-0.801	-0.822	-1.103	-1.148
	0.358	0.359	0.828	0.755	0.774	0.881
Presidential Regime	1.703***	1.705***	1.181*	1.009*	0.170	0.142
	0.382	0.395	0.674	0.603	0.766	0.810
Civil Dictatorship	1.322***	1.323***				
	0.453	0.457				
Military Dictatorship	1.776***	1.777***				
	0.478	0.486				
Royal Dictatorship	0.319	0.320				
	0.615	0.616				
Federal State	0.217	0.217	-1.275**	-1.427***	-3.165***	-3.245***
	0.576	0.615	0.551	0.546	0.983	1.068
Population (Natural Log.)	-0.152	-0.152	0.095	0.081	0.001	-0.007

	Model 1	Model 2	Model 3	Model 4	Model 5	Model 6
Purchasing Power Parity	0.096	0.106	0.150	0.147	0.122	0.123
	(0.000)	(0.000)	(0.000)	(0.000)	(−0.000**)	(−0.000**)
					(0.000)	(0.000)
GDP (Growth)	0.004	0.004	−0.114***	−0.109***	−0.106***	−0.107***
	(0.012)	(0.012)	(0.032)	(0.032)	(0.032)	(0.034)
Former Colony of GBR	−0.574*	−0.576	−4.477***	−3.804***	−2.882***	−2.941***
	(0.350)	(0.362)	(1.394)	(1.257)	(0.923)	(0.957)
Former Communist State	1.542***	1.543***	1.968***	1.823***	1.319**	1.312**
	(0.350)	(0.355)	(0.601)	(0.529)	(0.604)	(0.637)
MDDs around[a]	0.050**	0.050**	0.214***	0.211***	0.263***	0.270***
	(0.024)	(0.024)	(0.050)	(0.047)	(0.040)	(0.052)
Social Diversity	−0.578	−0.578	2.340	1.989	0.986	0.982
	(0.680)	(0.690)	(1.458)	(1.268)	(1.389)	(1.439)
Constant	−3.954***	−3.956***	−17.004***	−16.183***	−14.707***	−14.805***
	(0.679)	(0.679)	(3.238)	(3.051)	(3.209)	(3.274)
Wald chi²	111.75	111.42	256.72	394.32	255.40	246.73
Prob. >chi²	0.0000	0.0000	0.0000	0.0000	0.0000	0.0000
Number of obs.	4,404	4,404	4,404	4,404	4,379	4,379
Number of groups	186	186	186	186	185	185

Negative binomial population-averaged models with robust standard errors; coefficients and standard errors in parentheses.

[a] MDDs around in Models 1 and 2 correspond to all MDDs in geographically contingent countries regardless type. In Models 3 to 6, MDDs around correspond just to those CD-MDDs in geographically contingent countries.

*$P < 0.1$; **$P < 0.05$; ***$P < 0.01$.

although I expected this type of MDD to be negatively related to regime age, they are positively associated.

With regard to regime type, the results are self-evident: Presidential democracies and civil and military dictatorships use more TD-MDDs than do parliamentarian democracies (the omitted category/baseline group), and royal dictatorships' use of TD-MDDs are not statistically discernible from zero. As explained in the previous section, the greater the concentration of power in a dictatorship (i.e., the fewer veto players), the less one would expect the realization of MDDs. According to this logic, it is understandable why royal dictatorships use fewer MDDs than any other type of dictatorship. Another likely reason for this is that authoritarian monarchs perceive their actions as not needing any sort of popular legitimization because they are "legitimated" by an alternative set of standards.[30]

When I introduced the variables in the last section, I inferred that the economic situation would influence not only the results of MDDs but also the frequency with which they occur. Nonetheless, it is theoretically difficult to assess the directionality with which economic variables will affect the different uses of MDDs. On the one hand, it seems reasonable to infer that the more severe the economic constraints a country faces, the more frequently it will use MDDs to bypass formal institutions of representation in search of rapid economic decisions. On the other hand, it also seems plausible that the better a country is doing in economic terms, the stronger the temptation will be for leaders to increase or demonstrate the public's support for their agenda (taking advantage of the positive atmosphere) and increase their direct relationship with the citizens. Considering these potentially contradictory explanations, I examined the relationship between economic variables and the use of MDDs in an exploratory manner and found that neither PPP nor GDP growth is statistically significant.

Surprisingly, neither the federal character nor the population size of a country yielded results even close to statistical significance (I have also tried territorial surface with a similar result, though this is not shown). In addition, it is evident that strong and positive leverage is exerted by being a former communist country, whereas the impact of a British colonial background is negative – but weaker.

These models evidence a "domino effect" of the use of TD-MDDs. There is a positive and significant relationship between the use of MDDs in neighboring

positive + significant relationship
for MDDs in neighboring ctries

[30] There are just three evident cases of monarchs using top-down MDDs: King Hassan II (Morocco, 1984, 1989, 1992, 1995, and 1996), Sheikh Hamad bin Khalifa Al Thani (Qatar, 2003), and Emir Hamad ibn Isa Al Khalifah (Bahrain, 2001). In the last two cases, these ad hoc plebiscites brought in sweeping political reforms. For instance, in February 2001, then-Emir Hamad bin Eissa al-Khalifa, currently "King," decided to hold an ad hoc plebiscite to approve a new constitution that would be the basis for a constitutional monarchy with a two-chamber parliament and an independent system of justice.

countries (at time *t*) and the use of TD-MDDs in the considered country (at time $t + 1$).[31]

Finally, there is no evidence with regard to the positive or negative impact of social diversity and the use of direct democracy. I recognize, though, that this variable was included in a more exploratory fashion because theory was ambiguous in terms of expectations.

Models 3 to 6 test the most interesting subset of MDDs: those that are triggered by citizens and avoid official scrutiny (CI-MDDs). This has been the most motivating stage of the analysis, given the more democratic character of these institutions. These models clearly depart from Models 1 and 2 in that I am implicitly eliminating a subset of specific countries – non-democracies. Almost by definition, citizens cannot freely organize to trigger a CI-MDD in a nondemocratic country. Therefore, there is no theoretically driven reason to include the variables accounting for civil, royal, or military regimes in these models. Additionally, as mentioned in the introduction of this section, given the large fraction of all CI-MDDs that are provided by the Swiss (slightly more than 50 percent), it is crucial to revise the effect of dropping Switzerland from the data set on the estimated associations to avoid skewing the results to a Swiss-centered model. Accordingly, Models 5 and 6 replicate Models 3 and 4 but without considering the Swiss experience.

The statistical consistency between both pairs of models is notable. In all models, FREEPOL and regime age retain their statistical significance and expected signs. Also, there is a difference regardless of whether we are considering parliamentarian, mixed, or presidential democracies in Models 3 and 4[32] but not in Models 5 and 6, where Switzerland is not included. In Model 4, despite the lagged measure of the dependent variable being discernible from zero, it did not draw off statistical significance from its contenders at all.

With regard to the expectation that more veto players would result in more frequent use of MDDs, for the first time in the statistical analysis, federalism becomes significant in Model 3 and sustains its statistical significance and slope for the other three models (4 to 6), yet with a sign opposite to that suggested by the literature. Of course, we usually have Switzerland and California in mind when thinking about direct democracy, which clearly are federal entities. However, strongly unitarian and centralist states also use CI-MDDs, as is the case in Italy, Uruguay, and Lithuania.

Unlike Models 1 and 2 in terms of the economic variables, GDP growth acquires statistical significance with a negative slope in Models 3 through 6. Nevertheless, as in Models 1 and 2, in Models 3 and 4 there is no evidence that PPP is significantly different than zero. Interestingly, after we drop Switzerland

---

[31] I explored several possibilities for building the diffusion effect for this variable, all basically providing very similar results.

[32] Switzerland was codified as a presidential regime.

from the data, PPP becomes statistically significant, with a negative slope. Consequently, an intriguing picture arises: Poorer countries use more CI-MDDs, as do democracies facing a decreasing GDP per capita (in terms of PPP). Thus, we can conclude the opposite as well: The richer the country, or the more stable the economic situation in terms of GDP per capita, the less the use of CI-MDDs, all other factors being equal.

As with Model 1, the dummies accounting for the influences of the United Kingdom and the Soviet Union show the expected results. Population and social heterogeneity perform as in the models presented herein (Models 1 and 2). Both fail to attain statistical significance. Being a former British colony has a negative and significant influence on CI-MDDs, whereas having been a communist country has a positive impact. However, in my perspective, the most interesting findings of Models 3 through 6 are the diffusion-effect variables. In the four models, the coefficients are significant and have the expected sign, meaning that the use of CI-MDDs at time t in country y has a positive impact on the use of CI-MDDs in country z (its neighbor) at time $t + 1$.

We have learned a great deal about top-down and bottom-up MDDs and the factors that cause their occurrence. At this stage, one could be tempted to run a joint model accounting for all types of MDDs. However, I am skeptical of the analytical use of mixing all MDDs into the same model.

4. Conclusions

Direct democracy is a world unto itself, involving at least two very different sets of institutions: TD-MDDs and CI-MDDs. Whereas the former usually represent plebiscitary means to bypass other representative institutions or disengage from the responsibility of tough policies or simply are mobilization/legitimization populist tools, the bottom-up MDDs can be seen as truly democratic institutions in the hands of the citizenry. For that reason, this chapter has direct implications for those who study direct democracy from theoretical and normative perspectives. Even though it traditionally has not been a major topic of democratic theory, the debate between supporters and detractors of direct democracy has been extensive and is of increasing theoretical and practical relevance.

Furthermore, this chapter has direct implications for those who study direct democracy from a comparative perspective. Contrary to much of the conventional wisdom, I find evidence that direct democracy is strongly associated with the level of democracy, and that the more democratic a regime is, the higher its probability of having both TD-MDDs and CI-MDDs. Therefore, the idea that TD-MDDs are not employed in the *truly democratic world* is disconfirmed, and many of the arguments about the nondemocratic nature of MDDs are weakened.

From a worldwide perspective, the results show that size of the population of a country has no effect on the use of MDDs, as theory would assume. Along those lines, we fail to reject the null hypothesis with regard to social diversity

[handwritten note: Size had no effect → & Social Diversity]

and, consequently, we have no tools to affirm that diversity plays any role at all in the use of MDDs. As a general rule, we can affirm that the institutional inheritance of a country has important consequences on the uses of MDDs, as former British colonies resort less to these institutions and former communist states resort to them more, regardless of subtype of MDDs. The same can be said in terms of the age of the regime (whatever the regime is).

Regarding TD-MDDs, there is no evidence that the federal character of a country has a consequence on the uses of TD-MDDs. There is, however, a regime effect: Presidential regimes resort more to this type of MDD than parliamentary regimes, and civil and military regimes resort to these institutions in a positive and significant way.

My findings also help to redirect some of the hypotheses advanced either directly or indirectly by previous researchers, particularly in terms of CI-MDDs. It is clear that CI-MDDs are positively associated with the level of democracy and regime age and are more likely to be used in times of economic hardship. Contrary to theoretical predictions, federalism has a negative impact on the uses of this type of MDDs. Also, the models presented attempt to provide an unbiased account. When controlling for the Swiss case, presidentialism loses its significance, and PPP becomes significantly negatively different from zero.

This chapter has attempted to illuminate some of the reasons why certain countries use MDDs whereas others never do. The lack of previous studies dealing with similar research questions has at times made this a somewhat problematic endeavor. Nonetheless, my models and the findings of this chapter contribute to a recent and growing literature on direct democracy by providing more than a few select cases and anecdotal evidence.

Federal character irelevant
Presidential regimes use this more often

4

Direct Democracy within Nondemocratic Regimes

Chapter 3 demonstrates that MDDs are related to higher levels of democracy. This does not mean, however, that some dictatorships do not resort to TD-MDDs again and again. Actually, insights from the historical account on the use of MDDs show that it is plausible that their use in some autocracies plays an important role in contemporary politics. Some dictators have systematically resorted to plebiscites for advancing their political interest, demonstrated in the cases of Ceauşescu, Lukashenko, "Baby Doc," and Marcos. Yet not all autocrats resort to MDDs, as we see with the regimes of Hu Jintao, Somoza, Pol Pot, and Suharto. In different degrees and with different purposes, MDDs are political instruments used in any type of regime. This chapter highlights the importance of who controls the agenda in determining whether MDDs reinforce or undermine democracy.

Under nondemocratic systems, it is almost impossible to think about popular initiatives or referendums in the manner we have thus far (through sincere and clean signature gathering); instead, we would expect only top-down proposals. The dynamics of the political game are definitely different in an authoritarian regime (not to mention totalitarian) than those found in democracies. The underlying logic is that democracies allow their citizens to freely organize, mobilize, and press the government for changes (or the maintenance of the status quo). In democracies, citizens are more likely to influence, denounce, and punish their governments for their shortcomings, and the government's tenure depends on electoral politics. Yet free and fair signature gathering entails people exchanging ideas, trying to convince others, and meeting to coordinate collective action – actions that represent, for most autocracies, a deep undermining of their stability.

The study of MDDs in the context of no (or highly restricted) freedom poses several challenges to this research. In the context of totalitarian or authoritarian regimes, the evidence of a plebiscite's failure is provided only when government acknowledges its defeat. But if the (nondemocratic) government fairly succeeds in its plebiscitarian efforts, we may lack tools for knowing and empirically demonstrating that the plebiscite was truly fair. Moreover, even if the officially reported size of the majorities in a plebiscite is open to question, it may still be the case that it is backed by strong popular majorities. Nazi Germany at the prelude to World War II provides a useful example.

This chapter proceeds as follows. First, I underline the relevance of studying MDDs in a context of no liberties. I show the general trends and provide a few examples of the nefarious use of these mechanisms to exemplify how civic manipulation works. In the second section of this chapter, I move on to a small handful of examples that defy one of the most solid arguments in this regard: that *autocracies do not lose plebiscites*. Within a context of no freedom, I agree with Butler and Ranney, who argue that "the few cases where military have held referendums which yielded less than 90 percent support are much the most challenging to the analyst of nondemocratic governments" (Butler and Ranney 1994: 9).

1. Relevance of Mechanisms of Direct Democracy in Nondemocratic Regimes

Unfortunately, the list of nondemocratic regimes that abuse plebiscites is pathetically high, and the most plausible reason is the supposed façade of democratic legitimation they so obstinately pursue. For a description of the first nondemocratic use of an MDD, we have to travel back to the late 1700s. The first recorded plebiscite occurred in 1793 to obtain approval of the Montagnarde Constitution. From that time through the mid-nineteenth century, direct democracy was steadily used only in France (approximately ten times). One particular case helps to illuminate the nature of these votes. In May 1802, the senate recommended holding elections before they were scheduled, as a result of which Napoleon would have been consul until 1819. Napoleon was not satisfied with the pronouncement and forced an election to establish him consul for life. On that occasion, 3,568,885 (99.7 percent) voted for and only 8,374 (0.23 percent) rejected the idea.[1]

We must jump nearly a hundred years to see a completely new wave of plebiscites in Europe, whose implications are felt even today. In October 1933, then–Nazi Germany decided to withdraw from the League of Nations and end its participation in the Disarmament Conference. A full month after taking these actions, the government asked for popular approval. A plebiscite was held in conjunction with the parliamentary elections of November 12, 1933. The question was officially formulated as follows: "Do you, German man, and you, German woman, approve this policy of your government, and are you ready to declare it as the expression of your own views and your own will

---

[1] Retrieved from the Centre for Research on Direct Democracy (c2d) database.

Volksabstimmung und Großdeutscher Reichstag

Stimmzettel

Bist Du mit der am 13. März 1938 vollzogenen

Wiedervereinigung Österreichs mit dem Deutschen Reich

einverstanden und stimmst Du für die Liste unseres Führers

Adolf Hitler?

Ja

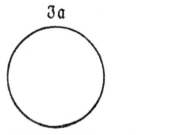

FIGURE 4.1. Voting Voucher – Nazi Germany 1938.[2]

and to joyously adhere to it?"[3] The results were rather clear: 95.02 percent agreed and only 4.92 percent rejected the question. From 1933 through 1938, Germans were called to vote three more times, with similar results both in participation rates and percentage of affirmative votes.

Professor Schiller considers that in the plebiscites of 1933 and 1934, it was possible to express dissent without proving much fraud. Despite intense propaganda and pressure to vote, there seems to have been substantial support for the Nazi government (which came to office in January 30, 1933). Yet the 1934 plebiscite was regarded as a failure by regime insiders and by underground opposition groups, given that the "no" option received 10.1 percent of the vote and, in some cities such as Hamburg and Berlin, was slightly below or above 20 percent. After that "failure," the regime lost – for a while – its interest in the plebiscite instrument. In the plebiscite of 1938 (see ballot paper in Figure 4.1),

---

[2] The ballot reads as follows: "Plebiscite and Greater German Parliament/Do you agree with the reunification of the Austrian and German State as carried out on the 13th of March 1938 and do you give you vote to our leader Adolf Hitler?" The large circle is labeled "Yes," the smaller "No." Source: Stadtarchiv Rottenburg Bestand A 70 Nr. 15 (Communal Archive of Rottenburg, archive fond A 70, No. 15).

[3] "Billigst Du, Deutscher Mann, und Du, Deutsche Frau, diese Politik Deiner Reichsregierung, und bist Du bereit, sie als den Ausdruck Deiner eigenen Auffassung und Deines eigenen Willens zu erklären und Dich feierlich zu ihr zu bekennen?" (Suksi 1993: 100).

the political support for the regime likely was very high, but propaganda and pressure to participate were also strong, and most likely a relevant rate of fraud existed (Interview with Theo Schiller, March 2009). Of course, this practice has not been restricted to Nazi Germany.

Rigging a direct vote could be done in miscellaneous ways, and one of the subtlest aspects of a potential manipulation involves the phrasing of the question in consideration, which could bias the answers in a hidden manner. Voters' attitudes could be skewed to a particular side of a question despite a fair electoral count of the votes.[4]

During the second half of the twentieth century, most (but not all) grotesque uses of direct democratic tools occurred in single-party regimes – in the Arab world, most often under Ba'thist regimes (e.g., Syria and Iraq), and in Egypt (under Nasser and the Sadat administrations), as well as under communist regimes of the East (most notably in Bulgaria and Romania). Of course, other types of regimes also tried to win a blue ribbon for their political agendas, exemplified by the plebiscites held under the military regimes in Latin America, the best known being the cases of Uruguay in 1980 and Chile in 1978 and 1980.

In general terms, it is possible to fit the purposes of plebiscites under non-democratic regimes into three broad categories or purposes: a) maintaining the illusion of an existing democratic process (an illusion both for those within and outside the country); b) cementing psychological and emotional bonds with the population through its mobilization and excitement (more likely to be witnessed under a totalitarian than an authoritarian regime; Douglas 2005:

---

[4] For instance, in March 2008, the conservative Hungarian Civic Union, an opposition party in Hungary, gathered enough votes to trigger three popular votes. Despite insufficient doubts about the democratic credentials of Hungary and its electoral system, the way the questions were presented to the public suggested a positive answer to each of them. László Kálmán, linguistic professor at the Hungarian Academy of Science, provided an alternative proposal for some of the questions in an indistinguishable setup with those of the opposition party, but interestingly enough, a positive answer to his questions would have connoted the opposite of those from before.

FIDESZ	László Kálmán
(Hungarian Civic Union – Leading opposition party)	(Professor of Linguistics, Hungarian Academy of Science)
Do you agree that...	
... public health care institutions should stay in the ownership of the – central or local – government?	... local governments should decide freely about methods of their health care duties?
... drugs could be sold only in pharmacies in the future?	... some non-prescription drugs could be sold in other outlets, not just in pharmacies?

Source: Réti (2009: 218–219).

42);[5] and c) showing the strength of the regime (also for those both within and outside the country).[6]

Around the world and on dozens of occasions, citizens in nondemocratic regimes were mobilized to "communicate" their will directly at the ballot box, and presumably the results have been systematically manipulated by autocrats who almost never have truly accepted the popular verdict. This type of manipulation of entire populations has nothing to do with petitions, signatures, demonstrations, or free citizens pushing for their interests. Governments thus are able to use a "vast array of resources and tactics to create the conditions for favorable outcomes" (Marques and Smith 1984: 98). To demonstrate the grotesque nature of this manipulation, for Table 4.1, I have selected those MDDs with the highest turnout and support from the worldwide database created for this research (they are sorted using a relatively simple measure of mobilization and support of MDDs that multiplies the ratio of participation and the ratio of approval of MDDs). Let's call this group of countries the *Nightmare Team* of direct democracy.

As seen in Table 4.1, in October 2002, Iraqis were called to determine whether or not Saddam Hussein should remain in power. It is hard to believe that the entire Kurdish population of northern Iraq, and all Shia Muslims for that matter, supported Hussein's intentions. Yet official results account for the unprecedented 100 percent support and 100 percent participation (Bertelsmann Stiftung 2003). The Romanian plebiscite called in 1986 was subtler and, despite absolute participation, Romanian authorities officially recognize that support was not unanimous – it was "just" 99.99 percent. As Wheatley recounts, in the former Soviet republics, plebiscites typically have been used to increase the power of the executive branch at the expense of the legislature (2008).

There is some truth in the generalization that plebiscites are systematically tergiversated by autocrats ("dictatorships do not lose plebiscites"). As such, we should be able to show this pattern through a simple scatter plot showing the democratic level of a country (FREEPOL) and the results of MDDs in terms of the percent of the electorate in support of the given initiative. In other words, I cross the support gathered by the executive's preferred outcome with the degree of democracy of all countries. I expect a heavy concentration of dots in the upper-left quadrant of the figure (where we see very low degrees of democracy and a high percentage of support) and almost no dots in the bottom left-quadrant. Figure 4.2 – turnout and approval rates of all MDDs controlling for degree of democracy – is quite telling; the enormous concentration of dots in the upper-left quadrant encourages us to imagine a dictator reclined, relaxing,

---

[5] See Nedelmann (1987) for a detailed analysis of contemporary political mobilization.

[6] I use Linz's definitions of authoritarian and totalitarian regimes (1975), later refined by Sondrol (1991). For Sondrol, totalitarian regimes are characterized by high charisma, public ends of power, low degrees of corruption, an official ideology, and a relatively high degree of legitimacy. Authoritarian regimes, however, are characterized as those regimes with low charisma, private ends of power, high degrees of corruption, no official ideology whatsoever, and a relative low degree of legitimacy (Sondrol 1991: 600).

TABLE 4.1. *The "Nightmare Team" of Direct Democracy Worldwide*

Country	Date (dd-mm-yyyy)	Turnout	Result	Turnout by Result	Issue or Question
Iraq	15-10-2002	100.0	100.0	100.0	"Do you agree that Saddam Hussein should remain President?"
Romania	23-11-1986	100.0	99.9	99.9	Reducing the size of the army, lowering the defense budget
Turkmenistan	15-01-1994	99.9	100.0	99.9	Prolonging President Niyasov's term to 2002
Syria	10-02-1985	99.8	100.0	99.8	President Hafez el-Assad and government policies
Iraq	15-10-1995	99.5	100.0	99.5	"Do you want Saddam Hussein to become the President?"
Bulgaria	16-05-1971	99.7	99.8	99.5	New constitution
Austria	10-04-1938	99.7	99.7	99.4	Adhesion to Germany
Togo	30-12-1979	99.4	99.9	99.2	New constitution
Syria	02-12-1991	99.1	100.0	99.1	Hafez el-Assad for president
Morocco	01-12-1989	98.8	100.0	98.8	Prolonging parliamentary terms by two years
Nazi Germany	10-04-1938	99.6	99.0	98.6	Adhesion of Austria
Togo	09-01-1972	98.7	99.9	98.6	Prolonging President Gnassingbé Eyadéma's term
Egypt	05-03-1965	98.5	100.0	98.5	Gamal Abdel Nasser for president
Mongolia	20-10-1945	98.5	100.0	98.5	Independence
Syria	10-02-1999	98.5	100.0	98.5	Hafez el-Assad for president
Egypt	11-09-1971	98.3	100.0	98.3	Constitution
Cameroon	20-05-1972	98.2	100.0	98.2	Constitution
Egypt	02-05-1968	98.2	100.0	98.2	"The Program of the 30th of March"
Egypt	01-09-1971	98.1	100.0	98.1	Founding of the United Arab Republic
Egypt	21-02-1958	98.1	99.9	98.0	Founding of the United Arab Republic
Egypt	21-02-1958	98.1	99.9	98.0	Gamal Abdel Nasser for president

(continued)

TABLE 4.1 (continued)

Country	Date (dd-mm-yyyy)	Turnout	Result	Turnout by Result	Issue or Question
Iceland	23-05-1944	98.4	99.5	97.8	Independence
Egypt	15-05-1974	97.8	100.0	97.7	"The October Paper"
Sudan	03-04-1977	98.3	99.3	97.6	Jaafar Nimeiri for president
Morocco	04-09-1992	97.3	100.0	97.3	More powers for government, proposed by King Hassan II
Portugal	19-03-1933	97.7	99.5	97.2	Constitution
Cuba	24-02-1976	98.0	99.0	97.0	Constitution
Morocco	31-08-1984	97.0	100.0	97.0	Union with Libya
Iceland	23-05-1944	98.4	98.5	96.9	Constitution
Syria	08-02-1978	97.0	99.9	96.9	Constitution, Hafez al-Assad for president
Italy	26-03-1934	96.6	99.8	96.4	Fascist government
Morocco	23-05-1980	96.8	99.6	96.4	Maturity of royal successor at sixteen
Niger	14-06-1987	96.8	99.6	96.4	National Charta
Egypt	10-02-1977	96.7	99.4	96.1	Measures for Public Law and Order
Guinea	23-12-1990	97.4	98.7	96.1	Constitution
Maldives	27-09-1968	99.0	97.0	96.0	Ibrahim Nasir for president
Egypt	16-09-1976	95.8	99.9	95.7	Anwar Sadat for president
Egypt	10-06-1976	95.7	99.9	95.6	President's term of six years
Germany (DR)	05-06-1951	99.4	96.0	95.4	Against remilitarization, for the Peace Treaty of 1951

Source: Author's database and historical record.

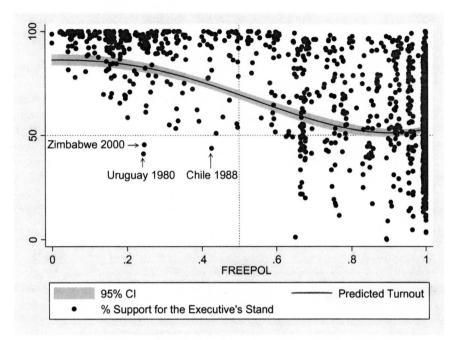

FIGURE 4.2. Direct Democracy Worldwide from the Power Holder Perspective.

and whispering Somoza's famous words: "Indeed, you won the elections, but I won the count" (cited in Eisenstadt 2004: 1).

Of the 254 MDDs that occurred in autocracies (about 15 percent of the universe of MDDs recorded), defeat was acknowledged in only three (i.e., Uruguay 1980, Chile 1988, and Zimbabwe 2000). This fact makes these cases extremely appealing for research. They had an enormous echo in the world; *Time* eloquently mentioned a "Resounding No" for the Uruguayan case; "Chile: Fall of the Patriarch"; and "Mugabe Regime Grows Old as Zimbabwe Grows Up."[7] Looking back, one can clearly see that two of the three cases have shaped the history of their countries (Chile and Uruguay), whereas the impact of the third case remains debatable. These three cases represent only 1.2 percent of all MDDs in autocracies and about 0.2 percent of all MDDs across all regime types.

In Figure 4.2, I have also included the pattern of participation (turnout). The farther we move to the right in the figure (the more democratic a regime), the lower the results (always seen from the power holder perspective); but also

[7] For these *Time* articles, see

Uruguay: http://www.time.com/time/magazine/article/0,9171,922215,00.html?iid=chix-sphere.

Chile: http://www.time.com/time/magazine/article/0,9171,968691,00.html.

Zimbabwe: http://www.time.com/time/nation/article/0,8599,39360,00.html.

the lower the participation rates, despite that the line stabilizes and starts to show an increase once the threshold of FreePol = 0.8 is reached. I use fractional polynomials (with their confidence intervals) as a sensible compromise between very complex curves and oversimplified straight lines (Royston and Altman 1997).

In no region of the world have plebiscites been abused as much as in the Commonwealth of Independent States, especially in Turkmenistan, Uzbekistan, Tajikistan, Kyrgyzstan, Kazakhstan, and Azerbaijan. Yet differences among these countries are easily found and, in discussing abuses, nobody better epitomizes the vulgar use of these mechanisms than former Turkmenistani president Saparmurat Atayévich Niyazov (1991–2006).

Former first secretary of the Communist Party, Niyazov founded the Turkmenistan Democratic Party (TDP), which ostensibly has dominated the political milieu of the country since its inception in an almost monopolistic way (most other parties are banned). In 1993, he adopted the title of *Türkmenbaşy* ("Father of the Turkmen"), inspired by the founder of the Turkish Republic, Kemal Atatürk. In a plebiscite that occurred on January 15, 1994, Niyazov extended his mandate until 2002, making a presidential election that would have occurred in 1997 unnecessary. Official numbers account for a 99.9 percent approval with 99.9 percent participation – amazing! On December 28, 1999, the Majlis (Parliament) unanimously approved a constitutional amendment extending Niyazov's mandate indefinitely, making him president for life. The eccentric leader of Turkmenistan had all media under his control and promoted a cult of his personality in a combination that incorporates the paternalistic and nationalist characteristics borrowed from the former Soviet Union and the current authoritarian Arab republics. Numerous statues of Niyazov are dispersed throughout the country, including one in the middle of the Karakum Desert and another – coated in gold – at the height of the tallest building in Aşgabat, the Arch of Neutrality. The latter statue has the particularity that it turns continuously so as to always be oriented toward the sun, that no shadow should fall on his face (Bertelsmann Stiftung 2007b).

If Niyazov predominates for vulgarity for his use of plebiscites in Turkmenistan, Kazakhstani leader Nursultan Nazarbayev excels in his "Machiavellian bid to amass power," as Wheatley (2008) affirms. Like Niyazov, Nazarbayev was a former Communist Party chief who had been at the helm since 1990. He managed to increase his power step by step, even using a regime change (from a parliamentary democracy to a presidential regime) with that aim in mind. Two events triggered the use of plebiscites in Kazakhstan. In 1994, parliamentary elections were held and, unsurprisingly, a majority of legislators supported Nazarbayev. Yet a few months later in the same year, a weak but still-viable Parliament triggered a vote of no confidence in the government. The president then dismissed Parliament on a rather artificial ruling of the Constitutional Court and ruled by decree for nine months until new elections were held. In April 1995, Nazarbayev's term in office was extended to 2000 by a plebiscite, where 96.21 percent of citizens accepted the measure (with a declared participation rate of 91.21 percent). A few months later, a new plebiscite reformed the constitution and signed the regime change, reshaping the government, and eroding the legislature's prerogatives (Bertelsmann Stiftung 2007a). Elections in December 2005 returned Nursultan Nazarbayev for an additional seven-year term with more than 90 percent of the vote, and on May 18, 2007, Kazakhstan's Parliament voted overwhelmingly to allow President Nazarbayev to stand for an unrestricted number of terms in office. Since 1991, the Organization for Security and Co-operation in Europe (OSCE) has sharply criticized the electoral processes that have taken place in Kazakhstan.

2. Disobeying History

The simplest and most obvious question is: Having roughly all the tools necessary to rig a plebiscite, why do authoritarian regimes accept a loss when they have held an MDD? Is this a political move pursuing other hidden results or a typical *nested game*?[8] Which factors determine the acceptance of the results of those plebiscites? Is it just a surprise, international leverage, or simply miscalculation? In the following pages, I more closely examine the only three cases that have defied history so far: Uruguay, Chile, and Zimbabwe.

a. Uruguay 1980: Setting the Precedent

History has its twists and turns, and Uruguay – one of the most democratic regimes in Latin America – succumbed, as most countries in the region did, to a brutal dictatorship that lasted for twelve years (1973–1985).[9] What makes Uruguay so special, for the purposes of this section, is the fact that "very few military regimes lose referendums, yet Uruguay was the exception to the rule" (Marques and Smith 1984: 92). Indeed, of all recorded MDDs worldwide, Uruguay constitutes the very first exception to the rule. Therefore, the maxim presented before must now be understood as "at times, dictators do lose plebiscites."

The causes of military coups d'état are beyond the scope of this research. The armed forces seized power in stages during the early 1970s after rising as a law-and-order counterforce to the urban guerrilla *Tupamaros* (Gillespie 1991: 33).[10] Acting in conjunction with the armed forces, President Bordaberry dissolved the nation's Congress on June 27, 1973. This was the conclusion of a steady erosion of democratic processes that began in the early to mid-1960s (Handelman 1981).

---

[8] See Tsebelis (1990).

[9] Indeed, this collapse defies an important part of the literature on "democratic consolidation" and its use within the political science discipline.

[10] For Ehud Sprinzak, a leading researcher on fighting groups, the Tupamaro Movement was one of the most sophisticated urban guerrillas in the twentieth century (personal communication). On the Tupamaro Movement, see Lessa (2002), Porzecanski (1973), Panizza (1990), and Garcé (2006).

Under the umbrella of what was known as the National Security Doctrine, the military governed and penetrated virtually every part of society. Despite the fact that the Uruguayan dictatorship was not as sanguinary as its regional counterparts (e.g., Chile and Argentina) in terms of killings, the social effects of the terror regime were enormous and evidently are felt even today. The Uruguayan military regime possesses the infamous record of having had the highest percentage of political prisoners in the world (Kaufman 1979) and, presumably, the highest percentage of torture as well (Edy Kaufman, personal communication). Kaufman, who spoke at the U.S. Congressional Hearings of 1976 on behalf of Amnesty International, estimated that one in every five Uruguayans went into exile, one in fifty were detained, and one in five hundred went to prison (most of them tortured).[11]

Enjoying the relatively positive economic performance of the country and having learned from the Chilean experience of 1978, the dictatorship, through a decree, called for a plebiscite to be held in November 1980. This was based on what has been called the *cronograma* (chronogram) of 1976 to 1977, a timetable intended for a democratic reinstallation. The military's objective was to sanction a new 238-article-long constitution, which would have given the military an even more all-encompassing role in the future political life of the country. The new constitution would have constituted the basis of some sort of a guarded (Torres Rivas 1997), controlled (Hinkelammert 1994), protected (Przeworski 1988), or even depoliticized (Whitehead 1992) democracy.

The text of the new constitution was released on the first day of that November. The Direccion Nacional de Relaciones Públicas (DINARP) started a colossal campaign, bombarding radio and television with massive amounts of propaganda.[12] The opportunities to campaign against the military proposal were severely curtailed, and very few windows for free expression were permitted (McDonald 1982). One weekly magazine, *Opinar,* provided a unique opportunity for the opposition forces and the "no" voice. Indeed, one of the founders of *Opinar,* José Enrique Tarigo, along with Eduardo Pons Etcheverry, was the protagonist of an already-mythic television debate on Channel 4 in Montevideo on November 14. The debate was mounted against colonel and lawyer Néstor Bolentini and Enrique Viana Reyes, defenders of the plebiscite, and, of course, the regime. This was the first time that the opposition had appeared in the media with relative freedom to express their negative opinion toward the regime and its constitutional aims. For some, the emergence of talk of a designed "structural fraud" was simply evidence of the unevenness

---

[11] In 1976, the Campaign against Torture in Uruguay was Amnesty International's first campaign devoted to a single country and not to individual cases from different parts of the world, becoming a model for the organization's future actions (Markarian 2004).

[12] The country was inundated with posters of happy children versus horrible images from the days of the Tupamaro actions. Also, every Uruguayan would remember the sticky jingle swamping radios throughout the country: "YES for the country / YES for Uruguay / YES for progress / And YES for peace / YES for the future / Let's vote / YES for greatness / YES for my Uruguay / (Voice-over: "Say YES to progress and peace, Say YES to Uruguay") / YES for my Uruguay."

in the campaign (Rilla 1997). Former President Sanguinetti (1985–1990 and 1995–2000) remembers the atmosphere:

I remember my friend, "Maneco" Flores,[13] told me a day before the plebiscite: "Tomorrow we will know whether we ever were the Switzerland of Latin America. Because everyone says, and it is known, that the plebiscites in dictatorships are lost." And I wish him hopefully to be right. But, what happened those days? Because "that" was never a campaign, it was simply the transmission of ideas mouth to mouth, it was going to bars, cafeterias, and friends' houses...But the great smack was watching Tarigo and Pons Etcheverry on TV. And that was very strong in a country where there was nothing, not discussing anything, nobody discussed with the government, and less on TV. It was a bomb! That hearing was decisive, especially in getting some fear out of people. (Interview with Julio María Sanguinetti, February 2008)

On the eve of the carefully orchestrated plebiscite, there were basically two expectations about its fate: a) the military regime rigging the election and lying about the results; and b) the victory of fear (because it was assumed that the widespread sensation of terror would have played a critical role in shaping the vote). Some people believed that the military was filming at the voting stations, gossips claimed that pensions would be suspended for those failing to give the support for the new constitution, and so forth. The opposition was permitted to hold merely three "no" rallies, although these had to be held in rented auditoriums, not in public squares or streets. In short, "opposition efforts were totally dwarfed by the government's massive propaganda campaign" (Handelman 1981).

Nonetheless, with a turnout exceeding 86 percent (voting in Uruguay is compulsory), 57.2 percent of the citizens rejected the reform and 42.8 percent supported it. The "no" vote crossed all strata of the country in a relatively similar pattern and had no correlation whatsoever with the economic performance of households.[14] After a long and essentially fraudulent course of action, the regime promptly declared political defeat (González 1983: 73).

Yet analysts likely would have predicted a completely different outcome and, as González himself stated, "it hardly seemed reasonable to expect fair play in the final stage of a process that had never been fair" (González 1983). What was the explanation for the recognition of defeat by the military regime? Some colleagues claim that the unexpected behavior of the military could be explained by the simple element of surprise. The military were absolutely stunned by the results and had been so convinced that the "yes" campaign would prevail that they did not believe any manipulation of the electoral process would be necessary, so they were caught unprepared.

Another potential explanation involves the political values of the military (Gillespie 1991: 72–73). Despite all the brutality that transpired during the

[13] Manuel Flores Mora, known as "Maneco," was an influential congressman of the Colorado Party and a writer.
[14] See also Aguiar (1985).

seven years of the dictatorship, the Uruguayan military, the product of a democracy itself, never became convinced of the merits of a complete dismantling of Uruguayan democracy. For example, from 1973 to 1976, President Juan María Bordaberry (a truly organicist politician à la Stepan 1978) attempted to forge the country into a kind of new Falangist, ultramontane movement without political parties, in which the major issues of determination would come from a militarily protected country. Yet even that was too much for the military, which deposed him in 1976. For them, democracy was not the problem; rather, corrupted politicians were the issue (Castiglioni 2005: 55–56).

The Uruguayan dictatorship was different from its regional counterparts in terms of the distribution of governmental authority, which also affected policy change (Castiglioni 2005: 7). Other military regimes of the region were led by one prominent individual (i.e., Hugo Banzer in Bolivia, Augusto Pinochet in Chile, Alfredo Stroessner in Paraguay, Juan Velasco Alvarado in Peru). In Uruguay, in contrast, the military functioned as a collegiate body that contributed to the policy-making process through an array of decision-making units. Indeed, characteristic features of military rule in Uruguay were "the lack of a centralized military intelligence service, the rotation of presidential and military posts, and the election of the head of the army by high-ranking officers" (Remmer 1989: 178–179). Moreover, throughout the period of military rule in Uruguay, the military was divided between hardliners and softliners over the questions of how and when Uruguay should transit to democracy. From this perspective, the plebiscite might have been used as a tool for resolving the contrasting positions of the officers, and its results would be accepted as a consequence of a previous agreement among the parties.[15]

A third consideration is the institutional framework of the Uruguayan electoral process. It is virtually impossible to falsify election results in Uruguay using its traditional vote system. The Electoral Court (La Corte Electoral) constitutes the fourth power of the country in constitutional terms and, surprisingly, it was not dissolved in 1973, only marginalized. After all, the Electoral Court provides each citizen with a civic credential, a document used not only for voting but also for other matters in the administration. Once the plebiscite was on the table, the military appealed to the Corte Electoral to trigger all the apparatuses needed for a vote, constituting the *mesas de votación* (polling stations) and appointing public servants (from schoolteachers to street cleaners) to observe and count the votes, and so forth.

The "secret" for the "no" victory comes from the decentralization of counting votes in Uruguay. In a typical election, more than five thousand polling stations are in operation in Uruguay. This figure implies that there are more than fifteen thousand people counting and observing the whole process. At the end of the election day, after the final vote count has been made, the three

---

[15] This argument is based on Magaloni (2006) and Londregan and Vindigni (2008). For these authors, even rigged elections provide valuable information to authoritarian rulers, regardless of whether the rulers accept the real results.

members of each polling station sign the act in duplicate: One is delivered to the departmental headquarters of the Corte Electoral and the other is retained by the president of the polling station (which she takes home). Thus, election fraud is made virtually impossible, unless – as Urruty said – a few thousand arrests are made the very same night to forge the acts (interview, September 2007).[16]

The plebiscite of 1980 is indisputably the springboard for democratic reinstallation in Uruguay. Despite the plebiscite having triggered a hardliner backlash in the country, the fate of the regime was already clear. The military did not enjoy the citizens' support, and sooner or later they would have to return the power to a civilian, elected government. The turnover occurred on March 1, 1985. The bottom line is that "in rejecting the regime's proposal, Uruguayan voters defied one of the most trusted political aphorisms, that 'authoritarian regimes never lose a plebiscite'" (Handelman 1981). No precedent existed in the world until that day.

b. Chile 1988: The Crucial Role of International Monitoring

In some countries in the region (e.g., Uruguay), armed forces seized power in stages during the early 1970s. However, the Chilean coup of September 11, 1973, lasted for just a few hours and included a massive rocket attack from military aircraft on the presidential palace in Santiago, the heart of the capital city. Of course, such a violent reaction against the democratic institutions must be understood in the context of the political and social polarization in which Chile had already been immersed for some time. As soon as the military regime came into power, it declared itself the embodiment of the executive, legislative, and constituent powers of the nation. Their purpose for including the constituent powers would soon be understood.

The socialist Salvador Allende was elected president by the Congress in November 1970[17] and, in fact, this was not the first time a committed socialist had become the president of a nation through democratic means. It was, however, one of the most symbolic leftist victories of the day in the Western world. Allende's coalition encompassed a variety of political groups, ranging from communists to moderate Catholics, and his policies constituted a drastic move toward the economic regulation of the country. The program of reforms was called *la vía chilena al socialismo* (the Chilean Path to Socialism). The economy was rapidly disjointed because of price controls, increased salaries, and the nationalization of industries (e.g., foreign copper firms) and of 60 percent of the private banks (Skidmore and Smith 2001: 127).[18] By mid-1972,

[16] Carlos Urruty (b. 1929) has worked at the Corte Electoral since 1944. Since 1996, he has been president of the Electoral Court.

[17] According to the Chilean Constitution at the time, if no presidential candidate obtained a majority of the popular vote, Congress would choose one of the two candidates with the highest number of votes as the winner. The tradition was that the Congress would vote for the candidate with the highest popular vote, regardless of margin.

[18] See also Vergara (1986: 90).

massive demonstrations for and against Allende were being staged, and signs of political violence began to increase drastically.

The Chilean military's main ideology was also – as in Uruguay – the doctrine of national security. On October 8, 1973, Decree Law 77 announced that the main goals of the new military government were "to extirpate Marxism from Chile, to restore the country morally and materially toward economic development and social justice, and to vitalize new institutional forms that bring about a modern democracy that is free from the vices that favored the actions of its enemies" (Vergara 1985: 20). In short, the military defined its goals in opposition to those that Allende's socialist government had embraced. The national security doctrine dominated the military government's early policy choices; it led to repressive measures and gross human rights violations throughout the regime. At the same time, "the military closed Congress, outlawed political parties, and stripped labor unions of their bargaining rights as well as their organizational base. Freedom of speech, press, and assembly were tightly restricted" (Stallings and Brock 1993: 81).

The strengthening of Pinochet's personal power at the expense of the military junta – a process known as "the coup within the coup" (Huneeus 2000) – and its consequences expanded the regime's room for maneuver. Pinochet sought to concentrate power not only by removing any officer loyal to Allende from the armed forces (using decrees 33 and 220) but also "to systematically neutralize and retire those officers who had engineered the coup" (Valenzuela 1991: 32–33). During the first years of the dictatorship, thousands were detained, tortured, and summarily executed or disappeared. Despite doubts regarding the concentration of power during the military regime (Barros 2002), it was unquestionably much more concentrated and powerful than its regional counterparts (Castiglioni 2001; 2005). Indeed, Pinochet's power was unprecedented among the region's other autocracies.

By 1977, four years after the military coup, the regime was gradually becoming less legitimate in the eyes of the international community. Systematic condemnations from the UN regarding the human rights situation in Chile contributed to the change in the tone of its relationship with the United States. This was a consequence in part of Carter's assumption of the American presidency but also of the murder of Orlando Letelier in Washington, which had been mandated by the Chilean National Intelligence Directorate (DINA).[19]

The accession of Jimmy Carter to the White House in early 1977 and the UN condemnation of Chile because of its systematic human rights violations pushed Pinochet to seek an aura of legitimacy through popular mobilization via a plebiscite. That plebiscite was held on January 4, 1978, in response to the increasingly frosty international environment facing Pinochet. The plebiscite was a gross imitation of something related to a vote, given the complete lack of

---

[19] On the occasion of the visit to Chile by the Assistant Secretary of State for Inter-American Affairs Terence Todman, the Chilean regime announced the dissolution of the DINA and the creation of the National Information Center (CNI).

Frente a la agresión internacional desatada en contra del Gobierno de nuestra Patria, respaldo al Presidente Pinochet en su defensa de la dignidad de Chile, y reafirmo la legitimidad del Gobierno de la República para encabezar soberanamente el proceso de institucionalización del país

— SI

—NO

FIGURE 4.3. Voting Voucher – Chile 1978.[20]

minimal conditions set for its transparency. Of course, as expected, Pinochet "won," with the support of almost 80 percent of the population (based on official records).[21]

It is extremely interesting to pause and think about the wording of the question – to not only observe the design of the ballot itself but also to grasp the nature of the regime's propaganda. The text of the 1978 plebiscite contained possibly the most propagandistic wording ever employed in this context: "In the face of international aggression unleashed against the government of our country, I support President Pinochet in his defense of the dignity of Chile, and I reaffirm the legitimate right of the Republic to conduct the process of institutionalization in a manner befitting its sovereignty."[22] The ballot itself portrayed the question and was followed by a Chilean flag; the "no" option was available far below on the right with a somehow smaller black flag to mark (Figure 4.3).[23]

---

[20] Faithful copy produced by author given low image quality of original ballot.

[21] Officially, the support for the regime was 78.69 percent and turnout was 91.43 percent.

[22] Translated from Spanish by the author.

[23] A twenty-two-second-long television spot by the regime transmitted images of tranquility in relation to the positive vote and then images of chaos associated with the "no" option. The commercial opened with an image of well-dressed television cooking show host Laura Amenábar sitting on a fashionable couch and asking the following question: "Do you know how to answer the national consult? We will teach you how to do it in a Patriotic way: With a big Yes to our national flag!" Then a hand appeared on the screen signaling how to mark the ballot. Immediately after the "lesson," there was a set of images of social disruptions, including workers throwing Molotov cocktails, firing guns, and throwing stones. A male voice off-screen said, "Chile says Yes to avoid chaos," and, finally, against the image of an all-black screen, the same voice exclaimed, "The Motherland's TRAITOR responds no!"

The "victory" achieved by the 1978 plebiscite – summoned by the dictatorship in response to the UN condemnations of the human rights violations – produced an aura of glory and legitimacy for the regime and General Pinochet (rather artificially). This served to catalyze the idea of the need to move forward with the institutionalization of the military regime. The plebiscite and the idea to approve a new constitution advancing the institutionalization of the regime – to secure a "protected democracy" – were captured by the "Chacarillas Plan" disclosed on September 9, 1977. These ideas were, in a way, a response to international pressure and controversy regarding the legitimacy of the regime. Thus, in the midst of an economic boom, on September 11, 1980, a new Chilean constitution was to be voted on.

As indicated, Pinochet's program was far more sophisticated than a mere survival against international or domestic pressures, and in a legalistic country such as Chile, this refounding purpose had to be amalgamated into a new constitution. The regime had already declared in 1973 that it embodied the executive, legislative, and constituent powers of the nation. The plebiscite of 1980, again on September 11, was held without any sort of international monitoring and with no freedom whatsoever. As expected, the regime "won" again. The new constitution stated, in transitory clause 14, that Pinochet would be president for eight years and that after those eight years (in 1988), Chileans would have to face another plebiscite (transitory clause 27) to decide whether Pinochet would remain (for another eight years, until 1994) or if a transition would be required. The plebiscite of 1988 was set in motion.

Chile is a case of an autocratic regime being bound by a constitution of its own making (Barros 2002: 1; Heiss and Navia 2007). According to Butler and Ranney, the constitution approved in 1980 was a ticking time bomb that would soon explode (1994:7). As in 1978, the constitutional plebiscite counted a high level of participation (6,271,868 citizens) and succeeded in obtaining an overwhelming 69 percent majority support for the new constitution (68.5 percent approval with a turnout of 92.9 percent).

With international cooperation, the opposition camp succeeded in building a parallel tallying system for the plebiscite.[24] Also by 1988, Chile was one of the last countries on the South American continent still under the control of a military regime; thus, global attention was focused on it. Unlike the Uruguayan experience of 1980, the 1988 plebiscite in Chile had a significantly long and, most important, relatively fair campaign by both camps.[25] Yet the day of the plebiscite did not pass free of tension. The day before the election, a blackout in Santiago predisposed the opposition camp to sharpen their senses; extreme

---

[24] Most notable among these were the National Endowment for Democracy and the German *stiftungs*.

[25] On February 2, 1988, thirteen political parties and movements signed an agreement calling for the "no" vote. This coalition was named Concertación de Partidos por el NO, which was the springboard for the Concertación de Partidos por la Democracia that has governed Chile since 1990.

caution was required at each of the more than twenty-two thousand polling stations throughout the country.

Notwithstanding the assistance of international cooperation for the 1988 plebiscite, Chileans were also learning from other international experiences, especially those within the region. During a personal interview of former Uruguayan president Sanguinetti, he stated that immediately after the military defeat in the Uruguayan plebiscite of 1980, a man (Genaro Arriagada) was sent to Montevideo on behalf of former Chilean president Eduardo Frei to learn about the Uruguayan experience and how the military had been defeated at the ballot boxes.[26]

On the day of the vote, a series of contradictory statements was released by both camps. Early in the evening, Arriagada announced from the "no" vote headquarters that the "no" vote was leading with 58.7 percent, with the "yes" vote trailing at slightly more than 41 percent. Police forces repressed some budding demonstrations in downtown Santiago, and the "no" headquarters was forced to evacuate. About an hour later, Cardemil provided the nation with a second outcome: 51.3 percent voting "yes" and 46.5 percent voting "no" based on six hundred polling stations. The Committee for Free Elections later indicated that the "yes" had obtained 44.6 percent of the vote versus the 55.2 percent "no" vote garnered by the opposition.

At that moment, a critical juncture had been reached by the leaders of the National Renovation (Renovación Nacional) party – a right-wing party that was a sympathizer of the coup d'état, which also had a parallel apparatus for tallying the votes and whose information was similar to that of the "no" vote headquarters. There was tension between those who wanted to wait and see and those who wanted to publicly acknowledge that their statistics were not convergent with those of the government. Allamand, a young leader of National Renovation, communicated to the presidential palace, La Moneda, that if a new distorted result were publicly announced, he would publicly acknowledge a rigging of the election (Allamand 1999: 164–165). A bit later, the Undersecretary of the Interior, Alberto Cardemil, informed Pinochet that it would be impossible for the "yes" to win. Arriagada again provided a new report: 40.2 percent for the "yes" and 57.8 percent for the "no." Subsequently, on a television program, the president of Renovacion Nacional, Sergio Onofre Jarpa, sat with Patricio Aylwin, one of the leaders of the opposition camp and the first posttransitional president of Chile, and recognized the "no" victory (Pinochet was supported by 44 percent, and turnout reached 97.5 percent).

A few minutes after midnight, Pinochet called a cabinet meeting and told his ministers, "Gentlemen, the plebiscite has been lost. I want your immediate resignation. That is all." Pinochet called all members of the Junta, and on his way to La Moneda, the Air Force commander, Fernando Matthei, told reporters,

[26] Genaro Arriagada was in charge of international cooperation for the 1988 plebiscite and later became the Ministro Secretario General de la Presidencia during the government of Eduardo Frei Ruiz-Tagle.

"It is fairly clear that the 'no' has won, but we are not concerned." This phrase was transmitted on air by Radio Cooperativa. The results were there for anyone to see (events reconstructed based on interviews with Arriagada and Godoy).[27]

c. Zimbabwe 2000: When Rule of Law Means Nothing

The first democratic election in Zimbabwe (formerly Rhodesia) occurred in February 1980 under the 1979 agreements of Lancaster House.[28] After winning the elections, Robert Mugabe and his movement, Zimbabwe African National Union (ZANU), abolished racist legislation and attempted to rebuild the country after many years of civil war and apartheid. The Lancaster House agreements stated, however, that white citizens would retain some of their former privileges. These privileges included the maintenance of a fixed number of seats in Congress as well as retention of their land, which quickly became the most heated issue at stake, though this had been an enduring policy issue since Zimbabwe's independence in 1980 (Pottie 2003). The early years of independence were times of reconstruction and had an aura of national reconciliation. Yet this atmosphere quickly changed, and Mugabe became perhaps one of the most evident kleptocratic, patrimonialist, and authoritarian leaders in the world.

The Commercial Farmers Union (CFU), mostly white and representing more than 90 percent of land-based production and 40 percent of the country's exports, became a hard veto point against the policy of land reform Mugabe's government was pursuing. The 1987 constitutional reforms eliminated the formerly reserved seats for whites in Congress and shifted the country toward a semipresidential regime, granting the president greater powers. By the end of that year, Mugabe had succeeded in broadening his base of support, incorporating the Zimbabwe African Peoples Union (ZAPU) – formerly competitors – into his party. The new coalition came to be known as ZANU-PF (Zimbabwe African National Union–Popular Front). Zimbabwe was rapidly approaching its leader's ideal of a single-party system. The year 1987 represented a crucial point in the drastic reduction of any vestige of democratic government.

In the 1990 elections, the ZANU-PF won 116 of the 120 seats in dispute. By the end of 1990, the legislature approved a land-reform law that authorized the expropriation of the land held by the white minority, with compensation fixed by the state, in order to redistribute this property among the black population. In 1999, a new 3 percent tax on salaries was created. The government claimed that the resources garnered from the new tax were aimed at the relief of the

---

[27] Interview with Oscar Godoy, March 2008, professor of political science and then-member of the Comité de Personalidades por las Elecciones Libres.

[28] During August 1979, the British government invited the leaders of the Patriotic Front to participate in a Constitutional Conference at Lancaster House, London. The purpose of the conference was to reach an agreement enabling Rhodesia to become independent and the parties to settle their differences by political means (see Preston 2004: 25–27).

HIV/AIDS pandemic. However, others (especially the National Constitutional Assembly [NCA])[29] saw the tax simply as a maneuver to finance the more than thirteen thousand troops Zimbabwe had sent to the Democratic Republic of the Congo in support of the Joseph Kabila regime (these soldiers, at the same time, were allowed to line their pockets with the Congo's cobalt and diamond wealth [Rotberg 2000]). "Prior to the abolition of apartheid, the economy served to ensure the survival of the regime was well as the privileged status of the white minority. [. . .] Mugabe essentially maintained this course from 1980 on, albeit modified such that government control of the economy was now to be used to reward the adherents of the ruling party and redistribute wealth in favor of country's black majority" (Bertelsmann Stiftung 2007c: 4).

That year, President Mugabe called for a Constitutional Convention that finally produced a draft constitution that was tailored to extend not only the executive's dominance of the country but also the government's power to seize farms owned by white farmers, without compensation, and transfer them to black farm owners as part of a scheme of land reform. This new constitution was to be voted on in a plebiscite in February 2000. The campaign was quite flawed: It involved some killings, and thousands were harassed, beaten, and forced to engage in partisan activities (Pottie 2002). However, despite the official confidence that these sweeping constitutional changes would be certified by a submissive body of voters, the new constitution was not approved by Zimbabweans. The "no" camp received 54.7 percent of the vote versus 45.3 percent for the "yes" vote. Participation was extremely low (about 26 percent of the eligible population) but, more interesting, the vote was unevenly distributed across the country. "[V]oters in the cities, like Harare and Bulawayo, voted No by three to one, whilst in the rural heartlands that were expected to vote Yes, there were widespread abstentions" (Slaughter and Nolan 2000).

Although the plebiscite's outcome had dashed the government's self-assurance and emphasized the magnitude of its unpopularity among the electorate (especially the unpopularity of Mugabe), the outcome was still not sufficient to quell the intentions behind it. To the contrary, Mugabe, who had never been seriously challenged before, grew more threatened and angry (Rotberg 2007), and "the government moved to unilaterally amend the constitution to include clauses enabling land confiscation to proceed, effectively negating the referendum result" (Venter 2005).

Although Mugabe did not entrust all his political power to the plebiscite, massive farm invasions and organized violence (including cold-blooded murders) were a direct consequence of the plebiscite of February (Compagnon 2000: 449–450). "The regime reacted to this defeat with overt repression, illegal expropriation of large-scale agricultural property and the dismantling of

repression

[29] Formed in 1997 to review the Zimbabwean constitution, the NCA is a coalition of opposition parties, churches, nongovernmental organizations (NGOs), and the Zimbabwe Congress of Trade Unions (ZCTU).

the constitutional order" (Bertelsmann Stiftung 2007c). Repression and manipulation allowed Mugabe to rig or otherwise steal the parliamentary elections
of 2000 and 2005 and the presidential poll of 2002. As Lindberg remarks,
"[i]n Zimbabwe, for example, there has been an inverse relationship between
the level of real competition and the trustworthiness of the official results.
The more competitive the struggle for political power in Zimbabwe, the more
unfair and violent the suppressive means applied by President Mugabe and his
regime" (Lindberg 2006: 36).

Since the plebiscite of February 2000, all aspects of life in Zimbabwe (political, social, and economic) have worsened. Zimbabwe, once one of the most
prosperous nations in Africa, is now on the brink of state failure, demonstrating precisely how manipulation and political obscenity sometimes can produce
much more than just popular verdicts.

3. Final Remarks

Nondemocratic regimes have resorted to plebiscites in miscellaneous ways –
from vulgar uses of these institutions, such as Niyazov in Turkmenistan,
to more sophisticated, almost Machiavellian uses, such as Nazarbayev in
Kazakhstan. These institutional features can be seen as a way of enhancing
the legality and legitimacy of the government, as well as giving "fresh popular
acclaim to the even more organic rule" (Suksi 1993: 101), as in Nazi Germany
during the late 1930s. Plebiscites in the no-freedoms context tend to simply
strengthen the government for a period of time in much the same manner as
any other event that mobilizes people (e.g., Olympic Games, World Football
Cups, or even a war). From this perspective, they do not particularly change
the political landscape whether or not they exist.

However, in a scattered way, they still may open a window of opportunity to
challenge nonelected leaders, especially if there is at least some measure of rule
of law in existence. There are three cases that challenge the almost axiomatic
rule: Uruguay in 1980, Chile in 1988, and Zimbabwe in 2000. Because the
reasons why each of these governments resorted to plebiscites vary, so do the
grounds for explaining why they accepted their outcomes. The cases of Uruguay
and Chile are almost the exception that proves the rule: MDDs in autocracies
are just a crude mimic of democratic practice, seeking unfounded legitimation
and mobilization without offering anything in return.

The Uruguayan case is fascinating, not only because it is the first plebiscite
performed under a crude dictatorship government in the twentieth century that
recognized it had lost, but also because it confirms how institutions can frame
and limit the actions of governments, even in a context of a lack of freedom.
Having had the use of different electoral tools to count votes, the Uruguayan
military could have rigged the results. Yet, had it done so, the legitimacy of the
plebiscite would have been negated even before the voting day, regardless of
the results. The Chilean case is also intriguing, but for two different reasons
than in Uruguay. Chile is an example of an autocratic regime being obligated

by a constitution of its own making and impacted by the crucial monitoring role that the international community filled. In both South American cases, these plebiscites forced the autocrats to begin a transitional bargaining process with democratic forces.

However, it is difficult to remain optimistic when analyzing the constitutional plebiscite of Zimbabwe. This case illustrates how governments can easily bypass the popular verdict with shocking degrees of impudence and no concern whatsoever about putting on a good show. Mugabe easily could have said, "Yes, I lost. So what?" and continued on with his own agenda.

5

Direct Democracy within Weak Democracies

Some Cases from Latin America

As we encountered in Chapter 4, the use of plebiscites in nondemocratic regimes is typically motivated by the creation or maintenance of the illusion of an existing democratic process (both within and outside the country). Additionally, plebiscites in non-democracies are employed to cement a psychological and emotional bond between the regime and the population through its mobilization. Yet facultative plebiscites and other types of MDDs can also be used by "low intensity" democracies, those that – despite being usually included in the democratic realm by most procedural criteria – present with shortcomings in terms of both horizontal and vertical accountability.[1]

As a rule, the more often facultative (unregulated) plebiscites are used by a given regime, the more evident are the signs that a low-intensity, low-quality democratic life exists in that particular country. However, a plebiscitarian atmosphere in a country is not necessarily due uniquely to the megalomaniacal propensity of a specific leader. Frankly, leaders tend to use all the prerogatives at their disposal to advance their political agendas – this is rational and expected. The question is why leaders have the leeway to use those prerogatives without the checks and balances that characterize a functioning representative democracy.

Although most new, posttransitional Latin American constitutions contain some kind of MDD, the literature shows an evident tension regarding their causes.[2] In short, the question remains open: Is the systematic use of MDDs the cause or the consequence of weak representative institutions? On the one hand, the inclusion of MDDs in constitutional charters in the region and their

---

[1] Most of the time, these shortcomings are due to the lack of a relatively established and institutionalized party system. On the debate about institutionalization of party systems, see Luna (2007).

[2] Of course, in many circumstances, this openness is no more than a mere declaration of will, given that no law stipulates or articulates how to proceed with the installation or execution of MDDs.

concomitant use seems to be more a corollary of plebiscitarian and delegative (à la O'Donnell) attitudes of governments and leaders rather than of demands from the citizenry "below."[3] Along these lines, Barczak explicitly argues that "the emergence of direct democracy may be both an indicator of and a cause behind weak representative institutions" (Barczak 2001: 39). She goes further, claiming that provisions for direct democracy in the new constitutions of the continent can be expected under two typical environments: when the reform for the new charter is constrained by those representing traditionally excluded political interests or, when under conditions of political *effervescence*, "traditionally excluded interests mobilize to capture a significant, but not controlling, share of the authority over the reforms-rewriting process" (Barczak 2001: 39).

On the other hand, Barczak's arguments could be questioned regarding the direction of causality. Whereas she claims that MDDs weaken representative institutions, my point is that weak representative institutions open the door for the use and abuse of MDDs because of the lack of the checks and balances characteristic of representative democracies – in other words, exactly the opposite could be argued. If the directionality of Barczak's theory is correct, how can we explain the strength of Uruguay's representative institutions considering that it uses MDDS more frequently than any other country in Latin American? Moreover, nobody can affirm that the Costa Rican plebiscite on the Central America Free Trade Agreement (CAFTA) was the cause of the worrisome decay of the party system in one of the most stable and solid democracies in Latin America and possibly the world.[4]

Barczak's arguments are appealing but fail the empirical test in at least two respects. MDDs have been in use in Latin America since before the process of constitutional reforms associated with the third wave of democratization. As a matter of fact, all of the countries Barczak includes in her research had MDD experiences before the breakdown of their democracies in the 1970s. Indeed, there are very few instances where her theory holds. Of the nineteen countries that comprise what we traditionally think of as Latin America, only five countries have never used (national and officially recognized) MDDs: the Dominican Republic, El Salvador, Honduras, Mexico, and Nicaragua. All others have experienced some kind of MDD. Of the remaining fourteen that have used MDDs since 1978, only three had not had previous experiences with any of these institutions during the twentieth century. These "newcomers" are Argentina, Costa Rica, and Ecuador. Of those with antecedents prior to

[3] The delegative type of democracy is one wherein "whoever wins election to the presidency is thereby entitled to governs as he or she sees fit" (O'Donnell 1994: 59), virtually unconstrained by horizontal checks and balances such as oppositional parliamentary control or judiciary supervision.

[4] The Costa Rican deinstitutionalization of its party system is a process that has shown signs since the elections of 2002 and even before (Alfaro Redondo 2006; Vargas Cullell 2007; 2008); the concatenation of events is crucial to understanding the phenomenon under consideration.

the third wave of democratization, only two (Cuba and Paraguay) have not employed MDDs at the national level since the late 1970s.[5]

Yet Barczak is right in one respect – most new Latin American constitutions have expanded the scope of direct democracy in their constitutions. Whether this is a consequence of citizens' disaffection or a matter of political fashion is still open for debate. The recent threat and use of plebiscites by presidents such as Chávez, Uribe, and Morales obscures the richer history of direct democracy that academicians and the mass media have in mind. Unlike some negative views of direct democracy advanced by the literature, I claim that the reasons behind the use of direct democracy in most of Latin America obscure a significant deterioration of those critical intermediate institutions that must exist in a given representative regime – namely, political parties and party systems.

1. Direct Democracy in Latin America

As shown in Chapter 3, the use of direct democratic devices has clearly increased worldwide, and Latin America is certainly part of this trend.[6] Although the continent has witnessed an augmentation in the use of MDDs, these institutions have generated relatively little interest within the realm of comparative political science, with the exception of a few single-country studies. What is worse, many of these studies are performed from a formal legal perspective, without considering the terminological implications of the categories of direct democracy (Rial 2000; Zovatto 2001; Zovatto, Marulanda, Lizarazo, and González 2004). The consequences of these agendas are evident, the result being an inconsistent and fragmented knowledge of this phenomenon (as discussed in Chapter 1). Before focusing on particular cases, I offer a broad picture of how MDDs have been used in Latin America (I consider just those MDDs after the start of the third wave of democratization in 1978).

In the last thirty years of democratic history in the continent (since those transitions in the Dominican Republic and Ecuador in the late 1970s), Latin

---

[5] Advocating for democratic political reforms within Cuba in 2002, about eleven thousand Cubans gathered signatures to trigger a constitutional popular initiative based on article 88(g) of the Constitution of 1976. This reformist movement is called the "Varela Project." The Cuban National Assembly's Constitution and Legal Affairs Committee suspended consideration of the Varela Project citizens' initiative and retorted with its own counterinitiative, providing that the Cuban Constitution be amended to make its socialist system of government untouchable (*intocable*). In a three-day marathon, the Cubans had the chance to endorse the legislative initiative and official reports state that 8,198,237 citizens (approximately 99 percent of the total citizenry) did so. But, as a BBC correspondent observed, the "opposition in Cuba has been stifled and many said they felt pressured into signing the petition" (*BBC News*, June 27, 2002). Subsequently, the amendment was unanimously approved by the deputies of the National Assembly in an extraordinary session held June 24–26, 2002. As interesting as these political events are, neither can be considered an MDD based on the definition provided in Chapter 1. Instead, they should be considered cases of legislative popular initiatives. See the full text of the note at http://news.bbc.co.uk/1/hi/world/americas/2069057.stm.

[6] With regard to the increased events of MDDs, see also Scarrow (2001) and Setälä (1999b).

Americans have participated in national direct voting more than a hundred times. Whereas some countries are characterized as frequent and recurrent users of MDDs, MDDs in other countries are just emerging and, in some, no MDDs have occurred at all. Of the nineteen countries of the continent, only seven have not had direct experiences of voting since the late 1970s (i.e., Cuba, Dominican Republic, El Salvador, Honduras, Mexico, Nicaragua, and Paraguay). The rest have had at least one experience of an MDD. However, only four countries in the region have experience with some form of CI-MDDs (i.e., Bolivia, Colombia, Uruguay, and Venezuela).

Although the spirit of popular initiative is incorporated into most Latin American constitutions, in most countries it is not more than a simple declaration of principles (i.e., is not regulated), and it is binding only in Colombia, Costa Rica, Paraguay, Uruguay, and Venezuela (Breuer 2009b). In most of these countries, the initiatives may not refer to tax or budgetary matters, and the signature threshold ranges between 5 percent of the census in Colombia and Costa Rica to 10 percent in Uruguay. However, in some countries, this mechanism is filtered by another institution (Congress, in most cases) that decides whether or not to proceed with the measure (e.g., Brazil, Guatemala, Nicaragua, and Peru).

Referendums also present important variations. Although they have been used only in Uruguay, there are constitutional provisions for them in Colombia, Costa Rica, and Venezuela. (In other countries they are just mentioned, but the constitutions do not specify the terms of their implementation.) The number of required signatures ranges from 5 percent of the electorate in Costa Rica to 25 percent in Uruguay. There are also requirements in terms of the time limits to gather signatures. The quorum is similar to popular initiatives.

Table 5.1 shows how different types of MDDs were used across countries in Latin America during the past thirty years. Within this universe, those "from above" constitute 85 percent of cases (of these, 54 percent are binding plebiscites, 21 percent are consultative plebiscites, and 25 percent are mandatory plebiscites). Only 15 percent of cases were initiated by citizens (of these, 56 percent responded to popular initiatives and consultative initiatives and 44 percent to referendums). Indeed, of these 15 percent, about 81 percent are concentrated in one country, Uruguay, which undoubtedly has the longest experience with direct democracy, dating back to the early twentieth century.

Table 5.1 also provides information about when the vote occurred, how many issues were in dispute, and how many were approved. For example, the first MDD shown in this table was conducted in Argentina under the administration of Raúl Alfonsín in November 1984, who, as we noted, sought the support of Argentine citizens on the Beagle negotiations with Chile. The vote was on a single issue and was approved. In the same column (consultative plebiscites), we found cases such as that of Ecuador in 1995, where a comprehensive questionnaire of eight MDDs occurred and none was approved (eight and zero, respectively).

TABLE 5.1. *National Mechanisms of Direct Democracy in Latin America (1978–2009)*

	Mandatory Plebiscites			Facultative Plebiscites (Consultative)			Facultative Plebiscites (Binding)			Popular Initiatives			Referendums			Events	Votes	Apro.	Aprox. Rate (%)
	Is.	Ap.	Date (dd-mm-yyyy)	Is.	Ap.	Date (dd-mm-yyyy)	Is.	Ap.	Date (dd-mm-yyyy)	Is.	Ap.	Date (dd-mm-yyyy)	Is.	Ap.	Date (dd-mm-yyyy)				
ARG				1	1	(25-11-1984)										1	1	1	100.0
BOL	2	2	(25-01-2009)				5	5	(18-07-2004)	1	0	(02-07-2006)				4	9	8	88.9
							1	1	(10-08-2008)										
BRA							2	2	(21-04-1993)							2	3	2	66.7
							1	0	(23-10-2005)										
CHI	1	1	(11-09-1980)				1	1	(04-01-1978)							4	4	3	75.0
	1	1	(30-06-1989)				1	0	(05-10-1988)										
COL							15	1	(25-10-2003)	1	1	(27-05-1990)*				4	18	4	22.2
							1	1	(09-12-1990)	1	1	(26-10-1997)*							
CRI							1	1	(08-10-2007)							1	1	1	100.0
ECU	1	1	(15-01-1978)	1	0	(02-06-1986)	3	0	(26-11-1995)							9	39	26	66.7
	1	1	(28-09-2008)	7	6	(28-08-1994)	14	14	(25-05-1997)										
				8	0	(26-11-1995)	1	1	(15-04-2007)										
				3	3	(26-11-2006)													
GUA	1	1	(30-01-1994)													2	5	1	20.0
	4	0	(16-05-1999)																
PAN	1	0	(15-11-1992)				1	1	(24-04-1983)							4	4	2	50.0
	1	0	(30-08-1998)																
	1	1	(22-10-2006)																
PER							1	1	(31-10-1993)							2	2	1	50.0
							1	0	(30-10-2005)										
URY	1	0	(30-11-1980)							1	1	(26-11-1989)	1	0	(16-04-1989)	16	18	7	38.9
	1	0	(28-08-1994)							2	1	(27-11-1994)	1	1	(13-12-1992)				
	1	1	(08-12-1996)							1	1	(31-10-2004)	1	0	(17-06-1998)				
	2	0	(31-10-1999)							1	0	(25-10-2009)	1	0	(20-09-1998)				
	1	0	(25-10-2009)										1	0	(18-02-2001)				
													1	1	(05-08-2002)				
													1	1	(07-12-2003)				
VEN	1	1	(15-12-1999)				2	2	(25-04-1999)	1	0	(15-8-2004)**				6	8	5	62.5
	2	0	(02-12-2007)				1	1	(03-12-2000)										
	1	1	(15-02-2009)																
Total	24	11	45.8%	20	10	50.0%	52	32	61.5%	9	5	55.6%	7	3	42.9%	55	112	61	54.5%

Note: Cuba, El Salvador, Honduras, Mexico, Nicaragua, Paraguay, and the Dominican Republic have never held an MDD during the considered period.

* Consultative popular initiative.

** Chávez's recall is included as a popular initiative.

Source: Author's database/C2D-Research and Documentation Centre on Direct Democracy, http://www.c2d.ch/; Keesing's Records of World Events, http://keesings.gvpi.net/; Suchmaschine für direkte Demokratie, http://www.sudd.ch/index.php?lang=de.

It is interesting to note that among the different types of MDDs, rates of approval are not as different as one might anticipate, with acceptance averages between 40 and 60 percent. To estimate approval rates more accurately, I calculated the average for the two major families of MDD, those from above and those initiated by the public. For the first, the average is 54.2 percent, and for the latter, it is about 50 percent. The slim difference indicates that they may not be as terribly manipulated as part of the literature suggests. In fact, if Lijphart was correct when he argued that "when governments control the referendum, they will use it only when they expect to win" (1984: 204), it is logical to expect governments to win much more than in the previously presented figures (Altman 2005). This is just a sign of how complicated the game of direct democracy – in a context of approval of slightly more than 50 percent of MDDs from above – can be.

Contrary to what happens elsewhere, the subjects of MDDs rarely deviate from institutional design or contingent politics. This overarching theme constitutes almost two-thirds of all MDDs in the reviewed period. Almost 50 percent (n = 53) of MDDs were related to reforms of institutional redesigns (topics ranging from the extension of mandates and presidential reelection [Venezuela in 2008], type of presidential election [Uruguay 1996], and legal status of parties in Congress [Ecuador 1997], among others). Also, within this group, which constitutes almost two-thirds of all MDDs, a subgroup of votes stands out because they seek the formation of Constituent Assemblies (n = 7) (e.g., Colombia 1990; Ecuador 1997, 2007; and Venezuela 1999).[7] Finally, among these countries are those that constitute a vote that expresses in one way or another (dis)trust in the previously elected authorities (n = 6) (i.e., Ecuador 1997, Venezuela 2004, and Bolivia 2008).

Whereas the rest of the MDDs form a sort of thematic potpourri, the presence of votes related to some basic services traditionally provided by the state, such as pensions and education, is distinct (n = 20). These are also accompanied by votes on diverse fields, as telecommunications, infrastructure, water, electricity, and health. Notably, nine of these twenty MDDs were conducted in Uruguay and the rest in Ecuador, Colombia, Bolivia, and Panama. As we will see in the following chapters, in Uruguay, most of these MDDs were initiated by unions of public enterprises to curb a possible process of privatization or outsourcing of these companies or by one of the most important lobbies in the country, the National Organization of Retirees and Pensioners (ONAJPU), which comprises approximately 28 percent of the national electorate. Indeed, in these opportunities, the mobilizing force of the main opposition's party (Frente Amplio) had a leading role in the vast majority of popular initiatives and referendums.

In Costa Rica, there was a crucial authorities' plebiscite conducted to check for popular support for a free trade agreement (FTA) between a group of small Central American countries and the United States. Perhaps this is the

---

[7] See also Breuer (2007).

best example of how direct democracy can be used to bridge deep cleavages between state powers (executive versus legislative). In this opportunity, the presidential position of allying with the FTA prevailed by a slim margin. In Brazil, despite its immense experience with other types of citizen involvement in public affairs – as in the world-famous example of participatory budgeting in Porto Alegre – the limited experience with direct democracy is still restricted to a few legislative plebiscites.

CI-MDDs have been scarce in the region in the last ten years, and with the exception of Uruguay, there have been only two instances of this type of MDD in the region: the Venezuelan presidential recall of 2004 and the Bolivian autonomic initiatives of 2006. In the Bolivian case, the popular initiative triggered a series of nonrecognized popular initiatives that have allowed conservative nationalistic groups to challenge the geographic boundaries of the country. With the exception of tiny Uruguay, CI-MDDs are almost nonexistent in the region, and even in this country of 3.3 million people, they face problems.

Except for the aforementioned examples, all uses of direct democracy have been plebiscitarian (i.e., coming from the authorities), and most of the time they have had the simple objective of institutional change for increasing or retaining power. Therefore, direct democracy has been mainly used against the basic normative ideal of empowering people. Overall, important lessons can be drawn from these miscellaneous experiences – experiences that generate a fertile background for checking important implications of theory on practical issues.

How can we compare and systematize the uses of MDDs in different countries? One way to grasp the degree of a country's experience with direct democracy (considering only the national level) is to multiply the number of times citizens have had to vote in this type of election by the number of questions decided. Of course, this provides only a small illustration of how acquainted citizens are with direct democracy. To operationalize this proxy, I consider, following Vatter (2007), a consultative MDD to be worth half the weight of a binding MDD. In a way, consultative MDDs are merely opinion polls, and the political leverage they exercise is less than that of binding MDDs.

Operationalizing direct democracy experience in this way, the continent is lead by Uruguay (with a score of 288), followed by Ecuador (138), Venezuela (48), Colombia (34), Bolivia (36), Chile and Panama (16), Guatemala (10), Brazil (6), Peru (4), Costa Rica (1), and Argentina (0.5). For example, Ecuador reaches 138 because twenty issues were decided on five occasions (twenty times five equals one hundred) and nineteen issues in four nonbinding decisions (nineteen times four divided by two equals thirty-eight). Despite this measure providing a glimpse of the direct democratic experienced by a country, it should not be concluded that Uruguay has 288 times more experience than Costa Rica, given the exponential shape that this operationalization produces. Figure 5.1 shows the weighted experience of each country on the continent regarding MDDs.

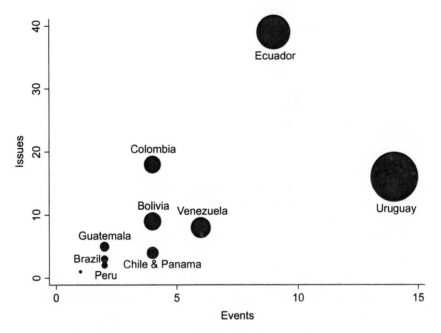

FIGURE 5.1. Measuring Experience with Direct Democracy in Latin America by Country (since 1978).

Although Ecuador and Uruguay are the frontrunners on the continent with respect to the systematic use of direct democracy, its use appears to be different in the two small countries. The former excels for having used omnibus questionnaires triggered by the executives, whereas the latter has not experienced this type of MDD. Uruguay stands alone for having primarily used citizen-initiated channels for direct democracy and for its limited use of mandated plebiscites. Indeed, in Uruguay, the executive power cannot use facultative plebiscites at all. Based on the previous index of direct democracy experience, in the following pages I present a succinct description of how MDDs have been used in Ecuador, Bolivia, Colombia, and Venezuela (I do not include Uruguay because it is the subject of Chapters 6 and 7).

a. Ecuador

Ecuador is one of the more experienced employers of direct democracy in Latin America. Yet the uses of these mechanisms are certainly far from the virtuous circle direct democrats would dream of; instead, they epitomize a desperate search by presidents for the legitimation of their policies and, more crudely, themselves. This country, perhaps more than any other in the region, epitomizes most the clichés of the maladies of Latin American democracies (e.g., political fragmentation and cronyism; presidential isolation; inability to build stable governing coalitions; distrusted Congress, political parties, and Justice Depart-ment; regional disparities; embedded poverty; and classism). Despite the fact that Ecuador is currently experiencing the longest period of democratic stability since its independence, such is the erratic evolution of its democracy, which, if plotted against time, looks more like an electrocardiogram than anything else. Three elected presidents (i.e., Bucaram, Mahuad, and Gutiérrez) were ousted, and their respective interim replacements (i.e., Alarcón, Noboa, and Palacios) did not have smooth administrations.

The plebiscite of January 1, 1978, constitutes the first evident political event in South America in the transition to democracy. Months before the plebiscite, the military junta (*Consejo Supremo de Gobierno*) created three committees, each in charge of a specific theme: 1) preparation of a new draft constitution of the republic; 2) development of a project for the reform of the political constitution of 1945; and 3) development of the electoral law, law of political parties, and a referendum act. The plebiscite of 1978 was passed between constitutions – one of which was newly proposed and the constitution of 1945 (Morales Viteri 2008).

The military was proud of the reform because it helped them to maintain certain power positions and prerogatives (e.g., at the national oil company and social security institute). Also, the junta was quite aware of the country's imminent economic collapse (a crisis that later impacted the Roldós–Hurtado presidency). In the end, this plebiscite implied a political agreement between the military, the political elite of the country, and some social groups (mostly workers' unions). "We give up the state and its institutions, but you will not try us for human rights violations," the military may well have said.

After the transition governments of Roldós and Hurtado, León Febres Cordero assumed office in 1984, and his popularity plummeted from the first day, in part because of his very conflicted relationship with Congress. His gov-ernment was perceived as an authoritarian government, embroiled in scandal and major human rights violations. To mobilize and legitimize his presidency, Febres Cordero resorted to a consultative plebiscite with the excuse that a minor electoral aspect of those Congress members who were independent had run outside the traditional party's slates. Of course, the plebiscite, on June 2, 1986, was not perceived as a proposal for citizen participation in public decisions but as a legitimating tool for the government (Morales Viteri 2008).

From 1988 to 1992, Ecuador seems to have begun a period of institutional tranquility under the government of Rodrigo Borja of *Izquierda Democrática*. A simple indicator was the stability of Borja's cabinet during those four years (turnover in ministerial posts was minimal, and no attempt was made to use any sort of plebiscitarian tool). Yet this stability was short-lived. President Sixto Durán Ballén (1992–1996) of Partido Unidad Republicana used MDDs in a fashion similar to that of Febres Cordero. On August 28, 1994, the citizenry was consulted on seven different subjects of constitutional reform. Despite participation of only an approximate 40 percent of the electorate, the triumph of the government was overwhelming and wisely capitalized on by Durán.

Nonetheless, one year later, after a large corruption scandal involving Durán Ballen's vice president, Alberto Dahik, the president sought to rebolster his image and advance his power in relation to a rather difficult and atomized Congress. He was confident that the triumph of 1994 could be reattained relatively easily, but he was wrong. In November 1995, Ballen posed eleven questions to the citizenry; the first eight were consultive, the last three binding. The range of questions was broader than those of the year before, and among all the questions, the most contentious issue was the proposal to allow the president to dissolve Congress (Breuer 2008b: 12). This omnibus consultative plebiscite was a disaster for the president's interests.

President Abdalá Bucaram's victory of 1996 is one of the few known examples of "outcome inversions," one of the crucial ingredients for a crisis between the branches of government (Pérez-Liñán 2007).[8] As explained by Pachano (1997), the president's "majority" was more of a negative coalition hostile to the Social Christian candidate who had prevailed in the first round (Pérez-Liñán 2000). In February 1997, the Ecuadorian unions opened a series of nationwide strikes opposing Bucaram's aim to liberalize the economy and eliminate subsidies for public services and prices. Under this stressful state of affairs, Congress reacted to the mass manifestations by impeaching President Bucaram on the justification of "mental incapacity" (Breuer 2007). Congress passed the measure with a simple majority instead of the two-thirds required by the constitution and appointed congressional chairman Fabián Alarcón in his place, bypassing the sitting vice president Rosalía Arteaga and, in so doing, bypassing the constitutional mandate (Pérez-Liñán 2007). At the time, Ecuadorians witnessed a severe constitutional crisis accompanied by high levels of civil unrest (Freidenberg 2006).

On May 25, 1997, the new interim yet weak president of Ecuador, Alarcón, sought to legitimize his presidency (and the maneuver for ousting Bucaram by Congress) through a plebiscite that consisted of fourteen somewhat related questions (Breuer 2007). The outcome gave a clear vote of confidence to Alarcón, with a participation level of about 60 percent and an average support level of 65 percent. As had become typical in Ecuador, chaos would not be postponed for long. Between 1998 and 2005, Ecuadorians witnessed one of the most politically volatile periods they had ever suffered. Two presidents were ousted by rather different coalitions and motivations (i.e., Jamil Mahuad and Lucio Gutiérrez). The final punch to the already-agonizing party system arrived with the elections of 2006.

The national elections of 2006 exemplify the collapse of the party system in Ecuador (Machado 2008). Rafael Correa of *Alianza País* was elected in November 2006, winning 57 percent of the vote in a runoff against Álvaro Noboa of the Partido Renovador Institucional Acción Nacional (PRIAN). Concomitantly with the presidential runoff, a series of relatively marginal questions was

---

[8] For Pérez-Liñán, an outcome inversion occurs when the victorious president in the runoff is not the one with the largest vote in the first round (2006: 136ff).

placed on the ballot (Machado 2007). Correa's platform for victory was rather simple: reform of the constitution and launching a constituent assembly for that purpose.

Correa, very much a political outsider, ran for the presidency even without any legislative ballot of his own. As soon he was elected, he triggered a plebiscite that called for a constituent assembly in April 2007. This act passed with the support of more than 85 percent of voters and with a relatively high participation of approximately 70 percent. Like most constituent assemblies, it suspended the sitting Congress and began to draft a new constitution in November 2007.[9]

The process of installing the constituent assembly encompassed a notably cumbersome fight between the president and the opposition camp. Spelling out the process goes beyond the scope of this research, but detailed analyses are found elsewhere (Machado 2008). Nonetheless, as Machado points out, in fewer than nine months, President Correa shifted to a system operating under the unfettered control of a fully empowered constitutional assembly.

On September 28, 2008, the new constitution (a product of the deliberations in Ciudad Alfaro) was presented to the citizenry. The relatively short electoral campaign (the draft constitution was approved in July 2008) pivoted around three major points: the joy that represents "opting for the change," the fear of losing all of the social benefits established by this regime, and, from the official standpoint, the anger of groups that would lose their benefits if the new constitution was ratified. From the government's perspective, "no" votes, abstentions, and annulling the vote were the same: They all meant a return to instability and chaos. The new constitution was approved by 69.4 percent, with a participation rate of 75.8 percent of the electoral body (Table 5.2).

b. Colombia

Unlike its neighbor, Ecuador, Colombia has a surprisingly stable constitutional order accompanied by an extremely violent society in which non-state armed groups (i.e., guerrillas, paramilitaries, and drug traffickers) deny the state the monopoly of coercion over the national territory. Colombia is one of the few countries in Latin America (along with Costa Rica and Venezuela) that did not have a military regime in the last half-century, and within the political science comparative literature, it stands out because it has one of the most stable and older party systems worldwide (Mainwaring and Scully 1995b). It is also unique for having had an electoral and governing coalition between the two major parties of the country, liberals and conservatives, between 1958 and 1974 (the National Front). With regard to the Frente Nacional, two facts are relevant: 1) its instauration was approved in a constitutional plebiscite in 1957 under the military government headed by Gustavo Rojas Pinilla, and in that plebiscite, 2) the citizenry renounced the right of becoming the constituent

---

[9] For a useful conceptual framework for analyzing the constitution-making process and its relationship with direct democracy, see Mendez and Triga (2009).

TABLE 5.2. *Mechanisms of Direct Democracy in Ecuador (since 1978)*

	Questions	Yes (%)	No (%)	Turnout (%)	Affirmative/ Registered
Sep. 28, 2008	Approval for the New Political Constitution of the Republic drafted by the constituent assembly	69.46	30.54	75.81	48.40
Apr. 15, 2007	Approval for convening of a constituent assembly with full powers to transform the institutional framework and develop a new state constitution	86.80	13.20	71.31	58.27
Nov. 26, 2006	Agreement with the Ten-Year Plan (2006–2015) for education to be regarded as state priority for public-sector investment	91.59	8.41	74.24	49.78
	Agreement that the National Congress should, within five months, debate and approve legislation to: a) target adequate resources to ensure the prevention and care of diseases; b) increase by 0.5 percent per annum the participation of health in relation to GDP until 2012 or until it reaches at least 4 percent of GDP	89.60	10.40	73.95	48.87
	Agreement that the National Congress should, within five months, issue laws aimed at ensuring that oil resources higher than budgeted should be aimed for social investment and revitalizing production	88.63	11.37	73.94	47.48
May 25, 1997	Dismissing President Abdalá Bucaram	75.76	24.24	59.25	36.12
	Fabián Alarcón Rivera for president during a transitional period lasting until August 10, 1998	68.37	31.63	59.22	32.53
	Creating a constituent assembly	64.58	35.42	59.19	27.63
	Popular election of a constituent assembly[a]	59.85	40.15	59.12	21.10
	Spending limits for campaigns	69.87	30.13	59.21	29.02
	Voting process: possibility of modifying the list of candidates*	48.27	51.73	59.13	16.99
	Presidential elections in one or two rounds*	61.30	38.70	59.13	21.32
	Striking parties from the register that failed to reach 5 percent twice in a row	68.45	31.55	59.20	27.46
	The Supreme Court consisting of representatives of the most influential parties	58.67	41.33	59.17	23.12
	Parliament appointing the leadership of the state enterprises by a two-thirds majority	50.75	49.25	59.16	19.94
	Modernization of the Justice	60.73	39.27	59.14	23.96

(continued)

TABLE 5.2 (continued)

	Questions	Yes (%)	No (%)	Turnout (%)	Affirmative/ Registered
Nov. 11, 1995	Appointment of the judicial authorities by the Supreme Court	55.97	44.03	59.14	21.95
	Dismissal of any elected official who breaks the law	60.25	39.75	59.13	23.44
	Parliament implementing the reforms within sixty days	66.88	33.12	59.11	25.98
	Equal distribution of public spending among the provinces	44.94	55.06	58.63	20.34
	Judicial reforms	44.53	55.47	58.64	20.10
	Privatization of social insurance	39.68	60.32	58.64	18.25
	Abolishing the right to strike in the public sector	39.69	60.31	58.62	18.00
	President's authority to dissolve parliament	39.69	60.31	58.62	18.00
	Four-year terms for local authorities	39.95	60.05	58.65	18.46
	Two-year terms for president and vice president of Parliament	43.17	56.83	58.66	19.87
	The president must implement these constitutional reforms within ninety days	43.57	56.43	58.63	19.93
	Decentralizing the social and health authorities	40.18	59.82	58.67	18.03
	Legal guarantees for civil servants	43.94	56.06	58.63	20.41
	Appointing a Constitutional Court	39.77	60.23	58.65	17.88
Aug. 28, 1994[b]	Revision of the constitution through Parliament	59.07	40.93	62.31	24.75
	Passive right to vote for non-party members	65.03	34.97	62.33	28.16
	Administration of the state budget through parliament	16.60	83.40	62.26	7.05
	Dividing the budget along districts or subject matters	54.03	45.97	62.30	20.15
	Unrestricted reelection for every post	52.77	47.23	62.30	22.30
	Parliamentary elections in the first or second round	55.73	44.27	62.28	21.13
	Recognizing citizens of double nationality	72.83	27.17	62.29	32.70
June 2, 1986	Agreement that independent citizens have the right to be elected without being affiliated with any political party?	30.51	69.49	64.43	16.11
Jan. 15, 1978	Approval of a new constitution draft	57.20	42.80	86.73	37.27

[a] Yes = simple direct popular election, No = partial appointment through private and public bodies.
[b] Data on registration from Idea International, http://www.tse.gov.ec.

for reforming the constitution, giving that right exclusively to the National Congress (Thomas Acuña 2007).

By the late 1980s, Colombians witnessed an apex in violence; constant failures of peace agreements among the state, the guerrillas, and the paramilitaries; a concomitant crisis within the political and party system; and an incredibly fragile economic situation. In the general elections of 1990, an amorphous social movement (led by the student unions of the country) succeeded in including an informal ballot calling for a constituent assembly to reform Colombia's archaic constitution. Massive support for the measure via opinion polls and pushes for inclusion of the ballot in their vote pushed the establishment to count the votes of the initiative. Then, in a legally questionable measure, the Supreme Court of Justice declared the initiative retrospectively binding.

The constituent assembly of 1991 signaled the end of bipartisan Colombia and the beginning of a complete metamorphosis of the country's party system (Bejarano and Pizarro 2005). The new electoral laws included in the charter – approved in two discussions of Congress in the same year – triggered the emergence of a multiplicity of political parties and movements whose result was a chaotic and unmanageable party system with serious implications for partisan discipline and cohesion (Rodríguez Raga and Botero 2006: 139).

At the brink of a complete collapse of the party system, Alvaro Uribe, a former member of the Liberal Party running as an independent based on the discourse typical of a political outsider (against politicians, politics, corruption, and the functioning of the institutions) won by a landslide, representing a clear conservative shift in the Colombian electorate (toward law, order, [neo]liberal economic orientation – everything that, for him, fit under the banner of the "democratic peace"). Uribe's platform underlined a refoundation effort calling for reform against the *corrupción y politiquería*, and there was no better way of achieving this than calling for a national plebiscite that would legitimize his tough policies, especially the abolition of "long-established personal privileges of legislators as well as the suppression of traditional pork barreling and vote buying practices" (Breuer 2008a).

Given that the executive authorities in Colombia cannot call for an ad hoc vote on matters of particular importance without the consent of the entire ministerial cabinet and the approval of the senate (article 50 of Law 134 of 1994), a painful negotiation with Congress began. Uribe softened the tone of his first draft to obtain legislative support. Whereas for Breuer this constitutes the "sole case of a reactive referendum [in my typology, plebiscite] triggered by the legislature on an executive proposal" (Breuer 2007: 567), this interpretation deserves further scrutiny.

Any time an executive sends a proposal to the legislature, it is likely to suffer some modification. In October 2003, just one year after being elected, Uribe successfully sent fifteen questions to the citizenry, including some hot-button economic and political reforms. Despite each question being written in a manner that was amazingly favorable to Uribe's interests, just one out of fifteen achieved the participation quorum for being legally binding (25 percent of the electorate). Regardless of this failure, Uribe advanced his agenda of austerity measures and political reforms, which included an FTA with the United States and enjoyed comfortable majorities in Congress.

Uribe's approach to conflict explains, at least partially, why he sustains constantly high popular approval ratings. In May 2006, Uribe was reelected for a consecutive term, and his second administration has had a constant presence in major newspapers all over the world because of its international implications. In March 2008, a Colombian cross-border strike into Ecuador that killed senior Revolutionary Armed Forces of Colombia (FARC) rebel Raúl Reyes sparked a diplomatic crisis with both Ecuador and Venezuela. Five months later, the successful rescue of fifteen hostages from the clutches of the FARC boosted Uribe's popularity to the unprecedented level of 90 percent of the Colombian electorate.

Such is the bandwagon effect of Uribe's presidency that more than 5 million signatures (5,021,873) were presented to the electoral authorities for a constitutional popular initiative that would allow him a second immediate reelection (third consecutive mandate).[10] The campaign took fewer than three months, and important questions have been raised with regard to the financing sources for such a campaign. These questions are justified by the presumably intimate relationship between drug trafficking and politics in the country. Evidently, the campaign cost significant sums of money, and there is no imaginable way of gathering an average of sixty thousand signatures a day (seven thousand signatures per hour!) without potential funding by traffickers. The speaker of the campaign for Uribe's reelection, Luis Guillermo Giraldo, stated that the signatures were gathered without the consent of President Uribe, though it is also true that Uribe did not deauthorize the campaign (*El Tiempo*, August 12, 2008).

In late February 2010, the Colombian Constitutional Court refused to allow a popular vote that would have decided whether President Uribe could run for a third consecutive term. Although Uribe enjoyed one of the highest approval rates of any Latin American president, seven of nine members of the court refused to accept the proposal because of clear procedural errors in the gathering of signatures supporting the popular vote as well as because of significant doubts concerning the constitutionality of the proposal itself (Table 5.3).

c. Bolivia
Bolivia constitutes a special case within the study of direct democracy in weak democracies. In this country, executives and local authorities have repeatedly

---

[10] These numbers notably exceed the required threshold (5 percent of the electoral register, or about 1.5 million) for signatures needed to trigger a popular initiative. As a note, the signatures were delivered to the *Registraduría* in two armored vehicles and escorted by the national police. Each of the 5 million signatures had to be checked in one month and for that purpose, more than eighty full-time workers were designated at a cost of about U.S.$500,000.

TABLE 5.3. *Mechanisms of Direct Democracy in Colombia (Since 1978)*

	Questions	Yes (%)	No (%)	Turnout (%)	Affirmative/ Registered
Oct. 25, 2003	Q1: Ban from holding public office any person previously convicted on corruption charges	93.33	6.67	25.11	23.43
	Q2: Introduction of nominal vote in Congress	94.35	5.65	24.82	23.42
	Q3: Abolition of substitute legislators	93.27	6.73	24.97	23.29
	Q4: Active participation of Congress, regional assemblies, and municipal councils in formulation and control of national budget	86.52	13.48	24.52	21.22
	Q5: Handing over the administrative functions of the legislature to an independent private or public independent body	93.60	6.40	24.16	22.61
	Q6: Dissolution of the 263-seat bicameral congressional body and convocation of new elections for a unicameral 150-seat body	93.00	7.00	22.85	21.26
	Q7: Strict ethical codes to govern the National Congress and regional and municipal councils (e.g., revocation mandate in case of reiterated absence from plenary sessions, infraction of campaign finance norms, vote buying, etc.)	94.71	5.29	22.76	21.55
	Q8: Limit public-sector salaries and pensions at a maximum of twenty-five minimum wages	90.06	9.94	24.82	22.35
	Q9: Abolition of municipal auditing authorities	90.57	9.43	24.48	22.17
	Q11: Prohibition of public budgetary allocations to specific projects promoted by legislators	93.57	6.43	24.36	22.80
	Q12: Destination of savings from abolition of municipal auditing offices and *personerías* to public education projects	93.87	6.13	24.09	22.61

(Continued)

TABLE 5.3 *(continued)*

Questions	Yes (%)	No (%)	Turnout (%)	Affirmative/ Registered
Q13: Reallocation of royalty transfers to educational services (53 percent), water and sanitation projects (36 percent), and national pension funds of the respective territorial units (7 percent)	93.39	6.61	24.68	23.05
Q14: Two-year freeze on operational spending in addition to a cap on public-sector pension and salary outlays, which exceed two minimum wages	80.28	19.72	24.38	19.57
Q15: Introduction of a 2 percent threshold as requirement for legal registration of political parties	91.06	8.94	23.91	21.77
Q18: Immediate legal enforcement upon promulgation of all reforms except numeral 6	93.71	6.29	23.31	21.84
Oct. 26, 1997 "I vote for Peace, Life, and Freedom"	91.49	8.51	47.88	43.81
Dec. 09, 1990 Appointment of the constitutional board (Because the Supreme Court had declared the results of student unions initiative legally binding, the newly elected President Gaviria decided to reinforce the legitimacy of the constitutional board by ratifying the results of the election to this body via a referendum.)	97.58	2.42	26.06	20.99
May 27, 1990 Convocation of a constitutional assembly (initiated by the student movement *Septima Papeleta* and later declared binding by the Supreme Court)	95.79	4.21	43.49	37.67

used MDDs; however, their use has exacerbated imbedded problems rather than deactivating them.

Bolivia is the poorest country in South America and one of the poorest in the world (more than 65 percent of its population lives below the national poverty line). Economic chaos, including high levels of hyperinflation and problems of political legitimization, characterized the first postauthoritarian governments of Bolivia. The government of Hernán Siles Zuazo from 1982 to 1985 faced severe obstacles in its attempts to stabilize the impoverished economy of Bolivia, where the hyperinflation rate reached 26,000 percent from 1984 to 1985. Two phenomena are germane to understanding the use of MDDs in the country: Presidential Decree 21,060 and the Law of Popular Participation of 1994. Both have fueled strikes, blockades, work stoppages, hunger strikes, marches, and takeovers, which in a way are the background noise of the chaos in which Bolivia seems immersed.[11]

In the early 1990s, Bolivia not only engaged in a radical structural liberalization program that served as an important testing ground for international organizations (Kohl 2002)[12] but also began one the most comprehensive political reforms in area of decentralization in Latin America in the last twenty years. The Popular Participation Law, Ley de Participación Popular (LPP), approved in Congress on April 20, 1994, subdivided Bolivian territory into 314 municipalities, each of which was each given a per-capita share of national resources.[13] As Lee Van Cott clearly demonstrates, "the LPP was in part a response to the failure of the political parties to integrate society and to aggregate and channel its demands" (2000: 170), and the consequences of such drastic reform are more evident today than ever.

Later known as the Gas War (La Guerra del Gas), a series of conflicts during October 2003 caused dozens of deaths and led the country to an absolute tragedy, fostered by President Sánchez de Lozada's idea of exporting Bolivian

---

[11] Early in 2000, the city of Cochabamba experienced the *Guerra del Agua* (Water War) because of the privatization of the public service of drinking water in the city and the authorization to raise tariffs from 40 to 300 percent. On this war, see Daroca Oller (n.d.).

[12] Paz Estenssoro from the Movimiento Nacionalista Revolucionario become president for the period of 1985 to 1989, and very early in his administration (August 29, 1985), he approved the Decree Nueva Política Económica (NPE) – New Economic Policy (Decree 21,060). This decree meant a liberalization of the economy, the "ascendance of the private sector as the central actor in economic development, recuperation of state control over key state enterprises that had been captured by factional cliques and labour groups" (Gamarra 1997: 373). As Mayorga states, it is interesting to note that the Decree 21,060 was the first structural adjustment program in Latin America to be carried out under democratic conditions (1997: 146).

[13] Known as the principle of coparticipación (coparticipation), 20 percent of national state expenditure is now disbursed among the local governments (municipalities) on a per-capita basis. Indigenous, peasant communities (campesinos), and neighborhood organizations gained legal status as formal representatives of their constituent populations through Grassroots Territorial Organizations (OTB). The OTBs from a single canton elect representatives for a municipal Vigilance Committee (Comité de Vigilancia, CV), whose role is to oversee municipal expenditures and budgets (Altman and Lalander 2003).

gas to the United States through Chile. This action touched deeply on two elements that, in combination, were explosive, reviving years-long anti-Chilean resentment by the historic maritime claim (Arrarás and Deheza 2005) and the flag of the Bolivian revolution of the 1950s (Mayorga 1997). By the end of that month, Sánchez de Lozada was forced to resign and flee the country. Carlos Mesa (the former vice president) was invested by Congress to finish Lozada's mandate. To deactivate the so-called *Octubre Negro* conflict, Mesa called for a binding national plebiscite on the gas policies of Sánchez de Lozada, calling for a constituent assembly and reforming the hydrocarbons law (*Ley de Hidrocarburos*).[14]

On July 18, 2004, Bolivians were asked five questions that basically amounted to whether gas should be exported; if the state should regain control of the gas sector, which was opened up to private investors in the mid-1990s; and whether gas sales should be used as a bargaining chip in negotiations with Chile in the territorial dispute over access to the Pacific.

After the abovementioned plebiscite (called *referendum del gas*), a deep discussion arose in Congress regarding the degree of taxation on the gas and oil industries. Whereas moderate groups sought to tax the industry at about 20 percent, the Movimiento al Socialismo (MAS), lead by Evo Morales, argued for raising it to 50 percent. Of course, even at this time, there was some discussion about how to interpret the MDD (for some it was illegal, containing contradictions among questions and using extremely sophisticated language). At the same time, rising fuel prices triggered further large-scale antigovernment mobilizations. Indeed, parties in Congress would eventually impede the conversion of the outcome of the plebiscite into a law (Uggla 2008). Before he had finished two years in office, Mesa resigned in June 2005, and Supreme Court head Eduardo Rodríguez Veltzé was sworn in as caretaker president. The chronic mobilization epitomized a never-ending problem of weak institutional capacity of the state, but between the plebiscite of 2004 and the resignation of Mesa in 2005, several actions occurred that are crucial for this study.

In February 2005, leaders of the Comité Cívico de Santa Cruz (Civic Committee of Santa Cruz), and business organizations (Cámara Agropecuaria del Oriente [CAO] and Cámara de Industria y Comercio [CAINCO]), delivered 6,000 books containing 421,000 signatures to the National Electoral Court, and commenced a popular initiative on autonomy. After much discussion, a lengthy and cumbersome question was finally agreed on. The Mesa government preliminarily set the date for the consult for August 2005 but was forced out of office in June.

With Mesa's exit came the call for general elections (president, vice president, senators, and deputies) for December 2005, and Evo Morales was elected president, with an unprecedented 54 percent of the vote. It was the first time a

---

[14] Until Mesa's takeover, Bolivia lacked the articulation of legal apparatus to make any sort of MDD and, following the regular procedures, would have allowed Mesa, at best, to be able to call for a plebiscite in 2007. Thus, an ad hoc procedure was used, stretching the spirit of the law with that purpose. See Arrarás and Deheza (2005: 164).

Native American had become president in a country where more than half of the population was Native American and the first time a president had enjoyed an absolute majority of votes since democratization in 1982.[15] These elections constituted the deepest reshaping of the party system Bolivia had experienced since the military regime.

The novel government recognized the legitimacy of the autonomic initiative and, in March 2006, after a convoluted negotiation process between the MAS and the opposition parties, Parliament approved an extraordinary law to simultaneously call for a constituent assembly and the vote on autonomies. The votes were held in July 2006. The representatives for the constituent assembly were elected, and the "no" to the autonomies won at the national level. However, the "yes" votes triumphed in the eastern departments of Pando, Beni, Santa Cruz, and Tarija. The combination of these four departments constitute the region of the Crescent Moon (Media Luna), the stronghold of opposition.

An enormous debate arose about how to interpret the outcome of the initiative (note that this problem is not new in the Bolivian context and will not be the last time Bolivians face such a problem). The lengthy and bizarre wording of the question itself was widely open to interpretation (Table 5.4). The departments where the "yes" vote won (and won by far) claimed that the result was binding for them. Yet article 2 of the Referendum Law is rather clear that results were contingent on the type of initiative. If the initiative is national, then national results have to be considered. If the initiative is local, then local results are relevant. Despite that the "no" vote was officially proclaimed the victorious side at the national level, that decision did little more than fuel the autonomic desires of the eastern departments of the Crescent Moon. Although Morales convened a constituent assembly to amend Bolivia's Constitution, unlike in Ecuador or Venezuela, this assembly coexisted with the sitting elected Congress, where the governing party lacked legislative majorities (especially in the Senate). Also, lacking a two-thirds majority in the constituent assembly, the MAS resorted to approving the new charter in a military barracks because of the violent opposition of some members of the assembly.

Yet the push for greater autonomy of regions in Bolivia persisted, despite the adverse results of the popular initiative of 2006. The opposition rejected the new constitution approved by the constituent assembly, and prefects from the Crescent Moon departments started a snowball wave of direct votes on greater autonomy from the central government. On May 4, 2008, a nonofficial popular initiative for greater autonomy was held again in Santa Cruz. That MDD was immediately followed by similar measures in Beni and Pando on June 1 and in Tarija on June 22. Unless the central government could deactivate the friction, the confrontation with the eastern prefectures threatened to engulf Bolivia in brutal clashes.

In a masterful play by Morales, in response to the four unofficial (and, for many, illegal) autonomy votes, he called for a plebiscite, putting his office on

---

[15] It has four official languages (Spanish, Quechua, Aymará, and Tupiguaraní), and only 40 percent of the population speaks Spanish as its mother tongue.

TABLE 5.4. *Mechanisms of Direct Democracy in Bolivia (since 1978)*

	Questions	Yes (%)	No (%)	Turnout (%)	Valid Vote/ Registered (%)
Aug. 10, 2008	Do you agree with the continuation of the process of change led by President Evo Morales Ayma and Vice President Álvaro García Linera?	67.41	32.59	83.28	51.98
Jul. 2, 2006	Do you agree, within the framework of national unity, with giving the constituent assembly the binding mandate to establish a regime of departmental autonomy, applicable immediately after the promulgation of the new Political Constitution of the State in the Departments where this Referendum has a majority, so that their authorities are chosen directly by the citizens and receive from the National Government executive authority, administrative power, and financial resources that the Political Constitution of the State and the Laws grant them?	42.41	57.59	84.51	33.32
Jul. 18, 2004	(1) Do you agree that the Hydrocarbons Law (No. 1689), enacted by Gonzalo Sánchez de Lozada, should be repealed?	86.64	13.36	60.08	40.12
	(2) Do you agree that the Bolivian State should recover ownership over all hydrocarbons at the wellhead?	92.19	7.81	59.89	42.92
	(3) Do you agree that Yacimientos Petrolíferos Fiscales Bolivianos [the state-owned oil company privatized under Sánchez de Lozada] should be reestablished, reclaiming state ownership of the Bolivian people's stakes in the part-privatized oil companies, so that it can take part in all stages of the hydrocarbon production chain?	87.31	12.69	59.89	40.23
	(4) Do you agree with President Carlos Mesa's policy of using gas as a strategic recourse to achieve a sovereign and viable route of access to the Pacific Ocean?	54.80	45.20	59.89	23.68
	(5) Do you or do you not agree that Bolivia should export gas as part of a national policy framework that ensures the gas needs of Bolivians; encourages the industrialization of gas in the nation's territory; levies taxes and/or royalties of up to 50% of the production value of oil and gas on oil companies, for the nation's benefit; and earmarks revenues from the export and industrialization of gas mainly for education, health, roads, and jobs?	61.74	38.26	59.87	26.47

Source: Author's calculations based on Consejo Nacional Electoral, http://www.cne.org.bo/.

the table. He defied all prefects to follow suit. It is important to note that the call for the plebiscite was endorsed by senators of the opposition (notably Quiroga, the former president), who aimed for two rather clear objectives: Having that confidence vote, opposition forces were delaying the vote for the new constitution for at least one year (by law, Bolivia can have only one vote of this kind per year), hoping that Morales had weakened his support base in the nation. The opposition's bet turned out to be a failure. Not only did Morales succeed in retaining his support, fortifying his base even in the Crescent Moon region, he also moved to set the vote of popular approval of the new constitution for December 7, 2008. Consequently, only two prefects (i.e., La Paz and Cochabamba) were revoked.

The votes on August 10, 2008, were widely known as fair and clean by national and international observers, despite the wording of the questions being notably ideologically biased in support of the president and against the governors. Nonetheless, it was unclear until just a few days prior to the election exactly how many votes were needed to remove the president or the governors from office (the constitution stated that the incumbent would have to be rejected by a greater percentage of the electorate than had initially voted him or her into office, whereas the electoral authorities [Corte Nacional Electoral] claimed that removal would occur with 50 percent of the vote plus one). In any case, no major problems arose in computing the numbers.

Both supporters and detractors of the measure declared themselves the victorious party. The result was an electoral victory for the government. The executive significantly increased its vote share in comparison with the election of 2005 and achieved noteworthy support even in departments controlled by the opposition. Paradoxically, it was also a success for Morales's main opponents, the prefects of the Crescent Moon. Most of the prefects were ratified, also with more votes than they had obtained in 2005. As Uggla writes, because both sides could claim a renewed and strengthened popular mandate on the basis of their respective votes, the consultation served only to further deepen the conflict rather than resolve it. In fact, the weeks after the pseudo recall were among the most troubled in recent years, leading to some twenty deaths in clashes between supporters and opponents of the government (Uggla 2008).

Although the Bolivian presidential and governors' recall vote of 2008 was indeed a typical plebiscite, it is extremely interesting in that it represents only the second-ever recall internationally for a presidential authority in its objectives. The way it was engendered looked more like a confidence vote than a censure vote. The political results of this vote remain to be seen, and they will hardly ease the divisive political tensions in Bolivia. Indeed, they may aggravate them.

d. Venezuela
Venezuela is a country whose democracy is at odds with the rest of the southern countries on the continent (Coppedge 2005). Although most Latin American regimes succumbed to obscure dictatorships during the 1970s, Venezuela enjoyed a relatively well-functioning democratic regime and served as a shelter

for thousands of South Americans seeking freedom. Later, while most Latin American countries were consolidating their respective democratic regimes in the 1990s, democracy in Venezuela was approaching collapse, with both government and opposition immersed in an arena where they were gambling their accumulated institutional capital in resorting to democratic and nondemocratic tools for political change (Alvarez and Acosta 2006).

As was the case for its neighbor Colombia, 1958 was a crucial year for Venezuela, which paradoxically is an extremely rich country with a poor society.[16] During that year, the *Pacto de Punto Fijo* was signed between the major parties of the time (i.e., Acción Democrática, COPEI, and the Unión Republicana Democrática). The pact marked the commencement of an enduring governability agreement, yet at the same time it implied an increasing "petrifaction" of political parties and leaders – within the pact was the seed of its own collapse. During the best years of *puntofijismo*, political parties were so overinstitutionalized that it was unnecessary to hold votes in Congress – it was enough simply to know the positions of the party leaders (Coppedge 1994: 24). In a way, Congress became a marginal – or, at best, the "rubber-stamp legitimizing" – institution of political parties.

During February 1989, a 100 percent increase in the price of petrol came into force across the country, as laid out in the program of macroeconomic adjustments announced on February 16 by the government of President Carlos Andrés Pérez (López Maya 2003: 120), an abrupt policy switch known as *Gran Viraje* (Great Turnaround). This policy reform produced a series of uprisings on February 27, 1989, in Caracas, and other cities "were the scene of barricades, road closures, the stoning of shops, shooting and widespread looting" (López Maya 2003: 117). This social explosion was known as the *Caracazo*,[17] a symbol that all agreements were undermined and that parties and unions had lost their ability to represent the people and especially to channel social discontent (Lissidini 2007).[18]

In February 1992, Hugo Chávez attempted to coordinate a (failed) military coup d'état and was sent to prison, yet this "catapulted him onto the centre stage of Venezuelan politics" (Ellner 2003: 143). Pérez was impeached a year later, and Congress selected Ramón Velásquez as interim president. The 1994 election of Rafael Caldera did little to improve the much-deteriorated democratic equilibrium, and in 1999, Venezuelans elected Hugo Chávez to the presidency (Lalander 2004).[19]

---

[16] As Karl has argued, Venezuela's oil has been a curse as well as a blessing (1985).

[17] On this topic, see Walton and Seddon (1994).

[18] Indeed, as discussed previously, Carlos Andrés Pérez epitomizes one of those presidents in the region who had betrayed his campaign promises (Stokes 2001).

[19] Recurrent opinion polls demonstrated that Venezuelans tend to impugn their economic disaster on the misuse of resources by dishonest politicians rather than the debt crises or the falling of oil prices (Coppedge 2005: 311).

Chávez is such a character that it is highly unlikely that his accession to the presidency would have produced indifference in any observer of Venezuelan or Latin American politics. For many, he represented a new beginning for Venezuela's institutions. His first measure, as promised in his campaign (Amorim Neto 2006: 162), was to convene a constituent assembly in 1999 to rewrite his country's constitution and eliminate any vestiges of its traditional "patriarchy." Unlike Bolivia, where the Constituent National Assembly coexisted with Parliament, the Venezuelan assembly – elected in 1999 – supplanted Congress and governed for a transitional phase after the new constitution was finally drafted. The new constitution was approved in a popular vote in December 1999.

Early in 2002, a nationwide strike and protests finalized the removal of the president by the military. "Business leader Pedro Carmona was installed as president, and promptly dissolved the Congress, refused to recognize the 1999 constitution, and tried to arrest elected Chavista governors and mayors. Within forty-eight hours, an outpouring of support for President Chávez in the streets, international condemnation, more deaths, and splits within the military led military officers to reverse course and reinstall the president to his post" (McCoy 2006: 64). The United States was one of the few governments (along with Spain, Ecuador, and Costa Rica) to salute the new government. Paradoxically, Chávez was defended using the Inter-American Democratic Charter – a charter he refused to sign in 2001.

Polarization grew in Venezuela, and the country was brought to a virtual standstill during 2003 and 2004. The refusal of the opposition to abide by constitutional rules until the coup of 2002 drastically changed (Alvarez 2007) and, paradoxically, employed the Chávez constitution of 1999 against him through the activation of a presidential recall – a constitutional right in the hands of the citizenry.

The signatures for a presidential recall were gathered during the summer of 2003, but the president of the national electoral council announced on September 12, 2003, that the petition had been rejected because the signatures had been gathered months before the August 19 midpoint of President Chávez's term in office and were inadmissible (the constitution was explicit that a president could not be impeached before his midterm, but it did not stipulate whether that same timetable would affect the gathering of signatures).[20]

---

[20] Article 72 of the 1999 Constitution states: "All [...] offices filled by popular vote are subject to revocation. Once one-half of the term of office to which an official has been elected has elapsed, a number of voters representing at least 20% of the registered voters in the affected constituency may petition for the calling of a referendum to revoke that official's mandate. When a number of voters equal to or greater than the number of those who elected the official vote in favor of the recall, provided that a number of voters equal to or greater than 25% of the total number of registered voters vote in the recall referendum, the official's mandate shall be deemed revoked and immediate action shall be taken to fill the permanent vacancy as provided for by this Constitution and by law."

One month later, the opposition mounted another attempt in the form of a four-day signature-gathering marathon that produced a new petition. This time, about 3.5 million signatures were collected, but the electoral council said that only 1.9 million were valid – the others either were invalid or dubious. For the second time in less than a year, the electoral authorities rejected a petition that was endorsed by a large portion of society. This rejection produced severe clashes between public forces, rioting in Caracas, and a long series of legalistic discussions. Venezuela was at the brink of a civil war. In an attempt to deflate the crisis, the electoral council set aside five days at the end of May 2004 to allow those citizens with disputed signatures to confirm that they were indeed theirs and that they did in fact back the referendum call.[21] At the end of that verification process, the electoral authorities said that the minimum required number of signatures had been obtained and, therefore, the referendum could take place.

Finally, on August 15, 2004, the recall was held, and Chávez (gathering almost 60 percent of the vote) successfully survived the confidence vote in a heavily internationally monitored popular vote that generally was accepted as cleanly conducted (McCoy 2005). Yet for some, the fairness of the process remains in serious doubt (Febres Cordero and Márquez 2006; Kornblith 2005). This doubt is somewhat founded because the question posed to citizens was odd in that it was asked somewhat counterintuitively; essentially, a "yes" vote was a "no to Chávez" vote – that is, a "yes to the recall" vote. The question was worded as follows: *Do you agree to revoke, for the current term, the popular mandate as President of the Bolivarian Republic of Venezuela conferred on citizen Hugo Rafael Chávez Frías through democratic and legitimate elections? NO or YES?*

In 2004, officialist parties won twenty-two of twenty-four states in the federation within a context of extremely low electoral participation and civic disaffection by the vast majority of citizens. Since 2005, the president has had absolute dominance over the legislature. Chávez was neatly reelected in 2006, and the moderate opposition recognized that the elections had occurred without fraud (Alvarez 2007).

Despite all of these victories for Chávez and his allies, he was defeated at the ballot box on December 2, 2007. He submitted to the citizenry a package of comprehensive constitutional amendments that failed to win the support of a majority of the electorate. This plebiscite was presented to voters in two separate groups ("Bloques"). Bloque A was composed by forty-six articles, of which thirty-three were directly proposed by the president; Bloque B included

---

[21] The names of the petition signers became public after the National Electoral Council presumably gave access to the Chavista member of the National Assembly, Luis Tascón, who created a Web site with all of the names, supposedly to help in the verification process. Some of those whose names appeared to be in the Tascón's List "could find themselves subjected to public derision; some in the public sector even lost their jobs" (Kornblith 2005:128).

twenty-three articles proposed by the National Assembly. Both Bloques were narrowly defeated by a margin of approximately 2 percent (Alvarez 2008).

As expected, the defeat at the ballot box was not welcomed by Chávez and his government, and on the very same night of the setback, he announced that he would repeat his try as many times as necessary. President Chávez alleged:

[The opposition] may know how to administer their victory, but they are filling it full of shit. It is a shitty victory! They call what happened to us a defeat, but it is a courageous defeat, filled with valor and dignity. Get ready because there is a new reform proposal offensive coming at us, may it be a transformation or a simplification, but I am sure it is coming. I have received letters from popular leaders, because the people know that if they collect enough signatures that this reform can be subject to a referendum again under other conditions, in another moment, in this same place that we call Venezuela. Therefore, gentlemen of the opposition, I would not be singing a victory song. (*El Universal*, December 6, 2007)

Finally, Chávez fulfilled his threats on February 2009. A plebiscite triggered by the National Assembly, allowing continuous reelection, among other reforms, was approved by 54.9 percent. In the end, Chávez's persistence paid off and he got his way (Table 5.5).

2. Direct Democracy within Inchoate Party Systems

The countries of Latin America serve as a lab experiment for studying the effects MDDs can have on the functioning of relatively young and not-so-consolidated democracies. Conventional wisdom has accused direct democracy of being one of the institutions that has created delegative leaders: "the practice whereby presidents use referendums [in my typology, *plebiscites*] to bypass legislative opposition has worked to the detriment of the horizontal dimension of accountability" (Breuer 2007: 554). However, the record of most Latin American countries shows something different – that minimized horizontal accountability was already functioning at the time MDDs were deployed. Hence, pointing to direct democracy as one of the causes of weak representative institutions is both confusing and erroneous.

Direct democracy is more a consequence than a cause of weak institutions. A political regime that does not deliver public goods is dismissed as corrupt, sustains inequalities, exhibits shortages in representation, and survives only because of banal pork barreling. It is expected that such a regime, sooner or later, will be subject to stressful situations. These situations usually bring about a complete reshuffling and sometimes even a complete metamorphosis of the political milieu. In these contexts, political parties are incapable of responding to the expectations of the citizenry, and these fluid times open the door for classic messianic visions of the political set, making these the best environments for political outsiders to exploit. These leaders are characterized by their search for rapid recovery without "wasting time on politics" and all other malaises of which the *ancien régimes* were "guilty." Venezuela's Chávez – an evident

TABLE 5.5. *Mechanisms of Direct Democracy in Venezuela (Since 1978)*

	Questions	Yes (%)	No (%)	Turnout (%)	Affirmative/ Registered (%)
Feb. 15, 2009	Approval of the amendment of articles 160, 162, 174, 192, and 230 of the Constitution of the Republic prepared by initiative of the National Assembly, which extends the political rights of the people in order to allow any citizen in exercise of a public office by popular election to become a candidate to the same office for the constitutionally established term, his election depending exclusively on the popular vote	54.87	45.13	70.35	37.9
Dec. 2, 2007	Approval of the draft of constitutional reform, presented in (Block A) two blocks and sanctioned by the National Assembly with the participation of the people and based on the initiative of (Block B) President Hugo Chávez	49.30 / 48.94	50.70 / 51.06	55.88 / 55.72	27.18 / 26.91
Aug. 8, 2004	Agreement to "revoke, for the current term, the popular mandate conferred on citizen Hugo Rafael Chávez Frías as President of the Bolivarian Republic of Venezuela through democratic and legitimate elections"	40.75	59.25	69.92	28.42
Dec. 3, 2000	Agreement with "the removal of existing trade union leaders from office mandate to totally replace the union leadership within the next 180 days" in elections supervised by the CNE	69.40	30.60	23.50	14.58
Dec. 15, 1999	Approval of the constitution draft prepared by the National Constituent Assembly	71.78	28.22	44.05	30.18
Apr. 25, 1999	Agreement with the Executive's proposal for the calling of a national constituent assembly according to the presidential decree examined and modified by the electoral authorities	86.50	13.50	37.37	30.68
Apr. 25, 1999	Convocation of a national constituent assembly to transform the state and create a new institutional order that would allow an effective functioning of a social and participatory democracy	92.36	7.64	37.47	32.94

Source: Author's calculations based on Consejo Nacional Electoral, http://www.cne.gov.ve/.

product of the Fourth Republic – best exemplified this type of leader. Indeed, it is impossible to understand the Venezuelan politics of today without taking into account the *Punto Fijo* agreement and the encapsulation of the country's party system since that time (Coppedge 2005).

These political outsiders, impatient to showcase their reforms, are tempted to bypass the classic institutions of checks and balances (O'Donnell 2002). These institutions (which traditionally have done the heavy lifting in the *ancien régime*) are usually blamed (as are the old politicians) and branded as corrupted, ineffective, and an incessant waste of time and resources. At times, these new leaders not only bypass representative institutions but also sometimes have incentives (and the power) to literally get rid of them. The recent moves to supplant sitting congresses by constituent assemblies in Venezuela and Ecuador exemplify this case. Thus, these leaders, though elected in relatively free and fair elections, have all of the incentives to go their own way, governing "directly with the people," because they believe they are the only ones who truly understand their citizens' needs. They are convinced they know exactly what to do: rearrange the rules of the game through a new order. This new order is accompanied by new adjectives that may be associated with their own form of democracy, whether participatory, popular, egalitarian, or revolutionary.

These leaders use all of the prerogatives at hand, and MDDs are just one of them. These institutions become more appealing in the context of amorphous groups of civic organizations, not only because of all the power resources that such a mobilization capabilities, but also because miscellaneous social groups that otherwise have little in common are molded into a more coherent one in the context of high political effervescence. When citizens expect a change but the (republican) institutional channels of representation are sterile, out of the way, or unreachable, political anxieties shift to other corridors. To be sure, sometimes this democratic hunger could easily, and paradoxically, derail into a democratic movement with undemocratic consequences. Ecuador, perhaps more than any other country in recent times, exemplifies how Congress was easily closed because, among those mobilized, there was not a broad-enough consensus on the importance of that institution for the reasons explained (Machado 2008). MDDs could be a practical instrument in the hands of political outsiders, becoming one of their preferred tools because they mobilize, they are "really" democratic, and they legitimize.

For oppositional forces, however, MDDs seldom create a window of opportunity, despite all the weaknesses inherent in these volatile democracies. By their very nature, MDDs create at least two clearly differentiated positions, yet if there is a hope for free and fair elections, they should also be embraced by the opposition. If free and fair elections are not the minimum minimorum, that particular regime cannot be considered a democracy at all and deserves to be included in Chapter 4 of this book. The Venezuelan plebiscite of 2007 represents how, despite the unevenness of the playing field, executive proposals sometimes can be derailed by the ballot.

3. Final Remarks

Given that MDDs leave ample room for manipulation by governments that either want to evade their liability for the political price of conflictive policies,[22] obtain additional legitimacy on their policies,[23] or neutralize other state institutions by, for example, bypassing parliamentary deliberations, existing laws, and constitutional rules,[24] plebiscites have produced a deeper aversion than any other type of MDD.[25] Such are the implications of plebiscites that some scholars would go so far as to exclude them from the direct democratic realm, yet this is based more on normative criteria than on strictly conceptual delimitation.

In a way, this chapter stresses the theoretical discussion of Chapter 2, which assumed that certain levels of horizontal and vertical accountability are present within the environment where MDDs are practiced. Unregulated or facultative plebiscites are blamed for triggering delegative democracies, but it has been shown that delegative democrats use MDDs, not necessarily the other way around. Even leaders of questionable legitimacy use MDDs to foster their particular interests. MDDs open a window of opportunity in the context of minimalist democratic guarantees.

When controversies about a political institution push a country to the verge of a civil war, incurring casualties and injuries in the process, the institution requires serious study. Such is the case with MDDs. Although these mechanisms are employed uneventfully in some countries, in others, the tension associated with MDDs may bring them to virtual political collapse (as occurred in the last months of 2002 and the first months of 2003 in Venezuela).

Have MDDs helped to further undermine the already-weak institutions that several of these countries have exhibited? I claim a reasonable amount of skepticism with regard to this argument. Latin American history is plagued with critical constitutional reforms over which citizens had no control. Most likely, if Venezuela had had a constitutional arrangement, as was the case in Chile in 2005 (where constitutional amendments were approved simply by the sitting Congress without consultation with any other actor), Chávez's 2007 constitution would have been adopted without major problems because of the absolute majority he enjoys in Congress.[26]

However, the counterargument works as well. Would the party system of Venezuela have collapsed had it used MDDs to channel social pressures? The answer to this is ambiguous because of the counterfactual nature of the question. In any case, it is perfectly possible to imagine that instead of a *Caracazo*,

---

[22] On this regard, see Setälä (2006a; 2006b), Butler and Ranney (1994), and Zimmerman (1986).

[23] For example, see Altman (2002b; 2005) and Gross (2002).

[24] As exemplified by Breuer (2007; 2008a).

[25] Kaufmann and Waters (2004) and Suksi (1993).

[26] After all, the Dominican (1994), Honduran (1982), Salvadorian (1983), and Nicaraguan (1987, 1995) constitutions, to mention just a few, suffered important alterations without any scrutiny by their respective citizens and within an environment of poor democratic performance.

citizens could have gathered signatures to shift the executive policies to their preferred ideal point. Furthermore, knowing that citizens have those prerogatives in their hands, the package advanced by the executive at the time might have been much more attenuated, making even the process of signature gathering unnecessary. This is pure speculation; however, it helps to build the argument advanced in the next two chapters. CI-MDDs are reasonable barometers for society; they force a finer tuning between party elites and citizens and serve as institutionalized intermittent safety valves for political pressure.

6

Direct Democracy within Democracies

The Case of Uruguay (Historic Evolution and Voting Behavior)

> Ciudadanos: el resultado de la campaña pasada me puso al frente de vosotros por el voto sagrado de vuestra voluntad general. [...] Mi autoridad emana de vosotros y ella cesa ante vuestra presencia soberana.
>
> José Gervasio Artigas, National Hero of Uruguay (April 5, 1813)[1]

Whereas Chapters 4 and 5 dealt with MDDs in the context of authoritarian and weak democratic regimes, respectively, this chapter shifts our attention to the use of these mechanisms in a relatively stable democratic regime. This and the following chapter tackle a unique case study: Uruguay. But why use a case study, and why Uruguay in particular? Three factors make Uruguay a particularly useful case study. First, Uruguay demonstrates significant variation in the dependent variable (referendums, plebiscites, popular initiatives, and legislative counterproposals). Second, Uruguay has a peculiar party system that makes it relatively easy to observe what is happening inside parties because the internal divisions are clear.[2] Finally, Uruguay is the most prodigious user of CI-MDDs in the global south; it does not belong to the "developed" north, neither is it a member of the OECD or the European Union. All these factors make it an "ideal case" for understanding direct democracy.

The intensive study of a case allows the decision-making process to be closely analyzed in order "to sift more finely through varied sources of evidence, and to pursue traces of politicians' reasoning and calculations in ways not possible when the field of observation spans many national settings" (Mershon 1996:

---

[1] "Citizens, during the last campaign you choose me to lead you through the sacred vote of your general will [...] My authority originates from you, and it ceases with your sovereign will."

[2] The institutional design of Uruguayan presidentialism has varied substantially since it became a democratic regime at the turn of the twentieth century; thus, we will be able to assess the impact that different institutional designs have on uses of direct democracy, holding constant other variables.

539). Also, "it allows us to take account of historical persistencies and different constellations of major causal factors, it identifies sequences that are potentially causally relevant, it establishes agency, and makes use of complex contextual knowledge in the operationalization of theoretical concepts" (Rueschemeyer, Huber, and Stephens 1992: 58).

Uruguay has had the most enduring democratic system of governance in Latin America (Smith 2004). Unlike other countries on the continent, there have been virtually no challenges to the state's monopoly of the use of force throughout the territory. Furthermore, by almost any set of criteria, the country has been an institutionalized liberal democracy for a significant part of the twentieth century, with political conflict and change following institutionalized and democratic procedures. Democratic institutions have been traditionally operational, and political decisions have been processed by the proper popularly elected authorities without any constraints on the free and fair nature of elections. Thus, I raise the question: What has made Uruguay so remarkable compared with other countries in this rather complex and convoluted region? The adoption of the aforementioned institutions in Uruguay is surprising not because of the country's uniqueness in the Latin American continent but because of its similarities with other countries in the region (i.e., like the majority of the countries in the region, Uruguay has Spanish colonial history; it has suffered violent confrontations in the process of organizing the state; its development was based on an agricultural-export economy; it was strongly dependent on the external market; and it had left-wing army groups and dictatorships).

However, despite being the Latin American country with the most years of democratic experience since the turn of the twentieth century, no constitution lasted more than eighteen years without suffering significant reforms. The country has seen continuous revision regarding electoral rules and the structure of the executive branch, having experienced semicollegiate, "pure" collegiate, and "classic" presidentialism, among others. Nonetheless, despite this institutional volatility, some frameworks have endured longer than others, even to the point of transforming themselves in institutions with strong roots in society. Among these, an institution has developed for citizens to have a voice regarding any major institutional and constitutional change. These have existed in several forms: first as obligatory referendums, then as popular initiatives, and finally as facultative referendums.

This chapter has two major sections. The first section accounts for the historical and legal context in which direct democracy has developed (tracing direct democracy in Uruguay since the constitutional discussions of the midteens of the twentieth century). The second section examines how the use of CI-MDDs challenges existing theories of voting behavior in Uruguay (finding that when Uruguayans go to the polls to vote on a popular initiative, their vote choice is primarily the result of their party loyalty rather than a reaction to economic conditions).

1. Historical and Legal Context of Direct Democracy

It is possible to trace direct democracy in Uruguay to the constitutional discussions of the mid-teens of the 1900s. Although constitutional plebiscites were included along with popular initiatives in the constitution of 1934, they already had been used in 1917 on issues such as whether the president could be reelected and what shape a potential National Council of Administration would have (semicollegiate),[3] universal enfranchisement for males, and the separation of church and state, among others. After 1934, obligatory referendums (also known as "constitutional plebiscites") and popular initiatives were used several times, but it was not until the constitution of 1967 that facultative referendums were included (through an obligatory referendum, of course).

It is not a coincidence that direct democracy arrived in Uruguay earlier than in most countries of the world. José Batlle y Ordóñez, a Colorado, assumed the presidency in 1903; the legacy of his two administrations (1903–1907 and 1911–1915) remains strong. Batlle's "project" represented the most radical challenge to the status quo presented by any Latin American reformer during or since this period. His two administrations ushered in a three-decade-long cycle of reform, the societal manifestations of which included modernity, democracy, and an indelible link between the state and *batllismo*. The strategy of batllismo focused on the incorporation of broad sectors of society (from workers to immigrants) without confronting the classic oligarchy or adopting a conservative order (Lissidini 1998: 173).[4] In his first presidency, Batlle focused largely on processes of state building and institutionalizing democratic norms. It was during his second presidency that the nation's welfare state gained its form and content.

batllismo

---

[3] The Constitution of 1917 resulted from this bargaining process. Extensive negotiations during the bargaining phase produced a draft constitution. The central foci of that draft were the creation of a bi-cephalous executive and the introduction of proportional representation for the Chamber of Deputies (Buquet and Castellano 1995). Uruguayan citizens approved the Constitution in an ad hoc presidential plebiscite (the first ever of its kind in Uruguay) held in November 1917. This established an executive power divided between two bodies: the President and the National Council of Administration (NCA). This Council was modeled on notions of power sharing and was composed of nine members, all of whom were directly elected by the citizenry through the use of a double simultaneous vote. Each member served a term of six years, with one-third (three members) of the Council elected every two years. At that time, Uruguayans went to the polls almost yearly. This fact worried those in the most conservative sectors of society but, at the same time, that practice rapidly solidified the electoral process as the main vehicle for political competition (Caetano and Rilla 1994: 129).

[4] Thus, Uruguay, along with Costa Rica and Chile, followed the Marshallian sequence of civil-political-social rights (Marshall 1992). O'Donnell argues that "Uruguay, on its part, with its very early welfare state, achieved social and political rights almost simultaneously. One way or the other, the pattern in these three countries is similar to those in the Northwest in the sense that, especially in the urban sectors, there existed a reasonably high degree of implantation of civil rights previously to the achievement of social and political ones" (O'Donnell 2001: 603). Interestingly enough, the three countries (i.e., Uruguay, Chile, and Costa Rica) are systematically pointed out as the most democratic regimes in Latin America.

During those years, several members of the Uruguayan political elite, beginning with Batlle himself, were strongly influenced by the liberal ideas coming from continental Europe. Batlle recognized this influence:

While my candidacy held fast, I was visiting France and Switzerland where I studied close the thousand aspects of their democratic political life, and compared the political forms of the European States with the archaic and very old Constitution of my country. I remembered that by our Constitution of 1830, we were constantly exposed to the bad luck of having a president of dubious intentions and with the sum of the really extraordinary faculties that our Constitution grants to him. That this person was free to took everything, to devastate the institutions and to sank the country in the most dark of the dictatorships (Batlle in Nahum 1994: 63).

Despite that one of the most contentious reforms championed by Batlle was the creation of a collegiate executive based on the Swiss experience (in Spanish, *colegiado*), there was an interparty consensus that elections, rather than civil wars, were the tool of political power par excellence.[5] Moreover, the first signs of MDDs can be traced to these constitutional discussions and evidently had their seed in the idea that sovereignty rests in the nation, which lies in each and every citizen in the country. For the reforms of 1917, Batlle championed the plebiscite as a measure in defense of freedom and against caprices of the state and public officials:

This measure will prevent the branches of government, acting in concert, from legally extending their own faculties, or voiding them, or destroying or eliminating the freedoms we will create. [. . .] The plebiscite will cut off at its roots the possibility of this manner of attacks (Batlle in El Día, May 30, 1916, quoted by Lissidini 1998: 179–180).

Yet the "European influence" is not a sufficiently strong explanation because the organization of other Latin American countries also follows this influence (but direct democracy was not developed in other Latin American countries as it was in Uruguay). Additionally, many European countries that debated the use of these mechanisms did not incorporate them, neither did they develop them as in Uruguay. Why, then, did Uruguay follow the Swiss model while the rest of the countries followed the North American, English, or French model? To answer this question, I maintain that despite Batlle's deep normative convictions (where the Swiss influences are evident), there were also notorious short-term partisan and political interests toward advancing with direct democracy. In cases where the legislature was adverse to some reforms (i.e., the collegiate executive), MDDs would offer the opportunity to transfer the political stalemate to a third arena: the citizenry. In a way, direct democracy was advanced by Batlle as a means for achieving the supreme political goal of the *colegiado*.

Despite Batlle's deep convictions, it is well known that there were also short-term partisan and political interests for advancing direct democracy. Hundreds

---

[5] The basic rationale underlying the logic of this change stemmed from the notion that the office of the presidency remained susceptible to the whims of individuals and exigencies of specific political situations.

of pages could be written analyzing the process of constitutional reforms of 1917; however, for our purposes, it is enough to point out that no MDD was incorporated in this charter (despite its approval through a plebiscite legitimized by an ad hoc law passed in February 1912).

The constitution of 1934 (article 284) spelled out several ways it could be reformed. Among those, it suggested – partially or in their entirety – the following procedures:

a) When a petition with the signatures of 20 percent of the citizens was presented to the president of the General Assembly, the petition's constitutional revisions would be submitted to popular decision in the next national (regular) election. In a joint session by both houses, the General Assembly could formulate alternative measures to be submitted to a popular vote, along with the original popular initiative.

b) When constitutional revisions supported by two-fifths of the members of the General Assembly were submitted to its president, the revisions were subject to a popular vote during the next election. In addition to points a) and b), to make the constitutional revisions binding, an absolute majority of the citizens voting would have to cast a "yes" ballot in the elections. If the required number of votes was obtained, the reform would be approved.

c) The Constitution also could be reformed by those constitutional laws that required, for their approval, two-thirds of the General Assembly. These laws did not need executive approval and were binding immediately after they were passed by the General Assembly. Nonetheless, these laws would be subject to popular approval in the first election held after their passing, and their final approval was contingent on the support of the majority of the citizenry. When these constitutional laws were about the election of officials, citizens would vote simultaneously for those positions using the proposed system and the previous one, and the final results would depend on the popular decision.

A new constitution was approved in 1942 with two major changes regarding MDDs (see article 281). First, the required percentage for triggering a petition was lowered from 20 to 10 percent; and, second, it incorporated a required quorum for approving constitutional reforms either by plebiscite or by popular initiative. In other words, to make the constitutional revisions binding, an absolute majority of the citizens voting would have to cast a "yes" ballot in the elections, and those voting "yes" would have to represent at least 35 percent of the total inscribed in the National Civic Register.[6] The constitution of 1942 consolidates the main features of the Uruguayan electoral

---

[6] Thus, strictly speaking, the constitution could be reformed with the support of 17.5% + 1 of citizens (50% + 1 of the 35% of the National Civic Register).

system and, for many, it represents the country's entrance to democratic adulthood.[7]

Since 1934, obligatory referendums (also known as "constitutional plebiscites") and constitutional popular initiatives have been used several times, but referendums were not included in the charter until the constitution of 1967. In this charter, devices of direct democracy are categorized as referendums, initiatives (article 304), or revocations of laws (article 79, part 2). The 1967 constitution also refers to the use of referendums in articles 79 and 331. Article 331 is a modified version of previous articles 284 and 281 and does not present significant changes. According to article 79, 25 percent of the electorate is required to employ the referendum mechanism against laws passed by the legislature within one year of their promulgation. The referendum, however, may not be used to revise or repeal laws that establish taxes or any legislation that falls within the "exclusive initiative" of executive power.[8]

This powerful institutional mechanism, the referendum, was used for the first time after the redemocratization in 1985. Yet complications arose on December 17, 1987, when the National Pro-Referendum Commission presented 634,792 signatures to the Electoral Court to dispute Law 15,848, which granted amnesty to those involved in human rights violations during the military dictatorship (1973–1985). At that point, the electoral authority realized that the constitutional right to hold a referendum had never been regulated (Cortés 1989). On January 4, 1989, the court set April 16, 1989, as the date for the referendum on Law 15,848. Nonetheless, the electoral authority claimed that it lacked suitable means for verifying the signatures of such a large number of citizens and, consequently, through Law 16,017 of January 13, 1989, a new mechanism was created to solve this problem.[9] Law 16,017 outlined the following: a) 0.5 percent of the citizens qualified to vote could present legislation to the Electoral Court – that is, more than 12,000 signatures (article 30); b) then, *two* calls would be made to validate the signatures – the first between sixty and ninety days after the signatures were validated – and, if validated, the second call within a year of the law's approval; and c) reached in the first or second call the concurrence and the affirmative vote of 25 percent of citizens, a referendum would be held within the following 120 days (article 37).

Call to approve B front

---

[7] From 1942 to 1999, the Uruguayan electoral system possessed characteristics that, taken together, made it very unusual in the democratic world. One of its most original characteristics was the double simultaneous vote. This device required that citizens vote simultaneously on two levels: intraparty and interparty. For the presidential election, the double simultaneous vote permitted party tickets (*lemas*) to divide into competitive factions (sub-*lemas*). The votes for these factions were then accumulated according to a party ticket without any possibility of making alliances among them. Thus, the winner of the presidency was the candidate of the faction who received the most votes within the party that received the most votes. Thus, by granting faction heads nomination control, the system sustained hierarchically organized factions that were able to act together on a consistent basis (see Morgenstern 2004).

[8] Unlike in other countries, the Uruguayan president cannot call for a plebiscite or referendum whatsoever.

[9] The full law is available at http://www.parlamento.gub.uy/leyes/ley16017.htm.

This device, of two pre-referendum calls, was a highly exceptional and expensive method for deciding whether or not a referendum was to be held. Only five of every one thousand citizens – a number far below the votes needed to win parliamentary representation – were required to trigger a mechanism that entailed at least two nonworking voting days and a huge amount of government expense. Essentially, Uruguayans voted twice to decide whether or not to vote. As could be expected, this manner of determining whether to have a referendum was fairly controversial. In fact, the legislature modified this law on July 30, 2000, with Law 17,244, wherein the legislature changed the required signatures to trigger a pre-referendum to 2 percent of the registered voters (instead of 0.5 percent) within 150 days (instead of a year) from the promulgation of the law in consideration. If the pre-referendum reached more than 25 percent of registered voters, a referendum would be required within the next 120 days.[10]

To trigger a referendum, a request must be made in writing to the Electoral Court and must include stamping the right thumbprints and providing the signatures of the promoters. The promoters of the referendum must be identifiable citizens providing the number and series of their civic document and an address (article 1–2, Law 17,244). In other words, one or more citizens are the trustees in terms of channeling the demands for a referendum to the electoral authorities. Note that they are trustees in the purest sense of the term and not delegates (as discussed in Chapter 2). This is crucial because in case the organizers of the referendum campaign, for whatever reason, decide that the referendum process must be halted – for example, during the stage when the Electoral Court is verifying the signatures – they are not entitled to take this action because they simply act as trustees and not delegates (Interview with Washington Salvo, February 2009).[11] This trustee/delegate tension was a subject of discussion during a referendum process in 2001 (Chapter 7 develops this point in further detail). In any case, this is one of the most crucial differences between the process of triggering a referendum in Uruguay and in Switzerland, where promoters act as delegates, not simply as trustees. As a citizen, supporting a referendum campaign is not terribly complicated; one simply has to file a form.

From 1967 until June 27, 1973 (the date of the coup d'état), the Uruguayan Constitution was, more or less, in a state of crisis given that the country was intermittently under emergency rule. Only with redemocratization in 1985 did the constitution of 1967 become "normalized" and fully applicable after seventeen years of unrest. On fifteen occasions from 1985 to 2007 – in addition to national elections for the executive and the legislature – Uruguayans have decided diverse issues at the polls (seven referendums, four popular initiatives, and four obligatory referendums).

---

[10] The full law is available at http://www.parlamento.gub.uy/Leyes/Ley17244.htm.
[11] Washington Salvo serves as minister of the Electoral Court of Uruguay.

Table 6.1 spells out all instances of MDDs (at the national level) that have arrived at the ballot box since 1917. Table 6.2 shows the instances since 1985.

During the last twenty years in Uruguay, citizens have had the opportunity to directly decide some of the most politically critical issues. For instance, through the use of popular initiatives, topics as diverse as the following have been decided: whether or not to try human rights violators; the scope of the privatization of public companies; the social security system; the budget for public education; regulations concerning the national electric company; and even time limits for labor claims. In short, any analysis of the Uruguayan period of redemocratization that does not take into account this powerful institutional arrangement ignores a crucial aspect of the country's political reality.

2. Confidence Votes on Government or Political Loyalties?[12]

As shown before, among stable democracies, Uruguay is one of the most prodigious users of CI-MDDs at the national level. In this section, I examine how the use of CI-MDDs in Uruguay challenges existing theories of voting behavior. I find that when Uruguayans go to the polls to vote on a popular initiative, their vote choice is primarily the result of their party loyalty, rather than their reaction to economic conditions. In testing my hypotheses, I rely on the following statistical methods: King's "Ecological Inference," multivariate regression, and path analysis.

In this section, I deal with cases in which organized citizens have proposed an alteration of the status quo through popular initiatives or have attempted to sustain status quo through the use of referendums. Both types of popular votes fall into the category of CI-MDDs. Because political parties generally have incentives to take positions on the issues at stake in CI-MDDs, these cases offer the scholar interesting insights into the citizen–party linkage. By studying CI-MDDs, we can analyze the effect that political parties' taking of positions has on the citizenry. Using the Uruguayan experience, this chapter addresses the relation between the recommendations of political party fractions and how citizens vote on MDDs.[13]

This section of the chapter deals only with the outcomes, leaving the CI-MDD process for the next chapter. The major question I am examining is what determines the electoral behavior of citizens with regard to CI-MDDs.

---

[12] This section draws on Altman (2002b).
[13] There is disagreement on whether to use the concept "fraction" or "faction" in the context of the Uruguayan party system. Some authors have called these political units factions (Coppedge 1994: 199; Mainwaring and Shugart 1997: 425). Following Sartori, I will not use the term *faction* because it has derogatory connotations: It is deemed "a political group bent on a disruptive and harmful *facere*" (1976). Also, I consider this definition misleading because fractions are more permanent than factions (e.g., the circumstantial "in" and "out" groups formed in Venezuelan parties [Coppedge 1994]). For a further discussion on this topic, see Altman, Buquet, and Luna (2006).

TABLE 6.1. *Mechanisms of Direct Democracy in Uruguay (1917–1980)*

Type	Date (dd/mm/yy)	Based On	Issue	Accepted	Yes (%)	Yes/ Electoral Register (%)	Registered Voters	Turnout (%)
Obligatory Referendum	25-11-17	Ad-hoc law of Feb. 1912	Semicollegiate executive, separation of church and state, creation of the National Civic Registry (including the secrecy of the suffrage), and other relatively minor points.	Yes	95.15	36.34	233,850	38.20
Plebiscite	19-04-34	Ad hoc presidential decree	Reestablishment of presidentialism, incorporation of constitutional plebiscites, change of representation at the Senate, creation of the Council of Ministries.	Yes	95.75	53.95	422,865	56.35
Obligatory Referendum	27-03-38	Art. 284 (C)	President elected through DSV, reorganization of the Senate.[a]	Yes[b]	93.45	52.47	636,171	56.15
Obligatory Referendum		Art. 284 (B)	Unique presidential candidate per *lema* and reorganization of the local administration.	Yes[b]	53.47			
Obligatory Referendum	29-11-42	Art. 284 (B)	Change to proportional representation	Yes	77.17	51.64	858,713	66.91
Plebiscite	24-11-46	Art. 281 (B)	Election of president and vice president without a *lema*	No	46.61	25.39	993,892	65.33
Plebiscite	26-11-50	Art. 281 (B)	Conformation of State Council	No	53.39	29.09		65.33
Popular Initiative		Art. 281 (A)	Several modifications	No	0.26	0.18	1,168,206	70.91
Obligatory Referendum	16-12-51	Art. 281 (D)	Reestablishment of collegiate executive	Yes	54.00	20.02	1,158,939	37.08
Plebiscite (Counter-prop.)[c]	30-11-58	Art. 331 (B)	Back to president elected without *lema*	No	23.47	16.74	1,409,372	71.33

				Yes/No				
Popular Initiative		Art. 331 (A)	Back to president elected with a DSV	No	15.28	10.90		71.33
Obligatory Referendum	25-11-62	Art. 331 (B)	Back to presidentialism	No	16.71[d]	12.81	1,526,868	76.69
Plebiscite (Counter-prop.)	27-11-66	Art. 331 (B)	"Orange" – regime of government	Yes	63.89	47.51	1,656,332	63.36
Popular Initiative		Art. 331 (A)	"Yellow" – regime of government	No	7.01	5.21		63.36
Plebiscite (Counter-prop.)		Art. 331 (B)	"Gray" – regime of government	No	14.22	10.57		63.36
Popular Initiative		Art. 331 (A)	"Pink" – regime of government	No	0.09	0.07		63.36
Popular Initiative	28-11-71	Art. 331 (A)	President's reelection	No	29.55	26.21	1,875,660	88.60
Popular Initiative		Art. 331 (A)	Interpellation of the president	No	0.11	0.10		88.60
Ad hoc Obligatory Referendum	30-11-80	Ad-hoc presidential decree (military regime)	New constitution	No	42.80	36.36	1,944,951	86.86

[a] The *double simultaneous vote* (DSV) permitted party tickets (*lema*) to divide into competitive factions, supporting different presidential candidates. The votes for these factions were then accumulated according to a party ticket. Thus, Uruguayan presidents were the most voted-for candidates from the most voted-for party, though they did not necessarily gain the largest vote share at the national level.

[b] On April 16, 1941, the Corte Electoral decides by 4:3 that because the two modes of presidential election contradict one another, both are declared null and void, and the old mode of election described in art. 149 of the constitution of 1934 is renewed.

[c] Depending on the typology used, this MDD could also be called an "authority's minority initiative."

[d] For constitutional reforms voted concurrently with the general elections, an absolute majority of the votes cast and a minimum of 35 percent of all eligible voters are required; thus, only votes for "yes" are possible.

TABLE 6.2. *Mechanisms of Direct Democracy in Uruguay (Since 1985)*

	Type	Date	Based On	Issue	Accepted	Yes (%)	Yes/ Electoral Register (%)	Registered Voters	Turnout (%)
Sanguinetti (PC)	FAC-Referendum	16-04-89	Art. 79	Amnesty Law (15.848)	No	42.47	34.99	2,283,597	84.72
	B-Popular Initiative	26-11-89	Art. 331 (A)	Adjustment of pensions to inflation	Yes	85.33[a]	72.51	2,319,022	88.67
Lacalle (PN)	FAC-Referendum	13-12-92	Art. 79	Partial withdrawal of the privatization law (16.211)	Yes	72.55	55.14	2,345,077	78.53
	OBLIG-Referendum	28-08-94	Art. 331 (C)	Constitutional reforms	No	31.08	24.55	2,278,375	81.38
	B-Popular Initiative	27-11-94	Art. 331 (A)	Stopping "hidden cuts" in pensions	Yes	69.16[a]	66.16	2,328,468	91.40
	B-Popular Initiative		Art. 331 (A)	27% of the national budget for public education	No	31.17[a]	29.82		91.40
Sanguinetti (PC)	OBLIG-Referendum	08-12-96	Art. 331 (D)	Constitutional reforms	Yes	52.20	43.34	2,343,920	85.90
	FAC-Referendum (pre-referendum call)	17-06-98	Art. 79	Opposing the Law of Energy Framework	No	22.10[a]	22.08	2,385,065	22.08
	FAC-Referendum (pre-referendum call)	20-09-98	Art. 79	Time available to workers to make claims against employers	No	4.64[a]	4.64	2,379,543	4.64

	B-LEG-Plebiscite	31-10-99	Art. 331 (B)	Limitation to executives of public services in running for office	No	38.09[a]	34.93	2,402,160	91.70
	B-LEG-Plebiscite		Art. 331 (B)	Financial autonomy for courts	No	43.09[a]	39.55		91.70
Battle (PC)	FAC-Referendum (pre-referendum call)	18-02-01	Art. 79	Derogation of thirteen articles of Law 17.243	No	20.66[a]	20.66	2,394,219	20.66
	FAC-Referendum	05-08-02	Art. 79	Derogation of arts. 612 and 613 of Law 17.296	Yes	–[b]	–		–
	FAC-Referendum	07-12-03	Art. 331 (A)	Derogation of Law 17.448	Yes	63.72	48.71	2,466,680	81.86
	B-Popular Initiative	31-10-04	Art. 79	Inclusion of water as a basic human right in the constitution	Yes	64.61[a]	57.90	2,488,004	89.61
Vázquez (FA)	OBLIG-Referendum	25-10-10	Art. 331 (D)	Voting rights for the Uruguayan diaspora	No	36.93[a]	33.19	2,303,336	89.85
	B-Popular Initiative	25-10-10	Art. 331 (A)	Nullification of the Expiration Act (Amnesty Law 15.848)	No	47.36[a]	42.56	2,303,336	89.85

[a] Only votes for "yes" are possible.

[b] This case constitutes the only successful case I have recorded of referendum threat, which took place in 2002 but was deactivated by the government days before the vote would have taken place. Despite that technically there was no vote, the threat was successful enough in derogating articles 612 and 613 of Law 17.296. This case will be discussed in Chapter 7.

Sources: Author's database, Venturini (1989), Caetano and Rilla (1994), Lissidini (1998), Marius and Bacigalupe (1998), Bottinelli *et al* (2000), Gros Espiell (2002), González-Rissoto (2007), and Corte Electoral (http://www.cortelectoral.gub.uy).

The motivating factors behind citizens' votes have produced an enormous amount of research (both in national candidate elections and in MDDs). In the most simplistic terms, two general schools, or models, of voting behavior have developed: the party identification model and the economic model. According to those subscribing to the economic model, economic variables, along with political factors, significantly influence an MDD's result.[14] As evidence, this model cites research on vote and popularity poll functions (sometimes called VP functions) in European democracies (Frey, Pommerehne, and Schneider 1981; Frey and Stutzer 2000; Nannestad and Paldman 1994; Schneider and Naumann 1982) and the United States (Bowler and Donovan 1998; Eulau and Lewis-Beck 1985; Hibbs 1979), among others, and a few studies in Latin America (Araos and Engel 1989; Panzer and Paredes 1991; Rius 1992). Drawing on this research, I test the hypothesis that economic conditions have a role in shaping voters' preferences on CI-MDDs. At the same time, based on the importance that party attachment has for Uruguayan citizens, I hypothesize that they vote primarily following fraction directions.[15] Consequently, I theorize that economic variables do not directly influence MDD results in Uruguay, as economic models of voting behavior would argue, but instead have only an indirect effect, if any.

If we analyze the relationship between the number of votes received by any CI-MDD and the number of votes received by those who politically supported it, we observe a strikingly high positive correlation of 0.90. This correlation requires an explanation. Three alternative hypotheses are plausible. First, such a correlation is a spurious association because of aggregation bias. Second, based on the VP functions, CI-MDD results may reflect economic conditions. A third hypothesis is that Uruguayans are extremely consistent in following their political parties' advice. This section seeks to disconfirm these alternative hypotheses.

This chapter proceeds in three parts. In the first, using King's ecological inference methods and software, I disconfirm the possibility that the high correlation between MDD results and the fraction's vote share is due to aggregation bias. In

---

[14] It has been demonstrated that, in general, the economic element in the vote-popularity function of the individual voter is sociotropic – based on the voter's perception of the behavior of the macroeconomy – instead of egotropic – based on the voter's own (or voter's households) economic conditions (Nannestad and Paldman 1994: 224).

[15] Political parties in Uruguay, one of the oldest party systems in the world (Sotelo Rico 1999), were shaped by class structure and class alliances. Uruguay's non–labor-intensive cattle-oriented economy fostered clientelistic parties, as in Argentina (Rueschemeyer, Huber, and Stephens 1992). The configuration of its parties – in the wake of a brutal civil war that led to a massive inclusion of inhabitants as citizens – resulted, as in Colombia (Coppedge 1998) , in clientelistic cross-class catchall parties, which tended to be strongly divided into competing fractions. Although its parties resembled fighting militias in the late 1830s, they succeeded in transforming themselves into party machines during the 1880s, and from then until the late 1990s, they have enjoyed almost 70 percent of the vote (Mainwaring and Scully 1995a). The presidential election of 2004 was, however, an historic event because for the very first time in Uruguay's 176 years as an independent state: Neither of the two traditional parties won the presidency. Instead, the winner was the center-left coalition Frente Amplio, which also won the 2009 elections.

TABLE 6.3. *Popular Initiative Dealing with the Supply of Electric Power (1998) Using King's Nomenclature*

	Frente Amplio	Other Parties	Total
Yes on PI	$\beta_i^w = ?$	$1 - \beta_i^w = ?$	$X_i = 22.10\%$
No on PI	$\beta_i^\beta = ?$	$1 - \beta_i^\beta = ?$	$1 - X_i = 77.90\%$
TOTAL	$T_i = 30.6\%$	$1 - T_i = 69.4\%$	100%

the second part, borrowing from the two previously addressed schools of voting behavior, I disconfirm the hypothesis of economic voting using multivariate regression and path analyses, testing empirically the impact of citizens' political loyalties and economic variables on MDD outcomes. Essentially, I am answering the following question: Are the factors contributing to CI-MDD outcomes essentially economic conditions, or are they political motivations? Finally, I conclude and interpret the findings. To do so, I use a database comprising the results of seven CI-MDDs in nineteen departments (electoral districts) in Uruguay, providing a total of 133 observations.

a. Citizen-Initiated Mechanisms of Direct Democracy Voting Behavior: Making Individual-Level Inferences from Aggregate Data

According to the "ecological fallacy," making individual-level inferences from aggregate data is problematic. Even if the number of votes for a CI-MDD and the number of votes obtained for those political fractions supporting that CI-MDD are almost identical, it is not implied that the people who voted in favor of the CI-MDD are the same people who voted in favor of the political parties supporting it. In other words, "the general ecological inference problem may be conceptualized as a standard contingency table with missing data. The marginals are known, since they are based on aggregate data, but the cell percentages are unknown" (Burden and Kimball 1998: 535).

For example, the popular initiative (PI) aimed at overturning legislation dealing with electric energy commercialization in 1998 was supported only by the leftist coalition, the Frente Amplio. All of the other parties openly opposed this CI-MDD. In Table 6.3, I show the aggregate CI-MDD results (rows) by the political support of the parties favoring and opposing the CI-MDD in the national elections (columns).

The most widely used statistical method in cases of ecological inference is Goodman's regression.[16] In Table 6.3, Goodman's method involves a

---

[16] King, Rosen, and Tanner argue, "The ecological inference literature before King (1997) was bifurcated between supporters of the method of bounds, originally proposed by Duncan and Davis (1953), and supporters of statistical approaches, proposed by Ogburn and Goltra (1919) but first formalized into a coherent statistical model by Goodman (1953, 1959)" (1999: 63–64).

regression of T_i (voters of the Frente Amplio)[17] on X_i (votes for the PI) and $1 - X_i$ (votes against PI), with no constant term. Goodman's regression is often wildly inaccurate, producing impossible results with regularity. For instance, King shows that the ecological regression predicts 111.05 percent of blacks voting in 1990 for the Democratic candidate in District 42 in Ohio (King 1997: 16). Running Goodman's regression on my entire data set suggests that a reasonable 94 percent of supporters of parties that backed a CI-MDD voted for it, yet a negative number (-2 percent) of supporters voted against it! Obviously, this method is inadequate.

King (1997) states that the ecological inference problem can be minimized by replacing the question marks in the body of the contingency table with estimates based on information from the marginals. For instance, the upper-left corner of Table 6.3 represents the (unknown) number of *Frentistas* that voted for the CI-MDD. Obviously, there is a wide range of different percentages that could be placed in this cell of the table without contradicting its row and column marginals. Based on Table 6.3, it seems reasonable to suppose that most of the supporters of the CI-MDD were *Frentistas*, and thus that the upper-left and lower-right cells are most likely large. By the same token, the opposite diagonal (lower left–upper right) cells probably should be small. Based on the election results, I know how many voters supported the CI-MDD (22.1 percent) and how many were *Frentistas* (30.6 percent), but I do not know how many of the supporters of the CI-MDD were *Frentistas*. For instance, I know that the number of supporters of the "no" option at the CI-MDD who were *Frentistas*, the lower-left cell, is between 8.2 percent (the Frente Amplio total minus the option "no" total) and 30.6 percent (assuming that all *Frentistas* were "no" voters). Granted, this is a broad range of vote percentages.

King's method begins with the method of bounds, identifying the complete set of values that might fill a table's cell (I have done this using EZI software).[18] The method of bounds is employed to restrict estimates of the upper- and lower-left cells, the cell quantities of interest, to a narrower region than the [0,1] interval. By calculating this function for each of the observations in the database, it is possible to build a *Tomography Plot* (see King 1997; Voss and Lublin 1998). A careful consideration of the tomography plot allows

---

[17] The Frente Amplio is the governing leftist coalition of Uruguay. In the national elections of 1994, it obtained 30.61 percent of the national vote (30.76 percent of the legislature). The Frente Amplio has a different organization than the traditional parties, partially because of its origins. This party was officially born on February 5, 1971, and it is currently (in 2009) the largest party in Congress. It comprises nineteen political groups (from mild social democrats to communists and former guerilla activists "tupamaros"). Since its creation, the Frente Amplio has had a dense network of activism closely related to labor unions (especially around the Communist Party). Although each fraction acts as the ultimate decision maker, as in the traditional parties, the Frente has central authorities and sophisticated decision-making processes. Each group has veto power, forcing binding decisions among the members of the coalition. This veto power is responsible for an increasing internal fractionalization.

[18] EZI is a program for Ecological Inference. This statistical software package can be obtained at http://gking.harvard.edu.

checking for the degree of aggregation bias (see King 1997: 283–4). With a 95 percent level of confidence, at the aggregate level, between 86.4 and 89.6 percent of those who belong to parties encouraging an affirmative vote followed their fraction's advice [88 ± 1.63]. Only between 5.7 and 8.3 percent [7 ± 1.28] of those citizens voted against a CI-MDD, contrary to their fraction's directions.[19]

b. The Effect of Economic Conditions on Citizen-Initiated Mechanisms of Direct Democracy Voting Behavior

Thus far, we know that the high correlation between CI-MDD results and the fraction's vote share is not a spurious association due to aggregation bias. This does not mean, however, that other variables have no effect on deciding a CI-MDD. A vast number of alternative hypotheses regarding the interaction between economic conditions and voting behavior have been put forward by a significant number of scholars (Key 1966; Kramer 1971; Lewis-Beck 1988). In their simplest form, these studies assume that voters withdraw support from incumbents when conditions worsen (Bowler and Donovan 1998: 71). However, limited attention has been directed toward the question of how these conditions might affect support for ballot propositions in countries other than Switzerland and some states in the United States. Because economic performance affects the government's reputation (which affects party loyalties and in turn affects their ability to mediate voting decisions), I conduct a pooled cross-sectional analysis to test for an association between economic conditions and voting on CI-MDDs.

The classical macroeconomic variables used in electoral behavior models are inflation, unemployment, and per-capita income rates. Although the inflation rate may vary somewhat across different regions in a small country like Uruguay, I do not use a regional measure because of the lack of accurate information and its presumably small variation. Instead, I follow Bowler and Donovan's work (1998: 75–6) and use economic trends measured by changes in unemployment and individual salaries. The relationship between the votes for a CI-MDD and the votes for those political parties supporting that CI-MDD and the economic situation are estimated using the following model:

$$\text{CI-MDD}_{dt} = \alpha + \beta_1 V_{dt} + \beta_2 U_{dt} + \beta_3 \Delta U_{dt} + \beta_4 S_{dt} + \beta_5 \Delta S_{dt} + \varepsilon$$

where

CI-MDD_{dt} = support for the CI-MDD in department d_i at time t_i;
V_{dt} = share of vote of political fractions that support CI-MDD in department d_i at time t_i;
U_{dt} = unemployment rate in department d_i at time t_i;
ΔU_{dt} = changes in the unemployment rate in department d_i at time t_i;

---

[19] King offers a group of methods to check for aggregation bias (1997: 283–5). I performed these techniques, and it seems that aggregation bias is not a problem in the data I am analyzing.

TABLE 6.4. *Multivariate (OLS) Analysis Assessing the "Yes" Vote*

Variable	B	Std. Error	Std. Coefficients	T-stat
Intercept	−4.875	(3.909)		−1.314
Political Fraction Vote	0.992	(0.021)	0.960***	46.573
Unemployment	0.0631	(0.164)	0.007	0.386
Δ-Unemployment	−0.829	(2.008)	−0.008	−0.413
Salary	−7.30 E-08	(0.000)	0.000	−0.012
Δ-Salary	6.078	(2.243)	0.051*	2.709
Prob > F	0.000			
R^2:	0.965			
Adjusted R^2:	0.964			
Root MSE	5.6217			
N:	133 (7 CI-MDDs by 19 departments)			

* $P < .01$; *** $P < .0001$.

S_{dt} = salary rate (in Uruguayan pesos) in department d_i at time t_i; and
ΔS_{dt} = changes in the salary rate in department d_i at time t_i.

The data used for this analysis were assembled in such a way that the position that the executive assumed in a given CI-MDD is consistent across all CI-MDDs.[20] I expect that CI-MDD will be determined primarily by fraction share (V_{dt}) and that the economic variables will have no effect on the CI-MDD outcome. In Table 6.4, I present the results of this multivariate regression analysis.

The empirical findings are somewhat surprising. Although the fit of the model, with an R^2 of 0.965, is close to ideal, three of the five independent variables (i.e., Unemployment, Δ-Unemployment, and Salary) are not statistically significant.[21] The only significant independent variables are Δ-Salary and

---

[20] "Consistent" refers to the position adopted by the president and his fraction. Because of the dynamics of the Uruguayan electoral system, political-party fractions control the nomination process and thus are the most prominent political agents. The elected president is no more than his fraction's leader (Buquet, Chasquetti, and Moraes 1998). He is only able to control the internal competition and nominations within his fraction. He is not capable of controlling the nominations and competition of other fractions, even in his own party. For this reason, in several instances, fractions from the governing party took positions that diverged from the president's. To make things more complicated, even within "opposition" parties, fractions do not have uniform positions regarding a CI-MDD.

[21] As previously mentioned, my universe of analysis is composed of 133 cases (seven CI-MDDs on nineteen electoral districts). Ideally, I should have had a database large enough to account for issue-type effects, performing the analysis on homogeneous issue groups, so as to have more confidence in the OLS estimates. However, more disaggregated economic and voting data were not available. Thus, I follow Bowler and Donovan's work on pooling all propositions, regardless of their content (1998: 76–81). Also, I am aware that an N of 133 cases might not be enough to make the maximum-likelihood estimates trustworthy. Nonetheless, some scholars believe that as long as some loading marker variables are high (>0.80), about 150 cases should

Political Fraction Share. On the one hand, based on the standardized coefficients, the impact of Δ-Salary on the dependent variable is almost null. On the other hand, Political Fraction Share is significant and has a powerful impact on voting for CI-MDDs. In fact, there is an almost one-to-one relationship between voting for a CI-MDD and voting for a political fraction.

For every additional percentage point of turnout for political parties supporting a CI-MDD, the vote for the CI-MDD will increase by about one percentage point (0.96) in any Uruguayan department. Based on OLS analysis, the percentage of votes for a CI-MDD at a given day, t, is almost the same percentage of votes that the political parties supporting the CI-MDD would have obtained if candidate elections had been held concurrently.

Because fraction loyalty has a substantial effect on political behavior in Uruguay, I hypothesized that citizens vote primarily according to political considerations and that economic variables do not *directly* influence CI-MDD results in Uruguay. My regression analysis confirms both of these expectations, particularly given the relative magnitude of the Political Fraction Share variable. However, this analysis does not mean that economic conditions are irrelevant to CI-MDD outcomes. So far, the evidence does not indicate that the total effect of economic considerations is null.

Because politics and economics are not necessarily tied together in any easy, straightforward, "functional" way, one way to analyze the impact of economic variables on CI-MDD outcomes is through a path analysis or structural equation model. This method allows for testing for the indirect and direct effects of variables. Path analysis is a confirmatory rather than an exploratory technique.

To model the potential indirect effect of economic variables on CI-MDD outcomes, two conditions must be met. First, independent variables (Unemployment, Δ-Unemployment, Salary, and Δ-Salary) must affect the mediating variable (Fraction's Vote Share); and, second, the mediating variable must affect the final endogenous variable (CI-MDD). The idea behind this model is that economic variables *do* have an effect on CI-MDD outcomes; however, these effects are mediated by Political Fraction Share.[22] Nonetheless, it may be the case that some of the independent variables impact CI-MDDs directly. Thus, I ran the path analysis, trying all possible combinations of direct and indirect effects of economic variables on CI-MDD outcomes. Figure 6.1 displays the output of this statistical model. The numbers along each arrow indicate the betas; the standard errors are given in parentheses. These empirical findings fit partially with my theoretical expectations. However, before discussing

be sufficient (Ullman, 1996: 640). Other scholars consider that approximately ten subjects per estimated parameter may be adequate (Ullman, 1996: 715). Doing a similar analysis, Bowler and Donovan (1998: 77–81) conduct several OLS regressions with diverse N (ranging from 21 to 268 cases). According to their analysis, an N of 133 cases, producing the reported coefficients, could be considered good enough to make the maximum-likelihood estimates reliable.

[22] Because in Uruguay political decisions are ultimately taken by party fractions, other things being equal, I expect fractions to take a more anti-incumbent position if economic conditions worsen.

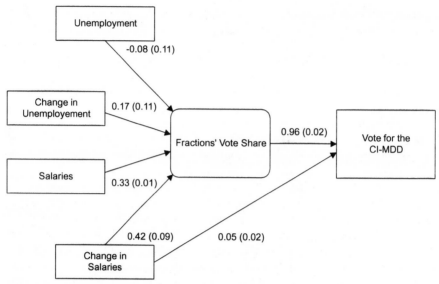

FIGURE 6.1. Path Analysis of Votes for the Mechanisms of Direct Democracy in Uruguay (Betas and Standard Errors).

the specific results, I must provide some evaluation of the model's overall performance.

To run a path analysis, one first considers a bivariate correlation matrix among all of the variables. One of the most important (and general) criteria for judging the results of a path analysis is whether it produces an estimated correlation matrix that is consistent with the original bivariate correlation matrix. "If the model is good, the parameter estimates produce an estimated matrix that is close to the sample covariance matrix. 'Closeness' is evaluated primarily with chi-square tests and fit indices" (Ullman 1996: 713). Because the goal is to develop a model that fits the data, a *nonsignificant* chi-square is desired. The chi-square in my model (with three degrees of freedom) is 0.24, with a *P* value of 0.97. Therefore, my model fits the data well. An adjusted goodness of fit index (AGFI) and a comparative fit index (CFI) with values greater than 0.90 also indicate a well-fitting model. In my model, these indices are equal to 1, providing further evidence that it performs well.[23]

I hypothesized that Unemployment, Δ-Unemployment, Salary, and Δ-Salary affect CI-MDD outcomes through Fraction's Vote Share. To test these hypotheses, the path coefficients going from each variable to Fraction's Vote Share need

[23] I also ran least squares with dummy variables (see Stimson 1985) for departments and CI-MDDs, and the conclusions are the same as those of the path analysis: The estimated standard errors became only marginally larger, but the political fraction vote coefficient remains highly significant. The change in salaries coefficient is the only variable that ever attains significance, and it is only weakly so. For simplicity, I decided to remain with the path analysis.

evaluation. Unemployment and Δ-Unemployment do not significantly affect Fraction's Vote Share. However, Salary and Δ-Salary do have a significant and substantial effect on Fraction's Vote Share. Their betas are 0.33 and 0.42, respectively (both with a *P* value <.01). However, only Δ-Salary has a direct effect on CI-MDD. Moreover, to find the indirect effect of Δ-Salary on CI-MDD through Fraction's Vote Share, the betas of the path Δ-Salary–Fraction's Vote Share and Fraction's Vote Share–CI-MDD are multiplied. Thus, the standardized coefficient of the indirect effect that Δ-Salary has on CI-MDD is 0.40 (0.42 times 0.96).

The impact of the change in the median levels of salaries (per department) on *Vote* is not explained theoretically. In fact, it is fairly counterintuitive. It should also be noted that I am working with *median* levels of salary, data that do not reflect more nuanced information (e.g., quintiles) about the evolution of salaries. For instance, the median salary per department could increase, even though a big part of the population was experiencing a decrease in their salaries. By definition, data about the median levels of salary do not take into account how wealth is distributed in a given region. One way to solve this problem is to work with more disaggregated data, but these data are not available for Uruguay because national surveys have not been done frequently or regularly.

c. Interpreting the Findings

This chapter addresses cases in which organized citizens in Uruguay have attempted to alter the political status quo through CI-MDDs. Because political parties have incentives to take positions on the issues at stake in popular initiatives, these cases offer the scholar interesting insights into the citizen-party linkage. This research combines two theories of voting behavior: the economic model and the party identification model. I have hypothesized that when Uruguayans go to the polls to vote on a CI-MDD, their vote choice is primarily the result of their party loyalty rather than their reaction to economic conditions.

CI-MDDs in Uruguay provide a valuable opportunity for the analysis of voting behavior, particularly with regard to instances of direct democracy. Using a variety of methods (i.e., EZI, multivariate regression, and path analysis), this study finds that the outcomes of popular initiatives are mainly determined by fraction loyalties. In Uruguay, citizens follow their party fraction's advice almost exactly, producing a striking correlation of 0.9 between the votes received by any CI-MDD and the number of votes received by those fractions that politically supported it. The reasons why fraction loyalty is so strong in Uruguay are beyond the scope of this piece of research and are open to debate. However, the parties' strong roots in society – a result of more than a hundred and sixty years of existence, conflict, and interparty political bargaining – must be part of the explanation.

This chapter shows that economic factors also influence CI-MDD outcomes but in an indirect fashion. When Uruguayans go to the polls to decide a

CI-MDD, they mainly take into consideration their political fraction's suggestion. Still, in making their recommendations on whether to support or oppose a proposed CI-MDD, political fractions are strongly affected by the economic performance of the country.

3. Final Remarks

In Uruguay, the introduction of direct democracy came "from above" in an attempt to bypass an inimical legislature that the reformers did not fully control. MDDs were slowly and silently incorporated into constitutions, and their inclusion brought only marginal discussions among constituents. Oddly enough, MDDs could be seen as bargaining chips among political elites vis-à-vis waves of greater concentration of power in the hands of the executive, not as demands from concrete groups in society for a broader participation in public decisions.

Of course, this inclusion deviates from the Swiss case (see Altman 2008). In Switzerland, MDDs "were introduced into the constitution under pressure from reform movements in the second half of the nineteenth century, after a number of cantons had accumulated some experience with them" (Papadopoulos 2001: 36); therefore, they may be seen as the product of a tremendously heterogeneous society attempting to create a series of political safety nets for minorities. Evidently, MDDs were implemented in Switzerland and Uruguay with diverse political goals, were used in different ways, and have produced dissimilar results.

Though not nearly to the degree of Switzerland, Uruguay is still one of the most prodigious users of CI-MDDs worldwide (Altman 2002b; 2005). Introduced several years ago, CI-MDDs were "discovered" by political parties mainly during the postauthoritarian period. Thus, using the Uruguayan experience, this chapter addresses the relation between political parties' recommendations and how citizens behave electorally on CI-MDDs.

This study argues that by knowing which fractions support a given CI-MDD and the economic conditions in the various regions of the country, we can predict with a fairly high level of confidence the outcome of a CI-MDD vote. For example, in the CI-MDD on September 20, 1998 (which was supported by only a few unions), I expected a very small percentage of citizens to vote in favor of the measure. As it turned out, only 4.72 percent of citizens voted for the CI-MDD. Alvaro Ferrín, one of the coordinators of the National Commission Pro Referendum, said, "We promoted the referendum regardless of any political consideration. We understand that not everything should obtain political backing. [. . .] There is a minority of the people that wants this issue to be submitted for popular approval. We did not consider it necessary to obtain any support from the political class" (Alvaro Ferrín, in "En Perspectiva," Radio El Espectador, September 24, 1998). Without being aware of the implications of his words, Ferrín supports the basic conclusion of this chapter: Without partisan backing, CI-MDDs are unlikely to succeed in obtaining citizen support.

The analysis in this section has been mostly procedural and did not take into account the specific topics on the table or the intentions of the CI-MDDs' promoters. In this sense, this section has been issue-free and topic-blind. Given that the specific issues at stake should not be left aside in a comprehensive assessment of how MDDs work, this is the focus of Chapter 7.

7

Uruguayan Citizen-Initiated Mechanisms of Direct Democracy as Agents of Vertical Accountability

This chapter has two main objectives. The first is to determine under which combination of institutional and political factors MDDs manage to limit the action and political desires of the government and thus become a weapon of political control in the hands of the citizenry. With this objective, this research selects from all MDD occurrences in Uruguay when the government and the promoters of the initiative held contrasting positions. Using the Uruguayan experience, this section explains what takes place when governments lose and organized citizens win – what combination of factors and conditions is necessary and/or sufficient to approve a CI-MDD. The second objective is to study the other side of the coin: how political elites relate to CI-MDDs – institutions that, for better or worse, literally have taken political decisions from politicians' hands. Given that these institutions help citizens "invade" the territory of elites, politicians presumably are likely to hold CI-MDDs in low regard, or at least view them in a rather negative manner.

1. Stressing the Complexity of Social Phenomena: Objectives, Methods, and Hypotheses

This section explores the combination of factors that are necessary and/or sufficient conditions to approve a CI-MDD (or for the government to lose) in Uruguay. Specifically, this research has as its dependent variable those MDDs in which the executive was averse to the objectives of the promoters of the measure. Usually, but not necessarily, there is a perfect correspondence between these cases and the use of a CI-MDD. Indeed, there are two cases of MDDs "from above" – constitutional plebiscites – that, despite being initiated by (a minority of) the legislature, did not count the support of the executive in Uruguay and consequently are included as well. Thus, the universe of analysis of this subset of MDDs is rather small (n = 13), wherein only seven of the thirteen cases saw the government losing at the ballot box.

The relevant causal conditions, or plausible explanations, can be derived from different theories and perspectives. Nonetheless, I do not intend to analyze the specific impact of a given independent variable over the dependent variable in a linear fashion, as I do in Chapter 6. Rather, I explicitly underline the complex combinatorial nature of social phenomena. In so doing, I rely on QCA.[1]

Substantively, in terms of explaining why some CI-MDDs fail while others pass, I hypothesize that the objectives of the promoters can be successful under two specific configurations, where some conditions are necessary and others are simply sufficient. The necessary condition in both scenarios relates to a strong group behind the MDD. As explained in previous chapters, the legal design of direct democracy has an enormous impact on the prospects of how MDDs are used and, in Uruguay, legal entrance requirements for triggering MDDs are rather "expensive," unlike in countries such as Switzerland. The presence of a strong mobilizing group is crucial; otherwise, it is unlikely (but not impossible) that they will overcome the legal thresholds imposed to trigger the action.

As we saw in Chapter 6, if the MDD happens to be held concurrently with national elections, it will tend to become a second-order election; therefore, citizens will follow political parties' advice. Yet, if we are assuming a strong group behind the initiative, it is likely that a majority of parties will support the measure (and parties tend to adopt much clearer stances regarding technical and economic issues than normative ones, regardless of whether the CI-MDD seeks to change the status quo). If the CI-MDD is held when the perceived economic situation of the country is negative, citizens' aversion to risk will flourish and they will naturally support the status quo, especially if the MDD touches on something related to economical expenses. Citizens are not ignorant and do not want to increase their expenses. Of course, in this second alternative scenario, I am assuming a strong group behind the initiative or referendum. In the following paragraphs, I discuss each variable in isolation to specify its operationalization – perhaps one of the Achilles' heels of QCA.[2]

---

[1] QCA has tremendous advantages; among them, it allows the researcher to deal with variables in isolation or in combination; it is sensitive to conjunctural causation; and it allows reconstructing chains of events. Nevertheless, I acknowledge the limitations of this analytical method. The main downside of QCA lies in variable codification and measurement, not in the neat, logical, parsimonious technique that it represents. Succinctly, QCA suffers from many of the weaknesses of linear analysis without many of its well-known advantages. But, to be fair, the following advantages must be highlighted: a) QCA forces a scholar to be explicit about his variables' definitions and operationalizations; b) QCA inhibits researchers from "fishing around" for miscellaneous variables; and c) QCA helps to confirm, even with very limited numbers of observations, how different combinations of independent variables affect certain values of the dependent variable. In this sense, QCA is a good complement to the other methods I use in this manuscript because it forces us to think in a way that linear analysis does not necessarily push us to do.

[2] As Ragin warns us, researchers "must carefully define their concepts before they can assess the degree of membership of cases in the sets corresponding to their concepts" (Ragin 2000: 310).

As the discussion on voting behavior in Chapter 6 acknowledges, perhaps the single-most-used variable in the literature predicting the motivations of triggering a CI-MDD and its results comes from what could broadly be called the *economic atmosphere*. Yet the motivating factors behind citizens' votes have produced an enormous amount of research (both in national-candidate elections and in CI-MDDs). One of the most recurrent discussions in the literature analyzing the results of CI-MDDs is on whether they imply an evaluation of the proposed measure or a confidence vote on the government (usually based on the economic situation). In this regard, and using the most simplistic terms, two general schools or models of voting behavior have developed: the party identification model and the economic model.

According to those endorsing the economic model, economic variables, along with political factors, significantly influence the results of CI-MDDs (see also Szczerbiak and Taggart 2004). Therefore, they can be understood as confidence votes for or against the government, regardless of the issue at stake (Hobolt 2006a).[3] Consequently, we can hypothesize that the better the economic atmosphere, the higher the support for the government's position on any given CI-MDD (almost by definition, this means lower support for the CI-MDD).

As noted in Chapter 3 (the cross-national analysis), the evident problem is how to determine the variable that best captures the prevailing "economic atmosphere" in a country, given that all classical variables of macroeconomics are highly correlated (e.g., inflation, unemployment, and salaries). In Uruguay, the debate has been centered on whether the relevant factor to assess the economic atmosphere is the variation of macroeconomic indicators or citizen's perceptions of the state of the economy (Luna 2002).[4] In one of the very few studies on this topic, Luna shows that Uruguayans respond sociotropically to objective economic conditions, especially to the interaction between unemployment and inflation (2002: 142–143). It has been shown that, in general, the economic element in the vote-popularity function of the individual voter is sociotropically based on the voter's perception of the behavior of the macro-economy – instead of egotropically based on the voter's own (or voter's household's) economic conditions (Nannestad and Paldman 1994).

---

[3] A clear example, before the referendum against a law allowing the association of the national petrol company of Uruguay with private companies (December 7 2003), is given by Senator Rafael Michelini, who claimed, "Votamos SI porque no queremos que haya un voto de confianza para este gobierno" ("We vote for this referendum because we do not want an affirmative confidence vote on the government") (*La República*, December 4, 2003).

[4] It must be said that whereas an analysis of the Uruguayan case seems to suggest that these two variables appear divorced (Altman 2002b), the case of Chile appears to support their linkage (Araos and Engel 1989). Although a single case study cannot disprove an entire theory (Munck 2003), it can shed light on why economic performance does or does not affect electoral outcomes in direct democracy. Also, this variable itself has produced diverse and sometimes contradictory theoretical arguments. For instance, Weyland (2002) argues that hyperinflation pushes citizens to the realm of losses and, consequently, they will tend to bet on magic solutions.

The question remaining, however, is which of these variables better reflects how people perceive the economic atmosphere. This perception may be reflected by growth, but this variable does not necessarily affect citizens' perceptions. Inflation, on the one hand, is a much more pervasive variable, directly affecting a citizen's well-being. But we could easily have an environment of inflation that does not lead to negative citizen perceptions, chiefly when personal income varies with inflation. Real wages, on the other hand, seem to be the best indicator (most citizens are workers), and even they can embrace some differences between sectors of employees (i.e., public versus private), it seems a reasonably good indicator of the economic atmosphere. People can perceive when they are able to buy more goods or services as well as when they cannot. I operationalize economic atmosphere as the impact that real wages have on the preceding months before the MDD. If the average real wage change in the last twelve months is positive, this variable acquires the value of 1; otherwise 0.[5]

Another determinant of the outcomes of CI-MDDs involves the issue that citizens have to decide. Some scholars have argued that citizens are economically conservative and usually tend not to support measures promoting an increment of public spending that eventually could imply tax increases (for a discussion on direct democracy and taxation, see Freitag and Vatter 2006). If this is correct, we also can hypothesize that CI-MDDs that involve rising public expenditures will have a lower chance of being approved, and even more so in a constrained economic atmosphere. Of course, it is possible to claim that almost any measure taken by citizens will have its related economic cost, so the previous hypothesis will be more difficult to operationalize. There are some political or normative instances that do not directly imply greater public expenditures because they are not related to budgetary issues. For instance, a CI-MDD on whether or not to judge the military for their human rights violations (as occurred in the first referendum held in Uruguay in 1989) has nothing to do with budgetary issues. Yet the approval of this initiative might have entailed devoting scarce resources.

Although some scholars would defend the idea that almost any change in the status quo would imply an increase in public expenditures (as in the previously mentioned example), I adopt a narrower vision of expenditures. For this work, public expenditures imply a larger budget for any specific measure. For instance, the popular initiative that sought to increase spending for public education in 1994 and the adjustment of pensions to inflation in 1989 directly involved an increase of expenditures. On the contrary, the defense of the status

---

[5] Those subscribing to the party identification model would also state something similar but based on the popularity of the government at the time of the CI-MDD instead of on the economic atmosphere. In this vein, the approval ratings of the executive also may affect the outcome of the CI-MDD. The higher the approval rates of the government, the higher the support for the government's position in regard to the CI-MDD. The problem is that this measure is also highly correlated with the previous one (Luna 2002) and, therefore, its inclusion would generate an enormous amount of noise.

quo does not imply an increase in public expenditures, as in the privatization referendum of 1992.[6] Based on these concerns, I propose a basic distinction between issues covered in a CI-MDD, identifying whether such CI-MDDs are directly related to economic (e.g., regulation and taxation) or political-institutional issues. This hypothesis is more exploratory than confirmatory, given that there is no clear theoretical clue as to whether economic issues tend to be rejected or accepted more often than political initiatives. However, we will presumably find that governments tend to lose more economic than political CI-MDDs.

Even though some studies and scholars are enthusiastic about the potential deliberation, participation, and competition that CI-MDDs involve, other scholars are aware of the conservative tendencies these mechanisms engender. Christin and colleagues (2002) discuss how the status quo is often advantaged, and other scholars, like Brunetti (1997), even talk about a status quo bias (in the context of Swiss referendums). In Switzerland, there is a typical pattern of direct democracy characterized by "a poor success rate for the initiatives and by good chances of success for the optional referendums (Hardmeier 2002: 1095–6). In this vein, "the literature suggests that poorly informed voters might reject innovations since existing policies are better known" (Christin, Hug, and Sciarini 2002: 760).[7]

Based on this debate – and on the assumption that voters are risk averse – we can put forward the hypothesis that not only are CI-MDDs inherently conservative, but also that citizens are inherently conservative. Consequently, facing any given CI-MDD, citizens will tend to support the status quo. To explain the operationalization of a measure that treats the maintenance or change of the status quo, I rely on several examples. We may be tempted to claim that any CI-MDD attempts to change the status quo. However, here I pay special attention to what the promoters of the CI-MDD envisioned. Two examples clarify this point.

In 1994, in Uruguay, a popular initiative sought to legislate (in the constitution) that 27 percent of the national budget should be allocated to public education. This popular initiative openly called for a change of the status quo (given that hitherto the educational budget was well below 27 percent). Then, consider the referendum against the privatization of publicly owned companies. This referendum tried to derogate an already approved law, so we could claim that the referendum also tried to alter the status quo. However, despite the law already having been approved, the intention of the promoters of the referendum was to revoke the law and maintain the companies in public hands, as they had been historically. Therefore, in contrast with the first example, I code this referendum as in defense of the status quo.

---

[6] Despite that many people would consider retaining in public hands the publically owned companies, this would actually increase the amount of public expenditures.

[7] See also Kirchgässner (2008).

Another plausible contributor for explaining CI-MDD outcomes comes from the study of electoral participation. It has been suggested that "yes" voters have a higher propensity to vote than "no" voters (Altman 2005: 224; Gilland 2002a; 2002b). Of course, if this is correct, organizers of CI-MDDs would seek a lower participation rate and obviously would expect most electors to endorse their CI-MDD. However, given that in many countries there is a minimum level of participation required for the CI-MDD to be binding, participation should be low but not so low that the CI-MDD is nonbinding. Thus, one could include turnout as a critical variable in the study of CI-MDDs. However, a problem arises when we realize that several measures (e.g., a popular initiative in Uruguay) involve only positive votes, so it is impossible to estimate real participation rates. Nonetheless, a related matter is what the literature calls the "contamination effect," which occurs whenever a CI-MDD is concurrent with another type of election (e.g., presidential). In relation to the contamination effect, it is plausible to think that in cases of concurrency of CI-MDDs with presidential elections, CI-MDD support is likely to be increased.

Finally, as shown in Chapter 6, the political support that organizers are able to attain (in terms of the political establishment and specifically political parties) seems to be relevant for the approval of the CI-MDD. This is not necessarily because legislators are politicians but rather because they have access to key power resources (e.g., appearances in the media and local committees) with the potential capacity of shifting public opinion (Lassen 2005). Political parties and legislators generally have incentives to take positions on the issues at stake in CI-MDDs (Freire and Baum 2003; Uleri 2002). Thus, the greater the political support enjoyed by the "yes" or "no" camp, the higher the "yes" or "no" vote. However, this support is, at least partially, a consequence of the strength of the organization triggering the CI-MDD. A strong union or lobby (by strong, I mean with high mobilization capabilities) backing the CI-MDD would bolster the probability of that CI-MDD's success. In Uruguay, the unions of publicly owned companies are the strongest among the union milieu. These companies (e.g., telecommunications, electricity, and trains) have the largest reach, and even in the most remote town of the country, these unions would have members predisposed to advancing union interests.[8]

2. Why Are Some Mechanisms of Direct Democracy Successful?[9]

The type of data and the scope of the universe of analysis (regarding the number of cases and countries) make this research especially suitable for using

---

[8] It is interesting to see how unions of the Inter-Union Workers Plenary–National Workers Convention (PIT-CNT) have divided critical corners of the city of Montevideo for gathering signatures. It is similar to the situation in New York when the Union of Physicians occupied the intersection between Fifth Avenue and 42nd Street on Monday and Wednesday, and the Union of City Cleaners on the other days of the week.

[9] The author is grateful to John Sonnet and Charles Ragin for their insightful suggestions on this section.

techniques of QCA. QCA uses Boolean algebra to shed light on combinations of causal conditions that produce an observed phenomenon. Therefore, it is a configurational approach that overcomes many of the limitations of linear (multivariate) statistics.

The first step in this type of analysis requires the reconstruction of the raw data matrix – that is, observable data with real events – into a *truth table* that displays all possible logical combinations of values on the independent variables (regardless of whether or not they constitute empirical cases). The truth table will be composed by 2^k cases, where k is the number of causal conditions. In this case, the truth table will be composed of thirty-two combinations because we are dealing with five causal conditions (i.e., 2^5), which is a rather manageable number of cases.

Following convention, an upper-case letter indicates the presence of a condition and a lower-case letter indicates its absence. Therefore, in the following Boolean equations, E = economic issues at stake; C = MDD concurrent with parliamentary and/or presidential elections, Q = MDD attempts to maintain status quo, W = positive evolution of real wages (*salario real*) in the past twelve months, and L = presence of a strong lobby or union with mobilization potential. Conversely, e, c, q, w, and l refer to the absence of these conditions, respectively.

The truth table (Table 7.1) shows all possible combinations of the relevant causal conditions. As seen, not all of the rows show empirical cases to analyze (the usual problem of "limited diversity"). Those rows without empirical cases are called "remainders," and the solution to the truth table will depend on how these remainders are dealt with (Ragin and Sonnett 2004).

QCA is a research design mined with counterfactuals (actually, each combination of causal conditions that shows no evidence constitutes a counterfactual). Remainders force us to think about the plausibility of cases for which we have no real-world examples. In this regard, the first critical question is whether it is theoretically reasonable to have a combination such as *ECQWl* (see row 2 in Table 7.1). What would happen in this scenario?

There are two major options for the researcher when treating remainders: a) ignoring them, which is the most conservative approach, or b) treating them as "don't cares." Ignoring those remainders is equivalent to treating them as "false" (i.e., = 0) when assessing the conditions for success = 1. Treating them as "don't cares" consequently equates the remainders with potentially simplifying assumptions; that is, they are included only insofar as their presence helps us find a simpler solution for the truth table (this is done in the next section, where I stress parsimony).

Table 7.1 shows that a CI-MDD against the desires of the executive has resulted from four combinations of the causal conditions (see rows in bold). The combinations in equation 1 show the unreduced (primitive) Boolean expressions for the outcome to occur:

$$\text{CI-MDD} = E.C.Q.W.L + E.C.Q.w.L + E.C.q.W.L + E.c.Q.w.L \quad (1)$$

TABLE 7.1. *Truth Table for Mechanisms of Direct Democracy Opposed by the Executive in Uruguay*

Row	E	C	Q	W	L	Frequency	Success	Cases
1	I	I	I	I	I	I	I	a. Including in the constitution that drinkable water constitutes a basic human right)
2	I	I	I	I	O	O		
3	I	I	I	O	I	I	I	b. Stopping "Hidden Cuts" of pensions
4	I	I	I	O	O	O		
5	I	I	O	I	I	I	I	c. Basing pensions on inflation rates
6	I	I	O	I	O	I	O	d. Conferring economic autonomy for courts
7	I	I	O	O	I	I	O	f. Transferring 27 percent of national budget to public education
8	I	I	O	O	O	O		
9	I	O	I	I	I	I	O	g. Opposing energy framework
10	I	O	I	I	O	I	O	h. Opposing investment law
11	I	O	I	O	I	3	I	i. Opposing privatization j. ANCAP k. 612–613
12	I	O	I	O	O	I	O	l. Opposing Urgency Law
13	I	O	O	I	I	O		
14	I	O	O	I	O	O		
15	I	O	O	O	I	O		
16	I	O	O	O	O	O		
17	O	I	I	I	I	O		
18	O	I	I	I	O	O		
19	O	I	I	O	I	O		
20	O	I	I	O	O	O		
21	O	I	O	I	I	O		
22	O	I	O	I	O	I	O	m. Directors of Public Companies cannot run for public office during following four years
23	O	I	O	O	I	O		
24	O	I	O	O	O	O		
25	O	O	I	I	I	O		
26	O	O	I	I	O	O		
27	O	O	I	O	O	O		
28	O	O	I	O	I	O		
29	O	O	O	I	O	O		
30	O	O	O	I	I	O		
31	O	O	O	O	I	I	O	n. Opposing Amnesty Law
32	O	O	O	O	O	O		

E: Economic issues at stake
C: MDD concurrent with parliamentary and or presidential elections
Q: MDD attempts to maintain the status quo
W: Positive evolution of real wage in the last twelve months
L: MDD triggered by a strong lobby or union
Success: Result is against the desires of the executive

Reducing the primitive Boolean equation produces a more parsimonious though still complex solution. It is possible to reduce equation 1 using simple Boolean algebra. In other words, "if two Boolean expressions differ in only one causal condition yet produce the same outcome, then the causal condition that distinguishes the two expressions can be considered irrelevant and can be removed to create a simpler, combined expression" (Ragin 1987: 93). Thus, the first term, $E.C.Q.W.L$, and the second, $E.C.Q.w.L$, could be combined into $E.C.Q.L$. This reduction has eliminated W and w, respectively. Also, the second term, $E.C.Q.w.L$, and the fourth one, $E.c.Q.w.L$, could be combined into $E.Q.w.L$. This reduction eliminates C and c, respectively.[10] Therefore, the reduced new equation looks like this:

$$\text{CI-MDD} = E.Q.w.L + E.C.W.L \tag{2}$$

From this, we can derive two settings wherein executives lose an MDD:

1) Economic issues are at stake, the MDD attempts to maintain the status quo, there is a negative evolution of real wages (see w in lower cases), and there is a strong lobby or union behind the MDD.
2) Economic issues are at stake, the MDD is concurrent with elections, there is a positive evolution of real wages (now see the W in upper cases), and there is a strong lobby or union behind the MDD.

Equation 2 states that adverse results for the executive occur under two alternative conjunctures of factors, and they fit in the hypothetical scenarios explained previously almost perfectly. Let me now explore the historical events that are the basis for these scenarios. A simple inspection of Table 7.1 and equation 2 shows that the only variables or causal conditions that appear in all combinations are the presence of a strong lobby or union behind the MDD and an economic issue at stake (every time success $= 1$, E and L are present). These are, however, necessary but not sufficient conditions. Although E and L are necessary for CI-MDD $= 1$; EL must still be accompanied by other conditions.

a. Successful Scenario (1): The Term E.Q.w.L

Although QCA is not sensitive to frequencies of events, it must be said that four of the six CI-MDDs where the government lost (two popular initiatives

[10] In fs/QCA 1.1, this solution is obtained by clicking Analyze, Crisp Sets, Quine; selecting the causal conditions and outcome variables; and then specifying the "Positive Cases" as "True," and all other cases as false (or exclude) (Ragin and Sonnett 2004: footnote 6). This way of treating remainders helps us to establish a complex and nuanced solution. Nonetheless, it may be the case that we are looking for a more parsimonious one. If we include the remainders – hypothetical counterfactuals – in the analysis, we might expect that the solution of the truth table would be simpler than without them. Therefore, to include remainders in the solution, we should proceed as follows: "Positive Cases" as "True," the "remainders" as "don't cares," and all others as false (or exclude) (Ragin and Sonnett 2004: footnote 7). The solution is as follows: CI-MDD $= Q.w.L + C.W.L$. Given that this simplification did not help us much in really simplifying the original solution, for the rest of the chapter I use equation 2.

and two referendums) shared the reduced term of $E.Q.w.L.$[11] This means that, in this configuration, a strong lobby or group pushing the MDD forward succeeded only when economic conditions were deteriorating (w), the measure attempted to preserve the status quo (Q), and the issue at stake belonged to the economic dimension (E). In this setting, whether the MDD was held concurrently (or not) with national elections is irrelevant. These four MDDs attempted (successfully) to defend some of the most valuable heritages of the Uruguayan *Batllista* state (which, as previously explained, was historically characterized by extensive support for public education, public ownership of public companies, and a universal pension system based on redistribution). The first successful referendum in Uruguayan history – the referendum against Articles 1, 2, 3, 10, and 32 of Law 16,211 that promoted the Privatization of State–Publicly Owned Companies (December 13, 1992) – was well known in Latin America because it was one of the very first democratic responses that sought to halt the (then) fashionable Washington Consensus in the region.

On November 27, 1989, Luis Alberto Lacalle (Blanco Party) won the presidency. Lacalle's electoral campaign was centered on promoting economic growth, stability, and deregulation of important areas of the huge Uruguayan state. After the legislative approval of a controversial privatization law in September 1991, the opposition had managed to force a referendum on the issue. Early in 1992, the labor union of the National Telecommunication Company (SUTEL) triggered a campaign to revoke the law. The Frente Amplio and two groups of the traditional parties immediately supported the campaign.[12]

During the first pre-referendum call on July 5, 1992, fewer than 19 percent supported the measure, and it was in the second attempt that the pro-referendum commission gathered more than the required 25 percent of signatures (32 percent) on October 1 of that year. By this time, other groups were already supporting the measure.[13] The Corte Electoral officially called the referendum for December 13, 1992, and President Luis Alberto Lacalle Herrera suffered a severe setback to his privatization program – a central component of his free-market economic policy – when five laws providing for the sale of public companies were overwhelmingly rejected by 72 percent of the citizenry. This situation was extremely similar to the referendum of 2003 that successfully revoked Law 17,448 (of January 4, 2002), which had eliminated the monopoly of the publicly owned company ANCAP on the importation, exportation, and refinement of oil.[14]

---

[11] This approach is "susceptible to the influence of one or two deviant cases and does not give appropriate emphasis to those causal combinations responsible for the largest number of the outcome of interest" (Chan 2003: 63).

[12] The "Polo Progresista" of the Nacional Party (Alberto Zumarán and Rodolfo Nin Novoa) and the "Movimiento de Renovacion Batllista" of the Colorado Party (Víctor Vaillant).

[13] Foro Batllista and the Cruzada 94 of the Partido Colorado, and the Nuevo Espacio.

[14] See the law at http://www.parlamento.gub.uy/Leyes/Ley17448.htm.

As previously stated, the configuration *E.Q.w.L* was also shared by two popular initiatives. Popular initiatives are, by definition, the quintessential proactive tool in the hands of citizens and therefore permit changes of the status quo. Paradoxically, in the opportunities analyzed here, popular initiatives were held to maintain the status quo. Interestingly enough, both popular initiatives went the way of constitutional reforms because organizers could not legally promote a referendum. Given that Uruguayans cannot call for a referendum on issues defined within the exclusive domain of the executive power (e.g., taxation, budget, and the like), these popular initiatives were the "back door" through which organizers could bypass the institutional constraints; otherwise, these MDDs would have been classic referendums. Remember also that as stated in Chapter 6, the "price" in terms of signatures is cheaper for a constitutional reform (10 percent) than for a referendum (25 percent);[15] therefore, attempting the constitutional reform instead of the referendum was absolutely rational.

On November 27, 1994, the popular initiative on social security, approved by Parliament through the Accountability Law of October 1992 (*rendición de cuentas*), attempted to partially revoke the social security system reform. With the law of 1992, pensions were adjusted periodically without taking into account the variation of the cost of living, which was rapidly rising. The promoters – the extremely powerful "gray coalition" – successfully included in the constitution the provision that pensions must be adjusted based on cost of living. As evidence of the power of this coalition, a local newspaper printed a picture of a retired woman proudly showing a banner stating *"We are more than 600,000 and we vote!"* (Figure 7.1). Those six hundred thousand account for about 28 percent of the national electorate of the country, and Parliament was besieged. Before this popular initiative, the number of undecided voters was rather large; however, public-opinion polls foresaw a majority in favor of the consultation. What appeared unusual in this initiative was the clear internal division of the traditional parties.

ONAJPU had a brilliant strategy for advancing its interests. It succeeded in convincing the general public that its proposals were not mere ideas of a particular sector of society but rather that they affected the whole population. The former minister of Labor and Social Security and vice president of the republic, Fernández Faingold, portrays this explicitly by stating that "in Uruguay distributional struggles were not among those that were organized against those who did not, or between rural and urban. The conflict was organized between elderly and the rest of society. And this was done with excellent public relations, because we all have some older adults at home and, eventually, all we will be aged and retired" (interviewed by Castiglioni; see 2005: 80).

Attention also must be paid to the only successful case I have recorded of a referendum threat, which took place in 2002. On February 21, 2001, Congress approved Law 17.296, in which Articles 612 and 613 opened the

---

[15] I asked three ministers of the Electoral Court, and none knew the reason.

FIGURE 7.1. "We Are More Than 600,000 and We Vote!" (Demonstrators outside the Uruguayan Parliament).

door for the creation of ANTEL S.A. in the realm of cellular telephony. Of course, ANTEL was still a 100-percent publicly owned company because of the 1992 referendum. Eventually, ANTEL S.A. would have a maximum of 40 percent of its actions in the hands of private shareholders, and the state would retain 60 percent control of the new company. SUTEL successfully gathered more than 25 percent of the signatures of the Registro Cívico Nacional (approximately 684,000), which were presented on February 19, 2002, to the Corte Electoral. In March 2002, public-opinion polls indicated that more than 70 percent of the electorate would be willing to vote in favor of the referendum, 20 percent would vote against it, and approximately 10 percent would be undecided. The fate of the referendum appeared as clear as it had been in 1992. In May 2002, before the referendum was called by the Corte Electoral, the government sent a bill to Congress through its finance minister, Alejandro Atchugarry, withdrawing Articles 612 and 613 of Law 17.296 to deactivate the referendum. Congress approved the bill and the referendum was not called.

b. Successful Scenario (2): The Term E.C.W.L

This term of equation 1 suggests that when the issue at stake is economic, the MDD is concurrent with elections, there is a positive evolution of real wages, and there is a strong lobby or union behind the MDD, governments lose at the ballot box. Two cases fall perfectly into this category: the popular initiatives on social security of November 26, 1989, and on the declaration of water as a basic human right in 2004. With regard to the social security initiative,

[...] during the first administration of President Sanguinetti (1985–1990) there were some attempts to reform the pension system that translated into only minor modifications. [...] In early 1987 the Executive introduced a bill to reform some aspects of the system that did not get legislative support but originated law 15,900 in October 1987. This law introduced some changes to the adjustment mechanisms for pensions, to the basic and maximum pension levels (Castiglioni 2005).

At the beginning of the 1989 electoral year, the issue of social security occupied a critical place on the electoral agenda. ONAJPU, with the support of the Frente Amplio and the Inter-Union Workers Plenary–National Workers Convention (PIT–CNT), started to collect signatures to support a constitutional reform with the aim of including a specific measure that would require pensions to follow the national salary index average. A constitutional reform was the only way in which ONAJPU could bypass a budget-related law (this was important because budgetary actions are the sole prerogative of the executive). ONAJPU claimed that the Sanguinetti administration had failed to adequately adjust pensions because of the executive's desire to reduce fiscal deficit (Castiglioni 2005).

This initiative, beyond the control of political parties, became a relevant issue because it achieved much more than the required 10 percent of signatures. The pensioners' movement asked for a clear definition of the support of each political group. Taking into account that pensioners were a significant portion of the electorate, almost every political group supported the initiative (even though this consideration was in clear contradiction with their ideological profiles). The Batllismo (Partido Colorado) was the only numerically relevant group that did not support the initiative; other small groups (i.e., MAS Batllista in the Partido Colorado and the MPP in the Frente Amplio) took the same position.

The result of the initiative was conclusive. Almost 85 percent of the electorate supported it, implying an imposition of the civil society over the political system, because the initiative and action were external to the traditional channels of public-matter procedures (political parties). In a popular initiative, concurrent with the presidential and legislative elections of 1989, 1,645,000 citizens voted for the introduction of a clause into the constitution allowing for the future correlation of all pensions to contemporary rates of salary increases.

This situation resembled what happened with the promoters of the constitutional reform that aimed to include drinkable water as a basic human right. The same reform also sought to retain all resources of water extraction, production, and commercialization in the hands of the state in 2004.[16] In both popular

---

[16] To finance the campaign for this constitutional reform, the organizers of the consult used extremely original mechanisms to collect money. For example, they orchestrated a lottery whose main prize was a farming package (which could be won by purchasing a $300 ticket – about U.S.$10 – available in three payments). The first prize consisted of a cow, two pigs, fifteen chickens, three calves, five ewes, 500 kilograms of rice, and 100 kilograms of apples.

initiatives, the causal configuration was identical. In 2004, concurrent with legislative and executive elections, Uruguayans voted on a constitutional reform following a popular initiative instigated by workers of the state-owned Water Company (OSE) along with the PIT–CNT, the Uruguayan labor federation. Enjoying the support of the Frente Amplio and half of the Blanco fractions, the reform was approved by 64.59 percent of the valid vote. Uruguayans again showed their confidence in the state as a provider of public services, as they had in the 1992 national referendum that prohibited privatization of the largest state-owned companies.[17]

3. Why Do Some Citizen-Initiated Mechanisms of Direct Democracy Fail?

From equation 1, one can deduce those combinations of conditions that produce adverse results for the executive facing a CI-MDD. This logical operation can be carried out by following De Morgan's law as described by Ragin (1987), resulting in the identification of conditions that are the negation of those variables that are supposed to cause the event in question (Chan 2003). "The application of De Morgan's law is straightforward. Elements that are coded present in the reduced equations are recoded to absent, and elements that are coded absent are recoded to present. Next, logical AND is recoded to logical OR, and logical OR is recoded to logical AND" (Ragin 1987: 99).

If the original solution for the truth table was:

$$\text{CI-MDD} = E.Q.w.L + E.C.W.L \tag{2}$$

then, applying De Morgan's Law:

$$\text{CI-MDD} = (e + q + W + l)(e + c + w + l) = \tag{3}$$

Several steps are held for simplifying equation 3, and the new minimized equation looks as follows:

$$\sim \text{CI-MDD} = e + l + q.c + w.q + W.c \tag{4}$$

Applying De Morgan's Law is a powerful logical mechanism to find the circumstances where the results follow a certain configuration. Equation 4 shows that a CI-MDD fails when:

a) the issue is not economic (e);
b) the organized group of citizens promoting the CI-MDD is weak (l);
c) the measure attempts to alter the status quo and is not concurrent with national elections ($q.c$);

---

[17] Ibarra (2005) considers that this popular initiative constituted a somewhat different approach to defending the state than that which Uruguayans had witnessed to that time. For him, the coalition behind this popular initiative was not limited to simply vetoing an eventual reform with regard to water services. Instead, this coalition had a more comprehensive vision of the provision of public services in general.

d) there is a deteriorating real wage and the measure attempts to alter the status quo ($w.q$); or

e) there is an improving real wage and the measure is not held simultaneously with national elections ($W.c$).

In the following paragraphs, I describe the reasons why certain CI-MDDs have failed (these are provided in chronological order).

a. Amnesty Law for Human Rights' Violators (April 19, 1989)

As soon as the new democratic government took office in 1985, a whole debate on what should be done with human rights violators during the military regime gained headlines, and Uruguayans were plunged into one of the country's most polarized and emotionally charged moments since the reinstallation of democracy. With the approval of the *Ley de Caducidad Punitiva del Estado* (Law 15.848) on December 22, 1986, direct democracy from below became a critical player in Uruguayan politics. The law was supported by all Colorados (then the executive party) and most Blancos and established that the state inhibit itself from applying its sanctioning faculty to the crimes committed during the dictatorship in connection to political repression (1973–1985). Immediately after the law was approved, a nonpartisan pro-referendum commission – presided over by the widows of two legislators assassinated in 1976 in Buenos Aires – started a campaign to promote a referendum against this law (the first of its kind in Uruguay), as was a constitutionally established right. The Frente Amplio was the first (but not the only) political group supporting the campaign and mobilizing its huge popular machinery toward this aim. Within the traditional parties, only a small number of legislators supported the measure. When almost 29 percent of the electorate supported the referendum request, the Electoral Court set the date of the referendum for April 16, 1989. The referendum was unsuccessful for the organizers, but it managed to gather 42.5 percent of the vote. This referendum had the Boolean configuration $ecqwL$ and, based on equation 4, despite being supported by a strong lobby (L), its failure could be explained simultaneously by several terms: $e, l, q.c,$ or $w.q$.

This referendum is perhaps one of the most emblematic cases of the tensions that can arise between popular sovereignty, on the one hand, and fundamental principles, on the other – in this particular case, a tension between justice and peace, in the words of Aryeh Neier. By popularly ratifying the law, Uruguayans went against the spirit of the American Convention of Human Rights, known as the "Pact of San José, Costa Rica" (1969), to which the country had subscribed since the first day the convention saw light (and later was ratified by Uruguay again on April 19, 1985). On this last occasion, the country acknowledged the competence of the Inter-American Commission on Human Rights indefinitely and the Inter-American Court of Human Rights for all cases related to the interpretation and application of the aforementioned convention.

Without a doubt, Law 15,848 stresses Articles 8 and 25 of the convention (right to a fair trial and right to judicial protection, respectively) and particularly emphasizes Article 29, which is rather explicit as to how this convention shall not be interpreted, specifically restraining the sanctioning obligations of the state (see sections a and b of this chapter). The convention maintains that crimes against humanity cannot be amnestied and that the state has the obligation to elucidate the truth and sanction those responsible for crimes. Despite the approval of this law transpiring through regular and democratic procedures, and despite that the vote on the referendum surely was free and fair, there is indeed an open file in the Inter-American Commission on the Uruguayan case, known as the "Informe N° 29/92," because the sovereign cannot impose its will on the victims.[18]

b. Allotting 27 Percent of the National Budget to Public Education (November 27, 1994)

Through this popular initiative, there was an attempt by the powerful teachers' unions to include in the constitution the requirement that a fixed amount of economic resources be aimed toward the public education system. The amount of resources the promoters requested was 4.5 percent of the GDP and no less than 27 percent of the national budget – this amount was based on the largest budget that education had ever received (1967). Incredibly, less than one week before the day of the initiative, public-opinion surveys indicated a majority in favor of the consultation. Yet only the center-left coalition, Encuentro Progresista, was in favor of the measure, whereas the rest of the political forces were openly against it. This initiative had the Boolean term $ECqwL$. De Morgan's explanation for the initiative's failure rests squarely with the term "wq." This measure attempted to alter the status quo while simultaneously experiencing a negative evolution of real wages in the previous twelve months of -2.5 percent (w).

c. Deregulation of the National System of Energy (June 17, 1998)

In 1998, there was a second important push against the law that created the regulatory framework for the national electrical system (i.e., transmission, transformation, and distribution of electric energy). In this case, the origin was clearly the union of the national electrical company UTE, the AUTE. Although the Frente Amplio supported the measure from the beginning and had an active participation, it was not until this second attempt that it committed strongly enough. At the first call for referendum, on March 8, 1998, the measure obtained 15 percent, whereas at the second, which took place on June 17, it nearly crossed the 25 percent threshold, obtaining only 23 percent. On this occasion, the leader of the Frente Amplio, Tabaré Vázquez, and the party machine worked strongly on behalf of the measure, even using televised publicity. This initiative had the Boolean term $EcQWL$. As predicted by De Morgan's Law, its failure lies specifically with the term Wc. This measure was nonconcurrent (c) in a context of a positive growth of the real wage of 1.53 percent (W).

---

[18] See the "Informe N° 29/92" at http://www.cidh.org/annualrep/92span/Uruguay10.029.htm.

d. Time Available to Workers to Make Claims Against Employers (January 7, 1999)

Of all the measures arriving at the polls, this attempt at referendum was one of the most likely to be designated a failure, given that the lobby pushing for the measure was weak (*l*) and growth of real wages was positive and nonconcurrent (*W.c*). Article 29 on the law of promotion and protection of investments was ratified at the ballot boxes when the second call for adhesion to the norm failed to obtain the needed support for a referendum. The promoters of the derogation of the law received the support of 9.31 percent of registered voters, a percentage that doubled the 4.64 percent obtained at the first call in September 1998 (albeit far from the required 25 percent of voters). Although the Frente Amplio supported the measure, it did not make any type of campaign, despite two instances in which Tabaré Vázquez appeared to publicly support the referendum. The Boolean explanation for the initiative failure is given by the terms *l* and *Wc* (from *EcQWl*).

e. Toward Economic Autonomy for the Courts (October 31, 1999)

This initiative attempted to alter the status quo (*q*), leaving in the hands of Parliament the possibility of accepting the required budget the judicial power claims every year while simultaneously inhibiting the possibility for the executive to veto it. This prerogative of the executive had caused controversies with the judiciary because the executive usually requested that Parliament approve a smaller budget for the judiciary than the one the judiciary claimed to be fair. Certainly, this measure had an economic issue at stake (*E*); however, unlike other CI-MDDs, where it was possible to see adherents pushing the measure in every corner of the country, the trigger for this measure was different. It was the first time in history that an interest group, instead of requesting citizens' support for its demand, succeeded in calling such a measure by obtaining the signatures of legislators (two-fifths of the General Assembly – that is, the combined deputies and senators). As a mandatory plebiscite, this had to be held concurrently with the next national election (*C*). There existed clear evidence of a group that, albeit highly educated and sophisticated as a lobby, lacked enough resources for mobilizing around its objective (*l*). At the time, there was also a positive evolution of real wages in the last twelve months to the tune of 2.3 percent (*W*). Enjoying the support of the Frente Amplio and half of the Blanco fractions, the reform was closer to being approved than the former one, obtaining a 43 percent support level.[19] The Boolean term for this instance is *ECqWl*.

---

[19] Neither Colorados nor Nuevo Espacio campaigned for this reform. One of the key issues in regard to the mobilization efforts by the interested group(s) is seen in whether the ballot for the CI-MDD is "attached" (ensobrada) – in case the CIMDD is held concurrently to the national elections – to the partisan and fractional ballot the citizen supports. In this case, the "white ballot" was included by all lists of the Frente Amplio–Encuentro Progresista, three of the six fractions of the National Party (Propuesta Nacional, 250); (Alianza Nacional/Manos a la Obra, 903); and (Todo por el Pueblo, 206). It is not found in any list of the Colorado Party or the Nuevo Espacio.

f. High Officials and Their Right to Run in Immediate Elections
(October 31, 1999)

Liberal-center-left party Nuevo Espacio (NE) triggered this initiative, basing its demand on the claim that high officials were using public resources to advance their personal political careers. This reform sought to disallow directors of publicly owned companies and decentralized services from running for office during the immediate presidential administration. As mentioned in footnote 19, in Uruguay it is possible to infer a party's position regarding MDD simply by whether they distribute the ballot for Election Day. The Colorado Party did not take a position regarding this measure, whereas the Blancos opposed it. The Frente Amplio only partially supported the measure, and 38 percent of citizens backed it.[20] This initiative has the Boolean term ($eCqWl$), and as a result, its failure may be blamed on the absence of a strong lobby (l) and the fact that there was no economic issue at stake (e).

g. Miscellaneous Articles of the So-Called First Urgency Law
(February 18, 2001)

This law was first approved in Uruguay with a declaration of urgency. The concept of "urgency," incorporated in the Constitution of 1967, does not refer to the urgency of the content of the law but rather to the parliamentary proceedings (constitutionally called "laws with declaration of urgent consideration"). The thirteen articles can be summarized in six subject headings:

1) Concessions to private firms for the use of the railway system.
2) The creation of a mixed (state-private) company for the use of the terminal for containers at the Montevideo port.
3) Opening freedoms for the investments of administrators of Pension's Saving Funds (AFAPs) and three other topics.
4) The restructuring of the Directorate of the National Cooperative of Milk Producers.
5) Taxes on the public lighting system.
6) Increasing the control of the executive over the autonomous entities of the state (*entes autonomos del estado*).[21]

This was the first referendum called under the new Law 17,244, which established a unique pre-referendum call. This referendum had the Boolean configuration $EcQwl$ and based on equation 4, and its failure could be explained simultaneously by two terms: l and $w.c.$

---

[20] Despite all parties having supported the measure in Congress, only the Nuevo Espacio and a few groups from the Frente Amplio distributed the ballot for this initiative. One official of the Nuevo Espacio, Ernesto Mateo, declared that his party distributed 450,000 ballots to other parties (El Observador).

[21] The autonomous entities and decentralized services of the state include most publicly owned companies (e.g., UTE, ANTEL, ANCAP), all public banks, and other services such as the national public university.

4. The Other Side of the Coin: Presidents' Views on Direct Democracy

The literature is rather clear on the fact that elected officials should not be indifferent to CI-MDDs. After all, as shown previously, these institutional arrangements have deviated political outcomes from the course originally elected in the assembly or the executive, and if we claim that politicians are rational maximizers of power, one could assert that CI-MDDs undermine the power of those elected (Hobolt 2006b). Consequently, it is reasonable to expect that representatives and presidents should at least be suspicious of CI-MDDs. At the same time, huge portions of the literature emphasize that citizens are "hungry" to get involved in governmental affairs.[22] However, again we encounter assumptions that are made – for which there is little evidence – regarding the strong positions that different sides should take in regard to direct democracy. This section tackles these assumptions and shows that we should not necessarily expect leaders to be on the "against" side.

Who would be better prepared to provide an assessment of CI-MDD than those who were, on several occasions, the "victims" of such institutions? Who were more victimized than those whose programs were derailed by citizens at the ballot box? On the following pages, I show how three presidents of Uruguay – Julio María Sanguinetti, Luis Alberto Lacalle, and Jorge Batlle – relate to the world of direct democracy and its diverse dimensions.

These presidents suffered important legislative flips because of the use of referendums and popular initiatives (see Table 6.2). If we would expect anyone to be really "at arms" with direct democracy, it would be these presidents. Yet, as we observe, Batlle and Sanguinetti are, in general, rather at peace with direct democracy, whereas Lacalle is notoriously less fond of these mechanisms. Of course, all three clearly demonstrate that the combination of representative democracy and direct democracy is not only plausible but also positive for the health of the democratic life of a country.

Sanguinetti, in his first presidency (1985–1990), faced the first national referendum that was held in Uruguay (Amnesty Law). Lacalle witnessed perhaps one of the most relevant referendums in Uruguayan history (against the privatization law), and Batlle (2000–2005) faced the popular initiative on water and had to derogate some laws to deactivate an evident referendum regarding telecommunications (see Chapter 6).

Inspired by the marvelous dialogues between the Critic and the Advocate, or among the Modernist, the Traditionalist, and the Pluralist, that Robert Dahl built for his book *Democracy and Its Critics* (1989), I too am building a dialogue among the last three presidents of Uruguay. Although these former presidents were not simultaneously seated at the same table, this exchange is based on the real answers they provided to me in face-to-face interviews. In creating this collage of their responses, I am confident that I have maintained the spirit of their thinking and words.

---

[22] See, for example, Hautala, Kaufmann, and Wallis (2002).

ALTMAN: *It is frequently argued that CI-MDDs undermine the power of the rulers and representatives elected by the citizenry. Do you agree?*

BATLLE: More than weaken it, they share it! The question is why at a certain moment was it understood that instruments of this nature had to exist? And it was for one quite simple reason – seems to me – because there are moments in which certain decisions have to find a broad consensus, larger than the one produced by simple elections contingent to a particular party structure, and a certain policy distribution of preferences. There are some subjects that require a greater consensus of citizenship, which is why when introducing the constitutional reforms, super-majorities are needed. I believe that there must be citizen participation.

The presence of these mechanisms does not weaken the power of the rulers; rather they represent a way of sharing power, which is also necessary. That is necessary because any democracy is a game of counterweights, it is a game of checks and balances – very difficult to manage and maintain; and, it is difficult to maintain because, generally speaking, all interacting actors love their own reasons more than the reasons of others. And they understand that their reasons are more profitable than the reasons of others, and if they have a considerable share of power, there will not be limits to these rational loves of their own reason, inhibiting the limits of the state action, which is the title of Humboldt's book: *The Limits of State Action*. So the limits of the state are recognized across the division of powers, through specific legislation, through the special majorities, through parliamentary action, and, of course, through the possibilities of direct democracy.

LACALLE: [What president Batlle says sounds great] but definitely they do affect political power. Because the popular approach to certain issues is in black and white, the process denatures much that could be a deep analysis of a topic. The referendum on the Law on Public Enterprises was the most typical case. Of the four articles under consideration there was little talk, the discussion turned to the "pirates," that "we were selling the assets," that "we were giving away the national heritage." It was politicized to such a degree that people believed they had been doing a campaign against the government; these naïve people were certainly convinced on "voting against the government," "voting against the economic policy," "health, housing, and education now" they have screamed. Yet, when they won, we did not change, nor did the housing policy, or economic policy, or health policy. We simply said: "These four articles are not in place anymore." That's it.

SANGUINETTI: As anything else, the risk with these mechanisms is their abusive use. When a right is used abusively, it ends up discrediting itself. Like all things, isn't it? Freedom of expression is sacred, but if one uses it for insult every day, it ends up discredited. The right to strike the same, the right to convene an MDD also the same.... Indeed, in previous years, CI-MDDs have been discredited; in particular during my second presidency because they were sought – and used for that matter – as a mechanism for popular mobilization, nothing more.

ALTMAN: *To what extent does the citizenry promote a mechanism of direct democracy more as a vote of censure of the government rather than as a vote on a particular topic?*

SANGUINETTI: That is always the risk with these institutions. That is why I felt very bad when the rules for referendums against laws were changed, were relaxed. I thought it was crazy . . . they became too easy. These are unique resources for exceptional situations, such as the revocation of the Amnesty Law. They are for problems that have to be solved by the citizenry, problems where values and emotions are at stake, very difficult elements. As Justino Jiménez de Arechaga said, "amnesties are a rational solution to an emotional problem."[23]

ALTMAN: *Do you not think that, for example, these MDDs systematically favor strong organized groups instead of the simple and ordinary citizen?*

BATLLE: Certainly – but it depends on the matters that are at stake. Because when the time of the vote arrives, organized groups – which are strong corporations that have strong tools to support an idea, an argument, a behavior – face new things in the political scenario. In the first instance, they have to face a situation in which citizens have a huge – a very large – amount of information. That is, every day people are more independent in terms of how they vote. During the nineteenth century, the vote was an act so out of the ordinary, where usually the results were not much respected, that voting citizens put on their best clothes as if they were going to Mass on Sunday. During those years, voting was an act of sovereignty, not very common, and where the individual also had the clear conscience that he had a limited knowledge of the events, usually he gave the vote to that person that he hoped to represent him before the authority either as a legislator or as a ruler himself.

Today with the invention of mobile phones, YouTube, the Internet, and anything else, there is sometimes, on the contrary, a sort of flooding of information of such magnitude and nature that it is possible in some cases it is easier to confound than before – to a degree the citizen does not know which information to choose. But the truth is that, speaking from a theoretical perspective, I'd rather be a citizen of the late twentieth century than a gentleman of the late nineteenth century. . . .

Currently, the individual who participates and who decides about a certain topic, rightly or wrongly, based on his or her own idea, decides with much more freedom, with much more information, and with much more independence from the sectors with which he or she integrates. Because the vote is secret, he might easily say "X" publicly, yet in the secrecy of the voting booth, between the shirt and the body there is another ballot paper, "Y," which he never showed to anyone, and that one is the one he places in the urn, not the one he received in his organization. With direct democracy, the circumstances are exactly the same because as there is an organization

---

[23] Arechaga was a notably influential Uruguayan university professor of constitutional law.

promoting a certain law, which apparently should be endorsed by a strong majority, the results are sometimes different than those expected.

ALTMAN: *Do CI-MDDs weaken, strengthen, or simply not affect representative democracy?*

LACALLE: I think they replace representative democracy. Indeed, I think that is something that someday, when the waters calm down, we will have to review in both instances: going against the laws, through the use of referendum, as in the shape of popular initiatives for constitutional reforms. They should be limited.

SANGUINETTI: They really have to be something exceptional; MDDs should not be the norm. They have to be exceptional mechanisms for what representative democracy could hardly resolve.

ALTMAN: *So, do you envision a reasonably "healthy" combination, that of representative democracy with mechanisms of direct democracy?*

BATLLE: Yes, there is no other choice. Otherwise, you do not let the steam exit the pressure of the boiler!

SANGUINETTI: I agree. Indeed, CI-MDDs also help to give legitimacy to representative democracy.

ALTMAN: *Some scholars have claimed that CI-MDDs serve as pedagogical tools. Are they?*

SANGUINETTI: Of course! Without a doubt! The civic exercise of it could be only learned through the exercise itself, but caution is required. On the one hand, because CI-MDDs generate an exercise of civic participation, they have an important role: They push citizens in front of the obligation to decide, to think for a while, to contemplate, to reflect, to feel that in their hands are many things. On the other hand, what we have is the potential for a negative and demagogic use, which are the forms of corrupt political systems that the teacher Aristotle already told us a while ago. Always there is a corrupt way of doing things. . . .

BATLLE: Well, well, I would not go so fast. I believe that civic virtues sometimes go forward, sometimes backward. The same thing happens with people, and it always has been so. People are victims of contingent situations with such amount of stochastic change that cannot be anticipated even by God. That is why you have to try to assemble all this in the long run, you cannot take a look in the short term, because you lose perspective given that things may go forward or backward. . . . Look, you read German philosophy, listen to German music, read German literature, and then you see this Hitler. And, of course, you then ask how the noble German people who were educated reading Schiller, Lessing, Goethe, and Heine come with this craziness of Hitler. Well, sometimes under certain circumstances there exists a majority of people that fall into a sort of mirage. Having said that, I believe that increased education, information, and enhanced forms of freedom do not guarantee but, at least, make it possible that people have a greater ability to discern the right from the wrong, the fair from the unfair.

ALTMAN: *When you sent a bill to Parliament, did you take into account that a*
   CI-MDD could potentially have been triggered?

BATLLE: Of course! What – the other players do not play? What is going
   to happen to your bill? How you will have majorities? We had an exceptionally difficult moment to manage in terms of the financial and banking
   crisis following the Argentinean "corralito."[24] We did not have majorities
   in the chambers, but nonetheless we dispatched some bills that needed to be
   approved, and we were confident that they were going to have the required
   majorities. At that time, the general shock was so immense that the possibility was the country would not reach anything that was really palpable, even
   as we were risking future elections with public disorder. This unfathomable
   financial and economic tragedy was so big that legislators said "this is not
   an electoral choice" and voted accordingly. Look, here the boat was sinking,
   let's row.... I did rely on common sense. But, I have to recognize that we
   also send other bills knowing that they are not going anywhere; they were
   simply testimonial bills....

SANGUINETTI: If one did not take into account that, he was almost committing
   suicide. It was decisive. Especially in very substantive reforms such as that
   of pensions, which is the mother of all battles in contemporary societies....

ALTMAN: *Yes, but other critical subjects were also disputed during your presi-*
   dency, such as the budget for public education....

SANGUINETTI: Yes, but none has the relevance, the size, and the difficulty of
   moving the structures imbedded within the subject of retirement. Changing
   the pension system is the most difficult task that could happen to a society.

ALTMAN: *Do you recognize that there is some sort of rollover of minorities*
   through majority rule, in a country that is characterized by consensus build-
   ing?

BATLLE: No, it's not the brutality of majoritarianism. The majoritarian aspect
   of direct democracy is precisely the democratic dimension of it. If you win the
   national election by one vote, you win it, that is it, and you take control of
   political power. The problem is that because no one has absolute majorities
   in Uruguay, during the last hundred years we had instituted policies of
   understanding in order to govern, otherwise we could not govern. Yet, real
   life makes from politics the art of the possible, and when you have to take
   a parliamentary decision, you have a system of majorities and minorities in
   some cases, special majorities in others – depending on the nature of the
   issues – but, generally speaking, if you have 50 votes against 49, then you
   have a regular law.[25] Exactly the same happens when people vote: If the
   people vote and the difference is just one vote, and the constitution does not
   require a special majority, the decision is reached.

---

[24] The "corralito" is a nickname for the 2001 deep financial crisis in Argentina.
[25] The Uruguayan Chamber of Deputies has ninety-nine members.

SANGUINETTI: Well, well, well...what are we going to do? It's democracy! Furthermore, it is never for a single vote. In the case of a referendum, this is not a whimsical question. In other words, once the referendum is on the road, it means that the constituted powers of the republic have acted: Representative democracy with all its machinery has reached a law, and that means we are facing a Law of the Republic. And, facing it, there is a group of citizens who feel they need to flip it. This mechanism is to pull down an arbitrary law, a law grinding with the sentiments of the people....

ALTMAN: *Are all subjects able to be dealt with on CI-MDDs?*

SANGUINETTI: I believe that topics that have another type of solution should not be subjects of popular decision because CI-MDDs could be easily abused. They should always be limited. For instance, since their origin, we have narrowed them in order to exclude issues about finance and taxation....

BATLLE: I agree 100 percent, not all topics are capable of being decided in a CI-MDD. Look, there are very large problems in this game: Do you believe that people would vote in favor of raising taxes? And, even in the event you say "sometimes," do you believe that people would not vote in favor of reducing taxes? Please, come on!

ALTMAN: *So, what about highly sensitive normative issues? What about abortion, for instance?*

SANGUINETTI: Those are the sort of issues and topics that should rightly be subject to these mechanisms!

ALTMAN: *In organizational terms, the price a group has to pay for triggering a CI-MDD in Uruguay is rather costly....*

BATLLE: But of course. First of all, you have to have an organization.... An organization with a larger caliber, and stronger than another organization will be more inclined to – and in a better position to – promote a process of direct democracy. Let me give you an example: the case of the popular initiative on the water [October 2004]. This case was handled through the workers' union officials of the OSE [national publicly owned company of water]. The first objective this union had was defending the interests of the civil servants of this autonomous body. Then, as a direct action of this nature – recognized by the Constitution and by law – done within a political context, it acquires the profile of being a tool against the ruling government. Once a corporation (a union in this case) triggers the mechanism – because it is a way of defending its (fair or unfair) interests – it is taken up by a party and used as a political tool against the government.

At that time, the Frente Amplio embraced the CI-MDD triggered by the OSE's Union as an instrument in the electoral mobilization against the government because it was said that "the government wants to leave us without water," because "it wanted to sell water to the imperialists." Yet, on this occasion, thinking that there will be not enough votes supporting the measure, the political forces against the supporters of the MDD did not mobilize. That was an evident miscalculation, but also they did not want to generate a national contention about the water that, to tell the truth, we felt that was something with no meaning at all. Well, the constitutional provision was enacted. It was overwhelmingly voted and supported, and today we cannot sell water to anyone, even the thirstiest on earth, unless the government dictates a measure authorizing legislation to do so for each specific case.

ALTMAN: *Could these mechanisms be improved in the Uruguayan case?*

SANGUINETTI: I think we would have to tweak the procedural mechanism, not the constitution itself. I think that the higher the levels of reflection they incorporate, the better. The problem here is when the sovereign acts are the subject of an emotional outburst, which is never the best way to govern. For example, the day that a psychopath rapes and kills women, and you submit the death penalty to an MDD, you almost ensure a win. If you set certain mechanisms of parsimony and some rationality, you have tempered things to a degree that the sovereign makes a rational use of power. And that is the deep and inherent reason for representative democracy....

ALTMAN: *Well, but then you are a "rare" president in that sense, as most presidents presumably would say, "No, I do not want direct democracy!"....*

BATLLE: You have to excuse me but I'm liberal, a defect that I have, you see? [laughs] I participate in the line of thought that has F-R-E-E-D-O-M as its center. And freedom must be arranged and organized because the law is the only thing that guarantees my freedom ... yes, yes ... I am as old as that.... I believe in the strength of formal freedoms, and the essence of formal liberties as a guarantee of fundamental freedoms.

5. Conclusions

Substantively, the first section of this chapter shows that when the executive opposes the objectives of the promoters of a measure, governments lose at the polls under specific configurations of circumstances. This occurs when: a) economic issues are at stake, the MDD attempts to maintain the status quo, there is a negative evolution of real wages, and there is a strong lobby or union behind the MDD; or b) economic issues are at stake, the MDD is concurrent with elections, there is a positive evolution of real wages, and there is a strong lobby or union behind the MDD. This is extremely solid in terms of theory building, but what happens when we observe how political elites approach direct democracy deserves some sort of analysis.

How can we explain the overall sympathy of Uruguayan former presidents toward direct democracy?[26] My answer is quite simple: It is a matter of political legitimization. As previously stated, direct democracy could not have been analyzed taking into account only those initiatives that reach the ballot box; sometimes the simple *threat* of activating and using a popular initiative or a referendum must be seriously taken into account. In a way, the Uruguayan experience can be related to the Swiss experiences with institutions of direct

---

[26] And, for this matter, also representatives (see Appendix 2).

democracy. In Switzerland, as in Uruguay, the *potential* of an MDD is already a relevant actor in the political arena. As Kobach explains, "Switzerland's Konkordanz-Demokratie is more firmly entrenched and more widely accepted than it might have been otherwise" (Kobach 1994: 151). Uruguay fits this logic perfectly. It is not strange that both Switzerland and Uruguay could be, in a way, characterized as the most consociational regimes in their respective regions (Western Europe and Latin America). In light of this realization, not only do citizen initiatives act as a system of political accountability, with a high degree of legitimization, but they also are the producers of political consensus.

At this point, it would be interesting to examine the flip side of the coin: citizens' support of CI-MDDs. Sadly, there are no public-opinion polls on this topic in Uruguay to contrast with the opinions of legislators and presidents. Nonetheless, some colleagues have already contemplated this issue in other settings and, despite evidence being inconclusive as of yet, most comparative analyses clearly support the idea that for citizens, referendums and initiatives are systematically and cross-nationally a "good thing" and "very important" (Donovan and Karp 2006). The discussion, though, focuses on the motivations for such opinions (Dalton, Bürklin, and Drummond 2001; Hibbing and Theiss-Morse 2001), but this topic is beyond the scope of this book.

8

Conclusions

Democracy requires a healthy blend of faith and skepticism: faith that if people are informed and caring, they can be trusted with self-government; and a persistent questioning of leaders and majorities.

(Cronin 1999: x).

1. Main Findings and Contributions

Direct Democracy Worldwide is a study of direct democracy, which is understood as a set of institutions that allow citizens to express their preferences at the ballot box through universal and secret suffrage about government issues other than who will represent them in the government. This book filled a lacuna in our understanding of MDDs in the contemporary world and the relationship between direct and representative democracy. It introduced a key distinction between forms of direct democracy, demonstrating that direct democracy is Janus-faced: Some mechanisms of direct democracy are forward looking, democratizing politics, whereas others are backward facing, enhancing the power of politicians who deliberately use them. Thus, although the practice of direct democracy sometimes gives *power to the people*, at other times it gives *people to the powerful*.

This book shows how the specific MDDs that are employed shape the relationship between direct and representative democracy. Eschewing the common view of direct democracy and representative democracy as mutually exclusive models that focuses on the false choice between one model or the other, *Direct Democracy Worldwide* pays special attention to how practices of direct and representative democracy interact under different institutional conditions and uncovers the specific conditions under which they can coexist in a mutually reinforcing manner.

Direct democracy has taken center stage around the world and is broadly seen as a potential answer to the challenges faced by contemporary democracies. But, as *Direct Democracy Worldwide* has argued, neither the critics nor the advocates of direct democracy have fully grasped how the variety of MDDs interact with representative institutions. As the book demonstrates, a country's embrace of direct democracy is costly, may generate uncertainties and inconsistencies, and can even be manipulated. Nonetheless, the promise of direct democracy should not be dismissed.

The book contains seven chapters that can be divided into two major groups. The first three chapters deal with larger normative and empirical questions on direct democracy. The last four chapters study how direct democracy interacts with other state institutions within three types of regimes (i.e., low-intensity democracies, and full democracies).

Direct democracy encompasses a plethora of different procedures, each of which relates to, and interacts differently with, representative institutions. In Chapter 1, *Direct Democracy Worldwide* developed a rather comprehensive yet user-friendly typology of the diverse MDDs. This typology avoids conceptual stretching by precisely delimiting what does and does not constitute direct democracy. At the same time, the concepts are as general as possible while simultaneously allowing nuances to evolve. The construction of this typology was critical to bypassing the existing semantic confusion given the concept's heterogeneity. This heterogeneity involves high degrees of conceptual stretching, which concomitantly constitute the first and perhaps most critical problem that this research faced. Research can proceed only if we escape the trap of words and remain disentangled from semantic confusion.

Chapter 2 focused on the normative views of direct democracy and presented an overview of the state of the debate. One of the intriguing aspects of this literature is that it lacks a broad comparative perspective. The bulk of the literature on direct democracy spotlights a few countries in the "north," particularly Switzerland (the world champion in the use of these mechanisms) (Fossedal 2002; Kobach 1993) and some states (e.g., California and Oregon) within the United States (Bowler and Donovan 1998; Gerber 1999; Matsusaka 2004). These two cases are sometimes accompanied by other countries (usually European) and are notably influenced by those MDDs related to very specific issues, such as the European Union (Hobolt 2009; Hug 2002) or policy options (Gallagher and Uleri 1996).

Whereas the European literature has been, in broad terms, optimistic (Qvortrup 2002; Setälä 1999a), the American literature has tended to be more negative (Cronin 1999; Haskell 2000; Magleby 1984), and there are reasons for these differing views. For instance, the American literature tends to suggest that by means of what Magleby calls the "initiative industry" (1984), economic interests or powerful social groups could easily use direct democracy for their own particular benefit, making it, in the end, harmful to representative democracy. Of course, there are extremely lucid and methodologically refined works of American scholars showing that, in the end, direct democracy is not as damaging to representative institutions as many would argue (see Gerber 1999; Matsusaka 2004).

By contrast, the continental literature – notably influenced by the Swiss experience – takes direct democracy to a place where it becomes a panacea for most, if not all, problems that representative democracies face (Kaufmann, Büchi, and Braun 2008; Verhulst and Nijeboer 2007). Yet again, there are voices of dissent, such as those of Freitag and Stadelmann-Steffen (2008), who claim that the more frequent the use of direct democracy, the lower the electoral participation in general elections, eroding one of the backbones of democracy itself.

At the same time, another hot debate focuses on the already "classic" argument between those who are notably concerned with the risk of a tyranny of the majority over the minority and the simultaneous and additional recurrent apprehension that is exactly the opposite – the impossibility of finding stable majorities at all. Moreover, there exists another recurrent group of challenges advanced by the literature against direct democracy: the (in)competence and alienation of citizens and the erosion of the power of elected officials. As shown in Chapter 2, not only are some of these arguments eroded as research continues and new methodological tools are used, but they also pose strong questions regarding the normative grounds of representative democracy itself. Evidently, many of these arguments are in tension with one another. Yet the evident contradictions in some of these positions do not imply that any one of them is without merit. It is highly unlikely that the use and relevance of direct democracy will decrease because of its theoretical and practical tensions with representative democracy.

I claim, however, that to understand the extremely complex world of direct democracy, research agendas must tackle at least three critical aspects of direct democracy: 1) the design, 2) the institutional milieu where they transpire and 3) the interaction between 1) and 2). The institutional design plays a key role in assessing how direct democracy will be used. For example, the entry hurdles in Italy often open the door for active boycott campaigns, which – as shown for other latitudes – could even violate the secrecy of the vote. In other words, some groups recurrently invited citizens not to participate in order for the MDD not to reach the required participation quorums, thereby disqualifying the MDD as a whole. In other countries, no participation quorums are required, so instead of abstaining from voting, everyone has incentives to take sides on the vote. Another evident example comes from the American milieu with regard to contributions and expenditures in ballot elections, where no limitations exist because of a series of decisions by the U.S. Supreme Court. This leads us to ask if direct democracy has to be left aside as a whole or if the Supreme Court must shift its position regarding contributions in these types of elections. Based on an extrapolation to regular elections, my point is that it would be highly beneficial to make some improvement to instrument design, and this is certainly preferable to eliminating the process as a whole. In short, although it is perfectly understandable why the American vision has been more negative than the European one, this book has shown that there is much room for skepticism regarding most concerns advanced in the literature.

Even when studying the very same subtype of MDD, important differences coexist at the procedural level in diverse countries that have a direct implication for their uses. Consequently, this research suggests that any assessment of direct democracy in general has to be done with extreme caution and argues that we must go beyond the either/or dichotomy, which most of the time is plagued with stereotypes of how representative and direct democracy work. The broad, oft-incorrect generalizations that the literature possesses and indeed fosters pushes researchers to ask the wrong questions and, consequently, to provide the wrong answers.[1]

One of the main objectives of Chapters 1 and 2 was to show that most arguments against direct democracy do not maintain equally and consistently for all instances of MDDs and all latitudes. As institutions, MDDs are closely related to other institutions; they do not occur in an institutional vacuum.[2] Thus, keeping in mind that most arguments about direct democracy are mediated by other factors, Chapter 3 offered an answer to the question of why some countries use MDDs exceptionally frequently whereas others seldom do and still others, never. In response to this question, the chapter compared all countries in the world over a twenty-five-year span (1985 to 2009). Thus far, no theory has offered a comprehensive answer to the former question, and most conjectures are usually based on anecdotal or impressionistic evidence from a few selected cases (Butler and Ranney 1994; LeDuc 2003; Suksi 1993). This study represents the first systematic attempt to explain this outstanding variation from a worldwide perspective.

Chapter 3 undermines many of the assumptions – sometimes explicit, sometimes implicit – about why different regimes use direct democracy in different ways. First, contrary to much of the conventional wisdom, this chapter showed that MDDs are not necessarily a recurrent strategy for either pure authoritarian regimes or solid democracies. It also showed that neither the size of the population nor the degree of social diversity of a country has any effect on the use of MDDs, as theory would assume. Concomitantly, this chapter has shown that countries' colonial pasts and institutional heritages do have a significant impact on the use of MDDs. Whereas former British colonies are much less likely to hold MDDs, those countries under the orbit of the former Soviet Union resort to MDDs much more frequently. Also, the durability of the regime under consideration seems to play a critical role in the uses of any type of MDD. The older the regimes, the more often they resort to MDDs. I believe, however, that one of the most interesting findings of this study lies with the diffusion effect

---

[1] Unlike another group of scholars, I hope to have provided enough arguments to eradicate oversimplifications about direct democracy; this tendency is best expressed by Broder for whom "[direct democracy] may be a noble sentiment, it invariably reduces complex policy issues to all-or-nothing, up-or-down choices between two extremes" (Broder 2000). I also have tried to refute crude explanations as to why, for example, direct democracy presents a threat to minority rights and promises only irresponsible and unaccountable governance based on a single case (Haskell 2000).

[2] For an interdisciplinary approach on the relevance of context, see Friemel (2008).

variables, as there is a positive and significant influence of the uses of MDDs in neighboring countries at time t over the considered one at time $t + 1$. These findings help to redirect some of the hypotheses advanced either directly or indirectly by previous researchers.

Chapters 4 through 7 studied the relationship of direct democracy along different levels of democratic development, from complete absence of democracy to full democracies, including low-intensity democratic regimes. Table 8.1 summarizes the main arguments expressed by these chapters. This 3*3 table collocates the three broad sections of the democratic continuum with the three broad types of MDDs (CI-MDDs, Mandatory TD-MDDs, and Facultative TD-MDDs).

a. Direct Democracy in Nondemocratic Regimes

In totalitarian regimes, MDDs are commonly used to reinforce a psychological and emotional connection between the regime and the population through its mobilization and excitement. The votes under Nazi Germany, as well as the grotesque uses of MDDs in one-party regimes, exemplify this point. In the context of authoritarian regimes (where voters do not have a free and genuine choice between at least two alternatives), plebiscites are usually just a formality for the government, enabling it to announce political or legal changes. By and large, they are used simply to maintain the illusion of an existing democratic process (both within and outside the country). Whether people like or loathe it, a plebiscite in this context, by hook or by crook, is usually accepted. Most of the time, these plebiscites are "approved" by bizarre majorities, and nobody believes they are true. This is exemplified in Table 4.1 by a group of countries that, in the absence of a more accurate name, I called the *Nightmare Team* of direct democracy. There, it is evident that the gross exploitation of MDDs occurred more often in totalitarian than in authoritarian regimes.

Plebiscites are frequently very narrow in terms of their objectives. They often aim to prolong presidential terms (e.g., Niyazov in Turkmenistan, Nazarbayev in Kazakhstan), or they may facilitate geopolitical maneuverings (e.g., Morocco in 1984, Egypt in 1971, Austria in 1938). There are almost no nuances – whether we are studying mandated or facultative plebiscites in the context of authoritarian regimes, it hardly makes any difference.

Rarely, in the toughest times, do plebiscites offer a window of opportunity, as in the cases of Uruguay, Chile, and Zimbabwe, but these are the exceptions that confirm the rule (as shown in Chapter 4). In statistical terms, just slightly more than 1 percent – 3 in 254 – of all MDDs held in nondemocratic regimes produced adverse results for governments. This handful of examples pushes us to ask the simplest and most obvious question: With roughly all of the tools necessary to rig a plebiscite, why do authoritarian regimes accept a loss when they have held an MDD?

The 1980 Uruguayan plebiscite is intriguing because it was the first MDD to violate the axiomatic rule that dictators do not lose at the urns. Also, this

TABLE 8.1. *Causes and Consequences of the Uses of Mechanisms of Direct Democracy in Different Contexts*

		Authoritarian Regimes	Democratic Regimes	
			Fluid/Inchoate Party System	Stable/Institutionalized Party System
Top-Down	Facultative (Unregulated)	Motivated by the maintenance of an illusion of an existing democratic process (to both internal and external observers); to strengthen a psychological and emotional relationship between the regime and the population through its mobilization and excitement; and showing the strength of the regime (also for both those within and outside the country). Usually are very narrow in terms of its objectives; such as prolongation of presidential terms – *Togo 1972, Turkmenistan 1994;* or geopolitical maneuverings – *Morocco 1984, Egypt 1971, Austria 1938.* This merits the warning: **Danger!**	Increasing legitimacy and political preferences of leaders, usually bypassing other democratic bodies (often Congress is bypassed by the executive). May exacerbate divisions and political conflict (*Bolivia 2004, 2008*) (*Ecuador 1997*). This merits the warning: **Danger!** But they may serve as consensus builders if two different bodies are in charge of triggering the unregulated plebiscite (*Colombia 2003*).	They may serve as a *hands-washing* mechanism. In general used as legitimizing tools for tough policies to avoid the political price for adopting such policies (*Costa Rica 2007*). Could serve as an escape valve for governing elites facing a bottom-up MDD (legislative counterproposal) (*Uruguay 1967*).

(continued)

TABLE 8.1 *(continued)*

| | | Democratic Regimes | |
	Authoritarian Regimes	Fluid/Inchoate Party System	Stable/Institutionalized Party System
Mandatory (Regulated)	At the very least, the outcome of these types of MDDs is similar to what would occur in their absence. At most, they provide a window of opportunity for challenging nonelected leaders (*Uruguay 1980*). **Risks:** Regime's backlash on identifiable democrats. Antiregime movements may be the springboard for future democratic parties (*Chile 1988*)	At most, a window of opportunity for challenging "edgy" executive leaders (*Venezuela 2007*), or "edgy" constitutional reforms (*Guatemala 1999*). Mandatory plebiscites do not facilitate the approval of new constitutions more than without them, as cases of reform happen without this type of MDD [Dominica (*1994*), Honduras (*1982*), El Salvador (*1983*), Nicaragua (*1987, 1995*)]. Thus, at the very least, outcomes may be the same in the absence of an MDD.	No major risks. Serves as a legitimization tool for constitutional changes. Help as a synchronization mechanism between politicians and citizens. Sometimes they fail (*Uruguay 1994*); sometimes they succeed (*Uruguay 1996*).

Bottom-Up	Citizen-Initiated	Almost by definition, they are unlikely to exist. CI-MDDs require citizens convincing fellow citizens to sign petitions; they have to talk, to convince, to gather, to organize. Thus, in case they do exist (no historical record exists as of this printing), they are likely to be totally manipulated by the regime.	Serve as intermittent safety valves against perverse or unresponsive behavior of representative institutions and politicians. Facing delicate political stress, it may let steam out of the boiler (*Venezuela 2004*). **Risks:** Manipulation by strong corporations or powerful groups in the absence of clear rules of the game. Could be used by current popular leaders that cannot – or do not – wish to call for an unregulated plebiscite (*Colombia 2008*).	A powerful synchronization between politicians and citizens (*Uruguay 1989, 1992,* etc.; *Switzerland*, dozens of examples). These MDDs help keep the political system from becoming a blight on society by grounding it in reality (calcium against potential party system osteoporosis [i.e., overinstitutionalization]. **Risks:** Major political and legal inconsistencies between citizenry and governing elites while synchronization occurs (*Uruguay, privatizations 1992*).

plebiscite shows how institutions can limit the actions of governments (decentralized system of vote counting) even in the context of a lack of freedom. Chile's 1988 plebiscite is also a case of an autocratic regime being obligated by a constitution of its own making and impacted by the crucial monitoring role that the international community filled. After all, most of the region had completed the transition to democracy, and the world's attention was centered there. Although institutions had a decisive responsibility in both South American countries, the Zimbabwean case exhibits the weakness of institutional explanatory power. This case exemplifies how regimes can, without difficulty, go around the popular choice without any concern as to putting on a good show.

Almost by definition, CI-MDDs are unlikely to exist in authoritarian or totalitarian regimes. CI-MDDs require citizens to convince fellow citizens to sign petitions; they have to talk, to convince, to gather, to organize. Thus, in case they do exist (there is no historical record at this time), they are likely to be totally manipulated by the regime.

b. *Direct Democracy within the Context of a Low-Intensity Democracy*

Within the context of a low-intensity democracy, the use of facultative plebiscites is mostly incidental, subsidiary to the ruling political elites desires, and is a means of molding and manipulating the electorate. The use of these institutions epitomizes a search for increased legitimacy and, more often than not, involves the bypassing of other democratic bodies (Congress is usually bypassed by the executive). Their use may exacerbate divisions and political conflict; this is evident from the Bolivian (2004, 2008) and Ecuadorian (1997) cases.

This subgroup of MDDs constitutes the preferred object of criticism within the realm of direct democracy. Scholars often pinpoint this subgroup of MDDs as responsible for what O'Donnell calls a delegative type of democracy. Yet extreme caution is warranted when making such an assessment. As shown in Chapter 5, these MDDs are mostly a consequence of the weakness of the representative institutions and the political system, not otherwise. Of course, not all countries with weak representative institutions resort to direct democracy, and not all countries with systematic use of direct democracy show a decaying strength in their party systems. Again, simply speaking about direct democracy does not help us much; we must go a step lower on the ladder of abstraction and differentiate among the diversity of MDDs and where they transpire.

Ecuador is notable as the country that most frequently uses plebiscites on the continent, even in its consultative (nonbinding) forms. With the exception of the center-left government of Borja, most administrations use TD-MDDs in an anxious search for the legitimation of both policies and leaders. No CI-MDD has ever been held in Ecuador, and the current resonant administration of Correa seems to maintain former practices in terms of direct democracy.

Bolivia also excels on the continent for its relatively recent wave of MDDs. Bolivia is a clear case of how MDDs can aggravate a situation that was complicated even before their use, and they regularly do, accruing more power to the executives. The absence of detailed procedures for MDDs creates doubt about their capacity to decide anything; here – more evident than in many other countries – the wording of questions brings into question the political-partisan ambitions of leaders.

Nonetheless, sometimes for oppositional forces, some MDDs – those mandated plebiscites – could open a window of opportunity (despite all of their weaknesses) in these volatile democracies. Because of their very nature, MDDs create at least two clearly differentiated positions, and if there is hope for free and fair elections, MDDs should not be automatically rejected by the opposition. They could be considered a window of opportunity for challenging "edgy" executive leaders (Venezuela 2007) or "edgy" constitutional reforms (Guatemala 1999). They are blamed for fostering leaders' orientations and giving them tools for civic manipulation. This may be correct, but historical records also show that MDDs do not facilitate the approval of new constitutions any more than in the absence of MDDs because the long list of constitutional reforms occurs in a context of no direct democracy whatsoever.

c. Direct Democracy in Mature Democracies

In a rather stable and mature democracy, the story is different. On the one hand, unregulated or facultative plebiscites serve as a hand-washing device given that, in general, these are used as legitimizing tools for a tough policy and to avoid the political price for adopting such policies (Costa Rica 2007). They also can serve as an escape valve for governing elites facing a CI-MDD (legislative counterproposal) (Uruguay 1966). On the other hand, no major risks are associated with mandated plebiscites, which are simply a legitimization tool for constitutional changes that occasionally serve as a synchronization mechanism between politicians and citizens (Uruguay 1994).

The question, and the paradox of this book, still remains: If democracy works reasonably well (i.e., is relatively institutionalized), why should it embrace institutions that might bring uncertainties, inconsistencies, and doubts; cost money; and be potentially manipulable? My answer is rather simple: Because institutionalized party systems may go one step further and become overinstitutionalized, they have serious dilemmas of channeling social demands, they lack the required flexibility for doing so, and ultimately they will be subject to massive demands for movement toward citizens' preferences.

CI-MDDs are reasonable barometers of society; they force a finer tuning – a synchronization – between party elites and citizens and serve as institutionalized intermittent safety valves for political pressure. Thus, CI-MDDs ground the political system in reality. They keep the political system accountable in a democratic context, generating homeostatic equilibria in polities.

Though they may produce legal vacuums and uncertainties, CI-MDDs offer a different arena where those who feel as though they have lost in the political game can win some political battles and articulate a coherent and differentiated political position. Arguably, in the absence of MDDs, the Uruguayan ideological and political turnover of 2005 would have been much cruder than it was, simply because MDDs (and their potential use) tempered both governing elites and opposition. Their existence also may explain why Uruguay has not experienced a large social crisis, such as those experienced by Argentina, Bolivia, and Ecuador; CI-MDDs created a channel through which citizens could express themselves and protest – for example, the neoliberal policies – in a formalized institutional framework.

Whereas politicians, academicians, and the media in many countries in Latin America have adopted a mantra that democracy is jeopardized, or at least under pressure, no relevant political actor in Uruguay seems to share these apprehensions, despite Uruguay having had all the ingredients for a petrification of its party system during the 1990s. Clientelism was the most frequently employed method of electoral co-optation, volatility was extremely low, and there was high political discontent. The question remains: Why did the Uruguayan party system not experience a crisis like those in Venezuela, Colombia, or even Costa Rica? As previously mentioned, this work suggests that CI-MDDs serve as institutionalized, sporadic safety valves of political pressure. In the words of President Batlle, "MDDs let the steam exit the pressure of the boiler!"

Reflecting on the process of steam exiting the pressure of the boiler, events progressed in the following manner. During the 1990s, discontented voters became alienated from governing parties as a result of economic decay, and the fiscal crisis hindered the ability of both traditional parties to feed their political machines. As a result, not only voters but also traditional party activists, and even some fraction leaders, became alienated from the Nacional and Colorados Parties. As traditional party leaders failed to fulfill clientelistic pacts with their constituents and brokers, the Frente Amplio made inroads with these groups (Altman, Castiglioni, and Luna 2008: 156). In this context, Frente Amplio gave political expression to a "veto coalition" to attract votes from the sectors that increasingly became alienated from the traditional system in the wake of the "happy Uruguay" crisis. Ideologically, this coalition put forth a statist platform advocating and enacting legislation through the use of CI-MDDs to roll back reformist legislation in favor of the status quo (strong state intervention in the domestic economy) (Altman, Buquet, and Luna 2006).

There are other collateral implications of the use of MDDs. Direct democratic mechanisms influence party–society relations and, in a way, they help to explain why Uruguay still has a relatively active union movement. When unions could not strike (because they provided essential public services), MDDs filled the empty space left by the non-strike by mobilizing and generating bonds. In Pribble's interviews with union members, they explicitly acknowledge that they would have disappeared in the 1990s without the "glue" provided by MDDs (Pribble 2008). Indeed, this also explains how much more difficult it would have been for the Frente Amplio to build its movement without that union action.

Still, the story is not completely black and white. MDDs in Uruguay have served narrow as well as broad interests in society but, again, they have helped organized citizens because of the enormous amount of social, political, and economic resources needed to stage a national campaign for a popular vote on any topic. Those underprivileged and unorganized inhabitants of Uruguay have very little chance to successfully advance their interests through CI-MDDs. Under these terms, direct democracy is fairly conservative in its essence. For example, the institutional design of MDDs explains why poverty in Uruguay is mainly concentrated in the population of children, not elders: ONAJPU constitutes maybe the most important lobby in Uruguayan politics – almost 30 percent of the electorate – and it plays accordingly. Children, on the contrary, do not vote or have a strong, organized lobby.

As this manuscript was written, a new attempt to nullify the Amnesty Law of Uruguay was on the horizon. PIT–CNT had organized a whole apparatus for the signature-gathering procedures conducted exclusively by volunteers belonging to the Union's movement. PIT–CNT has identified about ten hot spots (highly transited streets by pedestrians) for gathering the required signatures (about 250,000, given that it is a popular initiative to reform the constitution). An internal document says that on average, each spot gathers between eighty and one hundred signatures in a five-hour shift. Therefore, they call on all unions to help with that effort. Such was the coordination that each union was given a hot spot. For instance, the hot spot located at the entrance of the main bus station of Montevideo was given to the following unions based on a well-defined weekly calendar: Monday, Association of Postal Workers of Uruguay (AFPU); Tuesday, National Union of Workers of Consumer Cooperatives (AACC); Wednesday, Federation of Workers of OSE (state-owned water company, FFOSE); Thursday, Uruguayan Health Federation (FUS); and Friday, National Union of Workers of Private Education (SINTEP).

Figure 8.1 provides a glimpse of what a typical hot spot in the city of Montevideo looks like. It usually consists of a small table with a sign, a few small chairs, and two or more individuals asking pedestrians if they want to sign.

d. Summarizing

It is my intention that this book fill a lacuna in our understanding of the MDDs in the contemporary world and the poorly understood relationship between direct and representative democracy. Although CI-MDDs can serve as a catalyst for a synergetic relationship between citizens and political parties (penetrating parties and forcing them to seriously consider citizens' preferences or at least adopt a stance regarding the considered topic, maximizing their democratic potential), other MDDs usually help leaders to bypass other representative institutions and get rid of some of the republican check and balances.

Democracy certainly evolves both conceptually and in practical terms, and possibly "the time will come when nobody will remember that there were earlier times when the people were not able to decide their fate directly" (Verhulst and Nijeboer 2007: 12). They may be right but, again, it does not mean that representative government is to be supplanted by *any* sort of direct

FIGURE 8.1. Typical Signature-Gathering Hot Spot in Montevideo.[3]

democracy. MDDs complement, and sometimes correct, representative democracy. To facilitate this interaction, clear rules of the game must be established to avoid fratricidal disputes about how the process should take place (as we recently witnessed in Bolivia and Venezuela).

Like most institutions, practices of direct democracy have shown continuities, interruptions, abortions, and even setbacks. As demonstrated, its correspondence with other democratic institutions, such as female voting rights, is far from linear. Yet, having said that, CI-MDDs are much more than a simple, pragmatic second choice when representative democracy seems not to be working as expected.

[3] The sign reads as follows: "To Override the Expiration Law: Sign the Future."

2. The Road Ahead: Alternative Explanations and Avenues for New Research

Although this project contributes in several ways to our existing knowledge of direct democracy, it also has some important limitations. Considered as a whole, my results offer several new insights for future research and raise important implications about the theory behind direct democracy. Perhaps its main shortcoming is the issue of generalizability. In other words, to determine if this book's findings regarding the interaction between direct and representative institutions beyond the typical cases are generalizable, future research should either expand the universe of analysis or change the level of aggregation.

This research was mainly concentrated on MDDs held at the national level. It was not sensible to examine either subnational uses of MDDs or to look at the eventual transnational uses of these features (as proposed in the European Constitution with the Lisbon Treaty). Evidently, both spheres are gaining terrain, and eventually we will have to tackle them with a systematic perspective. Evidence shows, for example, that nonbinding, subnational popular initiatives could push national governments to notably stressful situations, as recently happened in Bolivia with the so-called autonomic referendums in several of the country's departments.

In the future, it may become necessary to develop a subtler operationalization of the dependent variable. In this work, I limited myself to a typology of direct democracy that was useful for answering my research questions. It is clear, however, that the world of direct democracy is perhaps much richer and more complicated than the proposed typology. Therefore, as different questions related to direct democracy are proposed, it may be preferable for different typologies to be used.

Because similar institutions (no matter which ones) may produce different results and evolve in distinctive ways, we should delve deeper into the institutional design of MDDs. Institutional design matters, and it matters a lot! Even considering rather similar institutions, small details imply quite different political consequences. Let me briefly summarize the case of constitutional popular initiatives and facultative referendums within the cases of Switzerland and Uruguay. In Uruguay, the "price" of launching a popular initiative, in terms of signature gathering, is no less than 10 percent of the electorate, and in Switzerland only one hundred thousand signatures are required, which represents approximately about 2 percent of the electorate (Table 8.2). In terms of facultative referendums, the gap between both countries is even larger. This fact might be explained on the grounds that in Switzerland, these mechanisms were designed as an instrument to protect very small groups within one of the most complex and heterogeneous contemporary societies, whereas in Uruguay, they were conceived as instruments of rather large groups in society in one of the most socially homogeneous countries on earth.

Finally, research can proceed only with more – and better – comparable data. To date, the database used in this research is one of the most comprehensive

TABLE 8.2. *Institutional Framework for Triggering Citizen-Initiated Mechanisms of Direct Democracy in Switzerland and Uruguay*

Year introduced	Popular Initiatives		Referendums	
	Switzerland 1891	Uruguay 1934	Switzerland 1874	Uruguay 1967
Signatures required (% of the electorate)	±2% (100.000)	10% (20% up to 1967)	±1% (50.000)	25%/2%
Time allotted to gather signatures	18 months	No limit	90 days	150 days
Time used and percentage of approval	160 (9%)	10 (20%)	155 (53%)	7 (29%)
Required participation	No	35%	No	No
Required majorities	Double majority (citizens and cantons)	50%+1	50%+1	50%+1
Qualifiers	Initiative could not go against basic humanitarian and international law	None	Cannot deal with national budget	May not be used to revise or repeal laws that establish taxes or any legislation that falls within the "exclusive initiative" of the executive power

cross-national databases ever assembled. Yet more information is required and more nuance needed. Spelling out direct democratic procedures will illuminate the current political and partisan use of direct democracy (e.g., which parties supported this or that MDD, who was in charge of triggering an MDD, which procedures were used, and so forth). Nevertheless, eventually we will have to tackle the different paths along which direct democracy has transited toward its constitutional status (where they are used in this manner). In so doing, a careful analysis of the actors involved, the institutional context (laws and rules), and the debates on direct democracy will shed light on the prospects for its future use and may help to better explain its consequences.

Appendix

1. Mechanisms of Direct Democracy Worldwide (1984–2009)

Country	Pop (2008)	Citizen-Initiated MDDs			Top-Down MDDs			All MDDs		
		Events	%	Yearly Average	Events	%	Yearly Average	Events	%	Yearly Average
Total		*328*	*100*	*12.62*	*621*	*100*	*23.88*	*949*	*100*	*36.50*
Albania	3.2				3	0.48	0.12	3	0.32	0.12
Algeria	34.4				6	0.97	0.23	6	0.63	0.23
Andorra	0.1				1	0.16	0.04	1	0.11	0.04
Argentina	39.9				1	0.16	0.04	1	0.11	0.04
Armenia	3.1				4	0.64	0.15	4	0.42	0.15
Australia	21.4				8	1.29	0.31	8	0.84	0.31
Austria	8.3				1	0.16	0.04	1	0.11	0.04
Azerbaijan	8.7				42	6.76	1.62	42	4.43	1.62
Bahamas	0.3				5	0.81	0.19	5	0.53	0.19
Bahrain	0.8				1	0.16	0.04	1	0.11	0.04
Bangladesh	160.0				2	0.32	0.08	2	0.21	0.08
Belarus	9.7				12	1.93	0.46	12	1.26	0.46
Belize	0.3				1	0.16	0.04	1	0.11	0.04
Benin	9.1				1	0.16	0.04	1	0.11	0.04
Bolivia	9.7	1	0.30	0.04	8	1.29	0.31	9	0.95	0.35
Bosnia Herzegovina	3.9				1	0.16	0.04	1	0.11	0.04
Botswana	1.9				12	1.93	0.46	12	1.26	0.46
Brazil	192.0				3	0.48	0.12	3	0.32	0.12
Burkina Faso	15.2				1	0.16	0.04	1	0.11	0.04
Burundi	8.1				3	0.48	0.12	3	0.32	0.12
Canada	33.3				1	0.16	0.04	1	0.11	0.04
Central African Rep.	4.4				3	0.48	0.12	3	0.32	0.12
Chad	11.0				3	0.48	0.12	3	0.32	0.12

Country										
Chile	16.8				2	0.32	0.08	2	0.21	0.08
Colombia	47.3	2	0.61	0.08	16	2.58	0.62	18	1.90	0.69
Congo, Dem Rep.	64.2				2	0.32	0.08	2	0.21	0.08
Congo, Rep.	4.2				2	0.32	0.08	2	0.21	0.08
Costa Rica	4.5				1	0.16	0.04	1	0.11	0.04
Cote d'Ivoire	20.6				1	0.16	0.04	1	0.11	0.04
Croatia	4.4				2	0.32	0.08	2	0.21	0.08
Cyprus	0.9				1	0.16	0.04	1	0.11	0.04
Czech Rep.	10.4				1	0.16	0.04	1	0.11	0.04
Denmark	5.5				6	0.97	0.23	6	0.63	0.23
Djibouti	0.9				2	0.32	0.08	2	0.21	0.08
Ecuador	13.7				38	6.12	1.46	38	4.00	1.46
Egypt	81.5				7	1.13	0.27	7	0.74	0.27
Equatorial Guinea	0.6				1	0.16	0.04	1	0.11	0.04
Eritrea	5.0				1	0.16	0.04	1	0.11	0.04
Estonia	1.3				4	0.64	0.15	4	0.42	0.15
Ethiopia	77.3				1	0.16	0.04	1	0.11	0.04
Finland	5.3				1	0.16	0.04	1	0.11	0.04
France	62.1				4	0.64	0.15	4	0.42	0.15
Gabon	1.5				1	0.16	0.04	1	0.11	0.04
Gambia	1.7				1	0.16	0.04	1	0.11	0.04
Georgia	4.4				4	0.64	0.15	4	0.42	0.15
Ghana	23.4				1	0.16	0.04	1	0.11	0.04
Guatemala	13.7				5	0.81	0.19	5	0.53	0.19
Guinea	9.8				2	0.32	0.08	2	0.21	0.08
Haiti	9.0				2	0.32	0.08	2	0.21	0.08
Hungary	10.0	5	1.52	0.19	7	1.13	0.27	12	1.26	0.46
Iran	70.7				1	0.16	0.04	1	0.11	0.04
Iraq	30.4				3	0.48	0.12	3	0.32	0.12

(continued)

Country	Pop (2008)	Citizen-Initiated MDDs			Top-Down MDDs			All MDDs		
		Events	%	Yearly Average	Events	%	Yearly Average	Events	%	Yearly Average
Ireland	4.5				22	3.54	0.85	22	2.32	0.85
Italy	59.9	52	15.85	2.00	5	0.81	0.19	57	6.01	2.19
Kazakhstan	15.7				2	0.32	0.08	2	0.21	0.08
Kenya	38.5				1	0.16	0.04	1	0.11	0.04
Korea, South	48.6				1	0.16	0.04	1	0.11	0.04
Kyrgyzstan	5.3				10	1.61	0.38	10	1.05	0.38
Latvia	2.3	6	1.83	0.23	2	0.32	0.08	8	0.84	0.31
Liberia	3.8				1	0.16	0.04	1	0.11	0.04
Liechtenstein	0.0	33	10.06	1.27	11	1.77	0.42	44	4.64	1.69
Lithuania	3.4	11	3.35	0.42	8	1.29	0.31	19	2.00	0.73
Luxembourg	0.5				1	0.16	0.04	1	0.11	0.04
Macedonia	2.0				2	0.32	0.08	2	0.21	0.08
Madagascar	19.1				4	0.64	0.15	4	0.42	0.15
Malawi	13.9				1	0.16	0.04	1	0.11	0.04
Maldives	0.3				5	0.81	0.19	5	0.53	0.19
Mali	14.6				1	0.16	0.04	1	0.11	0.04
Malta	0.4				1	0.16	0.04	1	0.11	0.04
Mauritania	3.3				2	0.32	0.08	2	0.21	0.08
Micronesia	0.1	2	0.61	0.08	52	8.37	2.00	54	5.69	2.08
Moldavia	4.1				3	0.48	0.12	3	0.32	0.12
Morocco	31.2				5	0.81	0.19	5	0.53	0.19
Myanmar	51.8				1	0.16	0.04	1	0.11	0.04
Netherland	16.4				1	0.16	0.04	1	0.11	0.04
New Zealand	4.3	4	1.22	0.15	5	0.81	0.19	9	0.95	0.35
Niger	15.4				6	0.97	0.23	6	0.63	0.23

Northern Cyprus	0.3				1	0.16	0.04	1	0.11	0.04
Norway	4.8				1	0.16	0.04	1	0.11	0.04
Pakistan	166.0				2	0.32	0.08	2	0.21	0.08
Palau	0.0	6	1.83	0.23	25	4.03	0.96	31	3.27	1.19
Panama	3.4				3	0.48	0.12	3	0.32	0.12
Peru	28.8				2	0.32	0.08	2	0.21	0.08
Philippines	90.4				2	0.32	0.08	2	0.21	0.08
Poland	38.1				9	1.45	0.35	9	0.95	0.35
Portugal	10.6				3	0.48	0.12	3	0.32	0.12
Qatar	1.3				1	0.16	0.04	1	0.11	0.04
Romania	21.5				7	1.13	0.27	7	0.74	0.27
Russian Fed.	141.8				6	0.97	0.23	6	0.63	0.23
Rwanda	9.7				1	0.16	0.04	1	0.11	0.04
Saint Kitts & Nevis	0.1				1	0.16	0.04	1	0.11	0.04
Samoa	0.2				2	0.32	0.08	2	0.21	0.08
San Marino	0.0	13	3.96	0.50	2	0.32	0.08	15	1.58	0.58
Sao Tome & Principe	0.2				1	0.16	0.04	1	0.11	0.04
Senegal	12.2				1	0.16	0.04	1	0.11	0.04
Serbia & Montenegro	7.4				3	0.48	0.12	3	0.32	0.12
Seychelles	0.1				2	0.32	0.08	2	0.21	0.08
Sierra Leone	6.0				1	0.16	0.04	1	0.11	0.04
Slovakia	5.4	5	1.52	0.19	4	0.64	0.15	9	0.95	0.35
Slovenia	2.0	3	0.91	0.12	10	1.61	0.38	13	1.37	0.50
Somalia	9.0				1	0.16	0.04	1	0.11	0.04
South Africa	48.7				1	0.16	0.04	1	0.11	0.04
Spain	45.6				2	0.32	0.08	2	0.21	0.08
St. Vincent & Grenadines	0.1				1	0.16	0.04	1	0.11	0.04
Sudan	41.4				1	0.16	0.04	1	0.11	0.04
Suriname	0.5				1	0.16	0.04	1	0.11	0.04

(continued)

Country	Pop (2008)	Citizen-Initiated MDDs			Top-Down MDDs			All MDDs		
		Events	%	Yearly Average	Events	%	Yearly Average	Events	%	Yearly Average
Sweden	9.2				2	0.32	0.08	2	0.21	0.08
Switzerland	7.6	167	50.91	6.42	70	11.27	2.69	237	24.97	9.12
Syrian Arab Rep.	21.2				5	0.81	0.19	5	0.53	0.19
Taiwan	23.0	1	0.30	0.04	6	0.97	0.23	7	0.74	0.27
Tajikistan	6.8				3	0.48	0.12	3	0.32	0.12
Tanzania	42.5				2	0.32	0.08	2	0.21	0.08
Thailand	67.4				1	0.16	0.04	1	0.11	0.04
Timor-Leste	1.1				1	0.16	0.04	1	0.11	0.04
Togo	6.5				1	0.16	0.04	1	0.11	0.04
Tunisia	10.3				1	0.16	0.04	1	0.11	0.04
Turkey	75.4				3	0.48	0.12	3	0.32	0.12
Turkmenistan	5.0				3	0.48	0.12	3	0.32	0.12
Tuvalu	0.0				2	0.32	0.08	2	0.21	0.08
Uganda	31.7				2	0.32	0.08	2	0.21	0.08
Ukraine	46.3	4	1.22	0.15	2	0.32	0.08	6	0.63	0.23
Uruguay	3.5	12	3.66	0.46	5	0.81	0.19	17	1.79	0.65
Uzbekistan	27.7				5	0.81	0.19	5	0.53	0.19
Venezuela	27.9	1	0.30	0.04	7	1.13	0.27	8	0.84	0.31
Yemen	23.1				2	0.32	0.08	2	0.21	0.08
Yugoslavia	7.5				4	0.64	0.15	4	0.42	0.15
Zimbabwe	13.0				1	0.16	0.04	1	0.11	0.04

Note: Sixty-eight countries did not have MDDs in the considered time whatsoever: Afghanistan; Angola; Antigua & Barbuda; Belgium; Bhutan; Brunei; Bulgaria; Cambodia; Cameroon; Cape Verde; China; Cuba; Czechoslovakia; Dominica; Dominican Republic; El Salvador; Fiji; Germany; Germany E.; Greece; Grenada; Guinea-Bissau; Guyana; Honduras; Iceland; India; Indonesia; Israel; Jamaica; Japan; Jordan; Kiribati; Korea, Dem. Rep; Kuwait; Lao PDR; Lebanon; Lesotho; Libya; Malaysia; Mauritius; Mexico; Monaco; Mongolia; Mozambique; Namibia; Nepal; Nicaragua; Nigeria; Oman; Papua New Guinea; Paraguay; Saudi Arabia; Singapore; Solomon Islands; Sri Lanka; St. Lucia; Swaziland; Tonga; Trinidad & Tobago; United Arab Emirates; United Kingdom; United States; Vanuatu; Vietnam; Yemen (N); Yemen (S); Zambia.

2. A Census of Uruguayan Legislators on Citizen-Initiated Mechanisms of Direct Democracy

Structured interviews with Uruguayan legislators were carried out to test the working hypothesis that power holders should be at least suspicious about CI-MDDs' potentialities.[1] Surprisingly, representatives in general do not have negative attitudes toward MDDs, as the literature might suggest. On the contrary, more than half of representatives consider MDDs from below to be mechanisms that strengthen representative democracy (see Question 1) and agree that there is no risk of a tyranny of the majority over the minority (Q2) (as stated in one argument put forth by many detractors of direct democracy). Not only do more than 60 percent of representatives deny the idea that MDDs from below weaken the power of congressmen (Q3), but 70 percent of representatives also consider that the presence of a potential referendum is a sufficient reason to look for a broad consensus within the political parties (Q4), an argument for which the Swiss experience is also robust.

Question (1): *What impact do popular initiatives have on representative democracy?* (% and n)

Party	Strengthen	No Effect	Erode	DK/NR[a]	Total
Colorado	34.5 (10)	37.9 (11)	20.7 (6)	6.9 (2)	100 (29)
Blanco	46.4 (13)	21.4 (6)	25.0 (7)	7.1 (2)	100 (28)
FA	77.8 (21)	18.5 (5)		3.7 (1)	100 (27)
NE	40.0 (2)		60.0 (3)		100 (5)
TOTAL	51.7 (46)	24.7 (22)	18.0 (16)	5.6 (5)	100 (89)

[a] (doesn't know/no response)

Question (2): *Is there a risk of a tyranny of the majority over the minority?* (% and n)

Party	Totally Agree	Moderately Agree	Neutral	Moderately Disagree	Totally Disagree	DK/NR[a]	Total
Colorado	6.9 (2)	13.8 (4)	10.3 (3)	20.7 (6)	48.3 (14)		100 (29)
Blanco	10.7 (3)	25.0 (7)	10.7 (3)	25.0 (7)	28.6 (8)		100 (28)
FA	13.8 (4)	6.9 (2)	13.8 (4)	20.7 (6)	41.4 (12)	3.4 (1)	100 (29)
NE			40.0 (2)	60.0 (3)			100 (5)
TOTAL	9.9 (9)	14.3 (13)	13.2 (12)	24.2 (22)	37.4 (34)		100 (91)

[a] (doesn't know/no response)

[1] During the months of June and July 1997, I interviewed ninety-one of ninety-nine Uruguayan representatives. That research was financed by the Kellogg Institute for International Studies at the University of Notre Dame.

Question (3): *Do you think that popular initiatives and referendums weaken the power of congressmen elected by the citizenry?*

Party	Totally Agree	Moderately Agree	Neutral	Moderately Disagree	Totally Disagree	DK/NR[a]	Total
Colorado	20.7 (6)	10.3 (3)	13.8 (4)	17.2 (5)	37.9 (11)		100 (29)
Blanco	10.7 (3)	7.1 (2)	28.6 (8)	32.1 (9)	17.9 (5)	3.6 (1)	100 (28)
FA		6.9 (2)	17.2 (5)	27.6 (8)	48.3 (14)		100 (29)
NE		20.0 (1)		40.0 (2)	40.0 (2)		100 (5)
TOTAL	9.9 (9)	8.8 (8)	18.7 (17)	26.4 (24)	35.2 (32)	1.1 (1)	100 (91)

[a] (doesn't know/no response)

Question (4): *Is the presence of a potential referendum a sufficient reason to look for a broader consensus among political parties?* (% and n)

Party	Totally Agree	Moderately Agree	Moderately Disagree	Totally Disagree	DK/NR[a]	Total
Colorado	17.2 (5)	51.7 (15)	13.8 (4)	10.3 (3)	6.9 (2)	100 (29)
Blanco	32.1 (9)	46.4 (13)	17.9 (5)	3.6 (1)		100 (28)
FA	13.8 (4)	55.2 (16)	31.0 (9)			100 (29)
NE	20.0 (1)	20.0 (1)	40.0 (2)	20.0 (1)		100 (5)
TOTAL	20.9 (19)	49.5 (45)	22.0 (20)	5.5 (5)	2.2 (2)	100 (91)

[a] (doesn't know/no response)

Even so, general support for MDDs shown by representatives is not entirely blind. In general terms, deputies recognized that MDDs are not applicable to every political situation. More than 70 percent oppose the idea that *all* issues at stake can be contemplated in popular initiatives and thus avoid the institutional intermediation (Q5).

Question (5): *Can all issues at stake be contemplated by popular initiatives and thus avoid the institutional intermediation?* (% and n)

Party	Totally Agree	Moderately Agree	Neutral	Moderately Disagree	Totally Disagree	DK/NR[a]	Total
Colorado	10.3 (3)	6.9 (2)	6.9 (2)	10.3 (3)	65.5 (19)		100 (29)
Blanco	3.6 (1)	14.3 (4)	25.0 (7)	10.7 (3)	46.4 (13)		100 (28)
FA	3.4 (1)	6.9 (2)	13.8 (4)	31.0 (9)	41.4 (12)	3.4 (1)	100 (29)
NE		20.0 (1)			60.0 (3)	20.0 (1)	100 (5)
TOTAL	5.5 (5)	9.9 (9)	14.3 (13)	19.8 (18)	49.5 (45)		100 (91)

[a] (doesn't know/no response)

Interestingly, almost half of the representatives were highly suspicious of the capacities of citizens to effectively weigh decisions using MDDs (Q6), although they simultaneously recognized that MDDs combat citizen alienation and apathy (Q7). Moreover, a broad majority believes that through MDDs, civic virtues are developed (Q8).

Question (6): *Do you agree that the common citizen lacks sufficient elements to decide on highly complex issues?* (% and n)

Party	Totally Agree	Moderately Agree	Neutral	Moderately Disagree	Totally Disagree	DK/NR[a]	Total
Colorado	41.4 (12)	20.7 (6)	3.4 (1)	6.9 (2)	27.6 (8)		100 (29)
Blanco	50.0 (14)	17.9 (5)	14.3 (4)	10.7 (3)	7.1 (2)		100 (28)
FA	13.8 (4)	17.2 (5)	10.3 (3)	27.6 (8)	31.0 (9)		100 (29)
NE	20.0 (1)	20.0 (1)	20.0 (1)	40.0 (2)			100 (5)
TOTAL	34.1 (31)	18.5 (17)	9.9 (9)	16.5 (15)	20.9 (19)		100 (91)

[a] (doesn't know/no response)

Question (7): *Do you think that popular initiatives combat apathy?* (% and n)

Party	Totally Agree	Moderately Agree	Neutral	Moderately Disagree	Totally Disagree	DK/NR[a]	Total
Colorado	20.7 (6)	44.8 (13)	10.3 (3)	17.2 (5)	6.9 (2)		100 (29)
Blanco	7.1 (2)	21.4 (6)	21.4 (6)	25.0 (7)	21.4 (6)	3.6 (1)	100 (28)
FA	24.1 (7)	51.7 (15)	6.9 (2)	3.4 (1)	13.8 (4)		100 (29)
NE	20.0 (1)	40.0 (2)	20.0 (1)	20.0 (1)			100 (5)
TOTAL	17.6 (16)	39.6 (36)	13.2 (12)	15.4 (14)	13.2 (12)	1.1 (1)	100 (91)

[a] (doesn't know/no response)

Question (8): *Do you think that through popular initiatives, civic virtues are developed?* (% and n)

Party	Totally Agree	Moderately Agree	Neutral	Moderately Disagree	Totally Disagree	DK/NR[a]	Total
Colorado	27.6 (8)	48.3 (14)	10.3 (3)	10.3 (3)		3.4 (1)	100 (29)
Blanco	25.0 (7)	39.3 (11)	21.4 (6)	10.7 (3)	3.6 (1)		100 (28)
FA	48.3 (14)	37.9 (11)	3.4 (1)	6.9 (2)		3.4 (1)	100 (29)
NE	40.0 (2)			40.0 (2)	20.0 (1)		100 (5)
TOTAL	34.1 (31)	39.6 (36)	11.0 (10)	11.0 (10)	2.2 (2)	2.2 (2)	100 (91)

[a] (doesn't know/no response)

The relationship between legislators' opinions on CI-MDDs and their party affiliation also deserves a few words. The relationship between their positions regarding MDDs and the development of their postmaterial values developed is remarkable. For this reason, I developed a series of elements that allowed me to create a direct-democracy index. The index was built based on ten questions, and a score on a scale of 1–10 was assigned to each response. I calculated the average and standard deviation of each party, with 10 representing the strongest sympathizers of direct democracy and 1 the strongest opponents of it. Perhaps the most interesting aspect of my findings is that the direct democracy index does not seem to belong to the "package" of postmaterialist values in the Uruguayan milieu (Pearson $r = 0.200$), but it is strongly related to the left-right position that each legislator declares (Pearson $r = -0.475$, significant at 0.01, 2-tailed). Having said that, the Pearson correlation between left-right and favorable opinions toward direct democracy is -0.474 (significant at 0.01, 2-tailed).

References

Achen, Christofer H. 2000. "Why Lagged Dependent Variables Can Suppress the Explanatory Power of Other Independent Variables." Presented at the *Annual Meeting of the Political Methodology Section of the American Political Science Association*, July 20–22, University of California, Los Angeles.

Ackerman, Bruce A. and James S. Fishkin. 2004. *Deliberation Day*. New Haven: Yale University Press.

Aguiar-Conraria, Luís and Pedro C. Magalhães. 2009. "Referendum Design, Quorum Rules and Turnout." *Public Choice* doi:10.1007/s11127-009-9504-1.

Aguiar-Conraria, Luís and Pedro C. Magalhães. 2010. "How Quorum Rules Distort Referendum Outcomes: Evidence from a Pivotal Voter Model." *European Journal of Political Economy* doi:10.1016/j.ejpoleco.2010.03.004.

Aguiar, César A. 1985. "Uruguay: Escenas Políticas y Subsistemas Electorales." *Desarrollo Económico* 24 (96): 517–541.

Aldrich, John. 1995. *Why Parties?* Chicago: Chicago University Press.

Alesina, Alberto, Arnaud Devleeschauwer, William Easterly, Sergio Kurlat, and Romain Wacziarg. 2003. "Fractionalization." *Journal of Economic Growth* 8 (2): 155–194.

Alfaro Redondo, Ronald. 2006. "Elecciones Nacionales 2006 en Costa Rica y la Recomposición del Sistema de Partidos Políticos." *Revista de Ciencia Política* 26 (1): 125–137.

Allamand, Andrés. 1999. *La Travesía del Desierto*. Santiago: Aguilar.

Almond, Gabriel and Sidney Verba. 1963. *The Civic Culture*. Princeton: Princeton University Press.

Altman, David. 2002a. "Increasing Horizontal and Social Accountability in Latin America: Satisfaction with Democracy, Social Accountability, and Direct Democracy." *International Review of Public Administration* 7 (2): 5–20.

Altman, David. 2002b. "Popular Initiatives in Uruguay: Confidence Votes on Government or Political Loyalties?" *Electoral Studies* 21 (4): 617–630.

Altman, David. 2005. "Democracia Directa en el Continente Americano: ¿Auto-Legitimación Gubernamental o Censura Ciudadana?" *Política y Gobierno* XII (2): 203–232.

Altman, David. 2008. "Collegiate Executives and Direct Democracy in Switzerland and Uruguay: Similar Institutions, Opposite Political Goals, Distinct Results." *Swiss Political Science Review* 14 (3): 483–520.

Altman, David, Daniel Buquet, and Juan Pablo Luna. 2006. "Constitutional Reforms and Political Turnover in Uruguay: Winning a Battle, Losing the War." Presented at the *Annual Meeting of the American Political Science Association*, August 31 – September 3, Philadelphia, PA.

Altman, David, Rossana Castiglioni, and Juan Pablo Luna. 2008. "Uruguay: A Role Model for the Left?" In *Leftovers: Tales of the Latin American Left*, edited by J. G. Castañeda and M. A. Morales. London-New York: Routledge, 151–173.

Altman, David and Rickard Lalander. 2003. "Bolivia's Popular Participation Law: An Undemocratic Democratisation Process?" In *Decentralisation and Democratic Governance: Experiences from India, Bolivia and South Africa*, edited by A. Hadenius. Stockholm: Expert Group on Development Issues – Almqvist & Wiksell International, 63–104.

Altman, David and Aníbal Pérez-Liñán. 2002. "Assessing the Quality of Democracy: Freedom, Competitiveness, and Participation in 18 Latin American Countries." *Democratization* 9 (2): 85–100.

Alvarez, Angel. 2007. "Venezuela 2007: Los Motores del Socialismo se Alimentan con Petróleo." *Revista de Ciencia Política* 27 (EE): 264–286.

Alvarez, Angel. 2008. "Venezuela: ¿La Revolución Pierde su Encanto?" *Revista de Ciencia Política* 28 (1): 405–432.

Alvarez, Angel and Yorelis Acosta. 2006. "The 2006 Presidential Elections in Venezuela: Electoral Competition and Regime Change." *Harvard Review of Latin America* V (1): 35–37.

Alvarez, R. Michael, Melanie Goodrich, Thad E. Hall, D. Roderick Kiewiet, and Sarah M. Sled. 2004. "The Complexity of the California Recall Election." *PS: Political Science & Politics* 37 (1): 23–26.

Amacher, Ryan C. and William J. Boyes. 1978. "Cycles in Senatorial Voting Behavior: Implications for the Optimal Frequency of Elections." *Public Choice* 33 (3): 5–13.

Amorim Neto, Octavio. 2006. *Presidencialismo e Governabilidade nas Américas*. Rio de Janeiro: Editora FGV.

Anckar, Dag. 2004. "Direct Democracy in Microstates and Small Island States." *World Development* 32 (2): 379–390.

Araos, María Raquel and Eduardo Engel. 1989. "Desempleo, Votación Histórica y el Plebiscito de 1988." *Estudios CIEPLAN* 27 (Diciembre): 5–17.

Arrarás, Astrid and Grace Deheza. 2005. "Referéndum del Gas en Bolivia: Mucho Más que un Referéndum." *Revista de Ciencia Política* 25 (2): 161–172.

Arrow, Kenneth J. 1950. "A Difficulty in the Concept of Social Welfare." *The Journal of Political Economy* 58 (4): 328–346.

Arrow, Kenneth J. 1963 (1st ed., 1951). *Social Choice and Individual Values*. New Haven: Yale University Press.

Auer, Andreas. 2005. "European Citizens' Initiative." *European Constitutional Law Review* 1 (1): 79–86.

Auer, Andreas. 2007. "National Referendums in the Process of European Integration: Time for Change." In *The European Constitution and National Constitutions: Ratification and Beyond*, edited by A. Albi and J. Ziller. Amsterdam: Kluwer Law International, 261–271.

Barczak, Monica. 2001. "Representation by Consultation? The Rise of Direct Democracy in Latin America." *Latin American Politics & Society* 43 (3): 37–59.

Barros, Robert. 2002. *Constitutionalism and Dictatorship: Pinochet, the Junta, and the 1980 Constitution*. Cambridge: Cambridge University Press.

Bejarano, Ana María and Eduardo Pizarro. 2005. "From "Restricted" to "Besieged": The Changing Nature of the Limits to Democracy in Colombia." In *The Third Wave of Democratization in Latin America: Advances and Setbacks*, edited by F. Hagopian and S. Mainwaring. Cambridge: Cambridge University Press, 235–260.

Bell, A. Derrick Jr. 1978. "The Referendum: Democracy's Barrier to Racial Equality." *Washington Law Review* 54 (1): 1–29.

Benhabib, Seyla. 1996. "Toward a Deliberative Model of Democratic Legitimacy." In *Democracy and Difference: Contesting the Boundaries of the Political*, edited by S. Benhabib. Princeton: Princeton University Press, 67–94.

Benz, Matthias and Alois Stutzer. 2004. "Are Voters Better Informed When They Have a Larger Say in Politics? Evidence for the European Union and Switzerland." *Public Choice* 119 (1–2): 31–59.

Bertelsmann Stiftung. 2003. *BTI 2003 Iraq Country Report*. Gütersloh: Bertelsmann Stiftung.

Bertelsmann Stiftung. 2007a. *BTI 2008 Kazakhstan Country Report*. Gütersloh: Bertelsmann Stiftung.

Bertelsmann Stiftung. 2007b. *BTI 2008 Turkmenistan Country Report*. Gütersloh: Bertelsmann Stiftung.

Bertelsmann Stiftung. 2007c. *BTI 2008 Zimbabwe Country Report*. Gütersloh: Bertelsmann Stiftung.

Black, Duncan. 1948. "On the Rationale of Group Decision-Making." *The Journal of Political Economy* 56 (1): 23–34.

Black, Duncan. 1958. *The Theory of Committees and Elections*. New York: Cambridge University Press.

Bobbio, Norberto. 1987. *The Future of Democracy: A Defence of the Rules of the Game*. New York: Polity.

Bollen, Kenneth A. 1979. "Political Democracy and the Timing of Development." *American Sociological Review* 44 (4): 572–587.

Bollen, Kenneth A. 1993. "Liberal Democracy: Validity and Sources Biases in Cross-National Measures." *American Journal of Political Science* 37 (4): 1207–1230.

Bollen, Kenneth A. and Robert W. Jackman. 1985. "Political Democracy and the Size Distribution of Income." *American Sociological Review* 50 (4): 438–457.

Bollen, Kenneth A. and Robert W. Jackman. 1995. "Income Inequality and Democratization Revisited: Comment on Muller." *American Sociological Review* 60 (6): 983–989.

Bollen, Kenneth A. and Pamela Paxton. 2000. "Subjective Measures of Liberal Democracy." *Comparative Political Studies* 33 (1): 58–86.

Bottinelli, Oscar, Daniel Buquet, Gerardo Caetano, Agustín Canzani, Antonio Cardarello, Daniel Chasquetti, Gustavo De Armas, Adolfo Garcé, Luis E. González, Aldo Guerrini, Jorge Lanzaro, Altair Magri, Constanza Moreira, Romeo Pérez Antón, Rosario Queirolo, and Jaime Yaffé (Ed.). 2000. *Elecciones 1999/2000*. Montevideo: Ediciones de la Banda Oriental – Instituto de Ciencia Politica.

Bowler, Shaun and Bruce Cain. 2004. "Introduction – Recalling the Recall: Reflections on California's Recent Political Adventure." *PS: Political Science & Politics* 37 (1): 7–10.

Bowler, Shaun and Todd Donovan. 1998. *Demanding Choices: Opinion, Voting, and Direct Democracy*. Ann Arbor: The University of Michigan Press.

Brasil De Lima, Olavo. 1983. "Electoral Participation in Brazil (1945–1978): The Legislation, the Party Systems and Electoral Turnouts." *Luso-Brazilian Review* 20 (1): 65–87.

Breuer, Anita. 2007. "Institutions of Direct Democracy and Accountability in Latin America's Presidential Democracies." *Democratization* 14 (4): 554–579.

Breuer, Anita. 2008a. "Policymaking by Referendum in Presidential Systems: Evidence from the Bolivian and Colombian Cases." *Latin American Politics & Society* 50 (4): 59–89.

Breuer, Anita. 2008b. "The Problematic Relation between Direct Democracy and Accountability in Latin America: Evidence from the Bolivian Case." *Bulletin of Latin American Research* 27 (1): 1–23.

Breuer, Anita. 2009a. "Costa Rica's 2007 Referendum on the Dominican Republic-Central America Free Trade Agreement (CAFTA-DR): Citizen Participation or Citizen Manipulation?" *Representation* 45 (4): 455–469.

Breuer, Anita. 2009b. "The Use of Government-Initiated Referendums in Latin America: Towards a Theory of Referendum Causes." *Revista de Ciencia Política* 29 (1): 23–55.

Brinks, Daniel and Michael Coppedge. 2006. "Diffusion Is No Illusion: Neighbor Emulation in the Third Wave of Democracy." *Comparative Political Studies* 39 (4): 463–489.

Broder, David S. 2000. *Democracy Derailed: Initiative Campaigns and the Power of Money.* Orlando: Harcourt.

Brunetti, Aymo. 1997. "Der Status Quo Bias und die bremsende Wirkung des fakultativen Referendums." In *Wieviel direkte Demokratie verträgt die Schweiz?*, edited by S. Borner and H. Rentsch. Zürich: Verlag Rüegger, 167–182.

Bühlmann, Marc and Markus Freitag. 2006. "Individual and Contextual Determinants of Electoral Participation." *Swiss Political Science Review* 12 (4): 13–47.

Bühlmann, Marc, Sarah Nicolet, and Peter Selb. 2006. "National Elections in Switzerland: An Introduction." *Swiss Political Science Review* 12 (4): 1–12.

Buquet, Daniel and Ernesto Castellano. 1995. "Representación Proporcional y Democracia en Uruguay." *Revista Uruguaya de Ciencia Política* 8: 107–123.

Buquet, Daniel, Daniel Chasquetti, and Juan Andrés Moraes. 1998. *Fragmentación Política y Gobierno en Uruguay: ¿Un Enfermo Imaginario?* Montevideo: Facultad de Ciencias Sociales.

Burden, Barry and David Kimball. 1998. "A New Approach to the Study of Ticket Splitting." *American Political Science Review* 92 (3): 533–544.

Butler, David and Austin Ranney (Eds.). 1978. *Referendums: A Comparative Study of Practice and Theory.* Washington, DC: AEI Press.

Butler, David and Austin Ranney (Eds.). 1994. *Referendums Around the World: The Growing Use of Direct Democracy.* Washington, DC: AEI Press.

Caetano, Gerardo and José Rilla. 1994. *Historia Contemporánea del Uruguay: De la Colonia al MERCOSUR.* Montevideo: Colección CLAEH/Editorial Fin de Siglo.

Cain, Bruce E., Russell J. Dalton, and Susan E. Scarrow. 2003. "New Forms of Democracy? Reform and Transformation of Democratic Institutions." In *Democracy Transformed? Expanding Political Opportunities in Advanced Industrial Democracies*, edited by B. E. Cain, R. J. Dalton, and S. E. Scarrow. New York: Oxford University Press, 1–22.

Cain, Bruce E., John Ferejohn, and Morris Fiorina. 1987. *The Personal Vote: Constituency Service and Electoral Independence.* Cambridge: Harvard University Press.

Cameron, Maxwell A. and Tulia G. Faletti. 2005. "Federalism and the Subnational Separation of Powers." *Publius. The Journal of Federalism* 35 (2): 245–271.

Campbell, Angus, Phillip Converse, Warren Miller, and Donald Stokes. 1960. *The American Voter*. New York: John Wiley and Sons.

Castiglioni, Rossana. 2001. "The Politics of Retrenchment: The Quandaries of Social Protection Under Military Rule in Chile 1973–1990." *Latin American Politics & Society* 43 (4): 37–66.

Castiglioni, Rossana. 2005. *The Politics of Social Policy Change in Chile and Uruguay: Retrenchment versus Maintenance 1973–1998*. New York & London: Routledge.

Cebula, Richard J. 2008. "Does Direct Democracy Increase Voter Turnout? Evidence from the 2004 General Election." *American Journal of Economics and Sociology* 67 (4): 629–644.

Chan, Steve. 2003. "Explaining War Termination: A Boolean Analysis of Causes." *Journal of Peace Research* 40 (1): 49–66.

Chasquetti, Daniel. 2001. "Democracia, Multipartidismo y Coaliciones en América Latina: Evaluando la Difícil Combinación." In *Tipos de Presidencialismo y Coaliciones Políticas en América Latina*, edited by J. Lanzaro. Buenos Aires: CLACSO, 319–359.

Cheibub, José Antonio. 2007. *Presidentialism, Parliamentarism, and Democracy*. New York: Cambridge University Press.

Cheibub, José Antonio and Jennifer Gandhi. 2004. "Classifying Political Regimes: A Six-Fold Measure of Democracies and Dictatorships." Presented at the Annual Meeting of the American Political Science Association, September 2–5, Chicago, IL.

Cheibub, José Antonio and Jennifer Gandhi. 2005. "Classifying Political Regimes: A Six Fold Classification of Democracies and Dictatorships (Database v.1–2006)." New Haven: Yale University.

Christin, Tomas, Simon Hug, and Pascal Sciarini. 2002. "Interests and Information in Referendum Voting: An Analysis of Swiss Voters." *European Journal of Political Research* 41 (6): 759–776.

Clarke, Harold D., Allan Kornberg, and Marianne C. Stewart. 2004. "Referendum Voting as Political Choice: The Case of Quebec." *British Journal of Political Science* 34 (2): 345–355.

Cleveland, William S. 1979. "Robust Locally Weighted Regression and Smoothing Scatterplots." *Journal of the American Statistical Association* 74 (368): 829–836.

Collier, David. 1991. "The Comparative Method: Two Decades of Change." In *Comparative Political Dynamics: Global Research Perspectives*, edited by D. A. Rustow and K. Paul. New York: HarperCollins, 7–31.

Collier, David and Steven Levitsky. 1997. "Democracy with Adjectives: Finding Conceptual Order in Recent Comparative Research." *World Politics* 49 (3): 430–451.

Compagnon, Daniel. 2000. "Briefing: Zimbabwe: Life After ZANU-PF." *African Affairs* 99 (396): 449–453.

Coppedge, Michael. 1994. *Strong Parties and Lame Ducks: Presidential Partyarchy and Factionalism in Venezuela*. Stanford: Stanford University Press.

Coppedge, Michael. 1998. "The Evolution of Latin American Party Systems." In *Politics, Society, and Democracy: Latin America*, edited by S. Mainwaring and A. Valenzuela. Boulder: Westview Press, 171–206.

Coppedge, Michael. 2004. "Quality of Democracy and Its Measurement." In *The Quality of Democracy: Theory and Applications*, edited by G. O'Donnell, J. V. Cullell, and O. M. Iazzetta. Notre Dame, IN: University of Notre Dame Press, 239–248.

Coppedge, Michael. 2005. "Explaining Democratic Deterioration in Venezuela through Nested Inference." In *The Third Wave of Democratization in Latin America: Advances and Setbacks*, edited by F. Hagopian and S. Mainwaring. Cambridge: Cambridge University Press, 289–320.

Coppedge, Michael. (n.d.) *Approaching Democracy: Research Methods in Comparative Politics*. Mimeographed.

Cortés, Cecilia (Ed.). 1989. *El Referendum Uruguayo del 16 de Abril de 1989*. San José: Instituto Interamericano de Derechos Humanos, Centro de Asesoría y Promoción Electoral.

Cox, Gary W. 1987. *The Efficient Secret: The Cabinet and the Development of Political Parties in Victorian England*. Cambridge: Cambridge University Press.

Cox, Gary W. 1998. "Closeness and Turnout: A Methodological Note." *Journal of Politics* 50 (3): 768–775.

Cox, Gary W. and Mathew D. McCubbins. 1993. *Legislative Leviathan: Party Government in the House*. Berkeley: University of California Press.

Cox, Gary W. and Michael C. Munger. 1989. "Closeness, Expenditures and Turnout in the 1982 House Elections." *American Political Science Review* 83 (1): 217–231.

Cronin, Thomas. 1999. *Direct Democracy: The Politics of Initiative, Referendum and Recall*. Cambridge: Harvard University Press.

Cunningham, Frank. 2002. *Theories of Democracy: A Critical Introduction*. London: Routledge.

Cutright, Phillip. 1963. "National Political Development: Measurement and Analysis." *American Sociological Review* 28 (2): 253–264.

Dahl, Robert. 1956. *A Preface to Democratic Theory*. Chicago: University of Chicago Press.

Dahl, Robert. 1971. *Polyarchy: Participation and Opposition*. New Haven: Yale University Press.

Dahl, Robert. 1989. *Democracy and Its Critics*. New Haven: Yale University Press.

Dalton, Russell, Wilhelm Bürklin, and Andrew Drummond. 2001. "Public Opinion and Direct Democracy." *Journal of Democracy* 12 (4): 141–153.

Danziger, James N. 1998. *Understanding the Political World: A Comparative Introduction to Political Science*. New York: Longman.

Daroca Oller, Santiago. n.d. "La Guerra del Agua: Protesta y Acción Social en Cochabamba." *Programa de Naciones Unidas para el Desarrollo (Bolivia)*.

de Vreese, Claes H. 2006. "Political Parties in Dire Straits? Consequences of National Referendums for Political Parties." *Party Politics* 12 (5): 581–598.

Diamond, Larry. 1999. *Developing Democracy: Toward Consolidation*. Baltimore: The Johns Hopkins University Press.

Diamond, Larry. 2003. "Advancing Democratic Governance: A Global Perspective on the Status of Democracy and Directions for International Assistance." Mimeographed.

Donovan, Todd and Shaun Bowler. 1998. "Direct Democracy and Minority Rights: An Extension." *American Journal of Political Science* 42 (3): 1020–1024.

Donovan, Todd and Jeffrey A. Karp. 2006. "Popular Support for Direct Democracy." *Party Politics* 12 (5): 671–688.

Doorenspleet, Renske. 2004. "The Structural Context of Recent Transitions to Democracy." *European Journal of Political Research* 43 (3): 309–335.

Douglas, Steve. 2005. "Referendum: Hitler's 'Democratic' Weapon to Forge Dictatorship." *Executive Intelligence Review* 4 (14): 40–43.

Downs, Anthony. 1957. *An Economic Theory of Democracy*. New York: Harper and Row.

Dunn, John. 1979. *Western Political Theory in the Face of the Future*. Cambridge: Cambridge University Press.

Eisenstadt, Todd A. 2004. *Courting Democracy in Mexico: Party Strategies and Electoral Institutions*. Cambridge: Cambridge University Press.

Elkins, Zachary. 2000. "Gradations of Democracy? Empirical Tests of Alternative Conceptualizations." *American Journal of Political Science* 44 (2): 293–300.

Elkins, Zachary and John Sides. 2007. "Can Institutions Build Unity in Multiethnic States?" *American Political Science Review* 101 (4): 693–708.

Ellner, Steve. 2003. "The Contrasting Variants of the Populism of Hugo Chávez and Alberto Fujimori." *Journal of Latin American Studies* 35 (1): 139–162.

Elster, John. 1998. "Emotions and Economic Theory." *Journal of Economic Literature* 36 (1): 47–74.

Epstein, David L., Robert Bates, Jack Goldstone, Ida Kristensen, and Sharyn O'Halloran. 2006. "Democratic Transitions." *American Journal of Political Science* 50 (3): 551–569.

Eulau, Heinz and Michael S. Lewis-Beck. 1985. *Economic Conditions and Electoral Outcomes: The United States and Western Europe*. New York: Agathon Press.

Fearon, James D. and David D. Laitin. 2003. "Ethnicity, Insurgency, and Civil War." *American Political Science Review* 97 (1): 75–90.

Febres Cordero, María M. and Bernardo Márquez. 2006. "A Statistical Approach to Assess Referendum Results: The Venezuelan Recall Referendum 2004." *International Statistical Review* 74 (3): 379–389.

Feld, Lars P. and Gebhard Kirchgässner. 2001. "The Political Economy of Direct Legislation: Direct Democracy and Local Decision-Making." *Economic Policy* 16 (33): 329–367.

Feld, Lars P. and Marcel R. Savioz. 1997. "Direct Democracy Matters for Economic Performance: An Empirical Investigation." *Kyklos* 50 (4): 507–538.

Feoli, Ludovico. 2009. "Costa Rica después del TLC: ¿La Calma que Sigue a la Tempestad?" *Revista de Ciencia Política* 29 (2): 355–379.

Fiorino, Nadia and Roberto Ricciuti. 2006. "Determinants of Direct Democracy across Europe." *Department of Public Policy and Public Choice – Universita del Piemonte Amedeo Avogadro* Working Paper 72.

Fiorino, Nadia and Roberto Ricciuti. 2007. "Determinants of Direct Democracy." *CESifo* Working Paper No. 2035.

Fishkin, James S. 1991. *Democracy and Deliberation: New Directions for Democratic Reform*. New Haven: Yale University Press.

Fossedal, Gregory A. 2002. *Direct Democracy in Switzerland*. New Brunswick, NJ: Transaction Publishers.

Franklin, Mark, Cees Van DerEijk, and Michael Marsh. 1995. "Referendum Outcomes and Trust in Government: Public Support for Europe in the Wake of Maastricht." *West European Politics* 18 (3): 101–117.

Franklin, Mark N. 2002. "Learning from the Danish Case: A Comment on Palle Svensson's Critique of the Franklin Thesis." *European Journal of Political Research* 41 (6): 751–757.

Freidenberg, Flabia. 2006. "Izquierda vs. Derecha: Polarización Ideológica y Competencia en el Sistema de Partidos Ecuatoriano." *Política y Gobierno* XIII (2): 237–278.

Freidenberg, Flavia. 2003. "Selección de Candidatos y Democracia Interna en los Partidos de América Latina." Instituto Interuniversitario de Estudios de Iberoamérica y Portugal, Universidad de Salamanca, Salamanca.

Freire, André and Michael A. Baum. 2003. "Referenda Voting in Portugal, 1998: The Effects of Party Sympathies, Social Structure and Pressure Groups." *European Journal of Political Research* 42 (1): 135–161.

Freitag, Markus and Isabelle Stadelmann-Steffen. 2008. "Stumbling Block or Stepping Stone? The Influence of Direct Democracy on Individual Participation in Parliamentary Elections." Mimeographed.

Freitag, Markus and Adrian Vatter. 2006. "Initiatives, Referendums, and the Tax State." *Journal of European Public Policy* 13 (1): 89–112.

Frey, Bruno S., Marcel Kucher, and Alois Stutzer. 2001. "Outcome, Process and Power in Direct Democracy – New Econometric Results." *Public Choice* 107 (3–4): 271–293.

Frey, Bruno S. and Lorenz Goette. 1998. "Does the Popular Vote Destroy Civil Rights?" *American Journal of Political Science* 42 (4): 1343–1348.

Frey, Bruno S., Werner Pommerehne, and Friedrich Schneider. 1981. "Politico-Economic Interdependence in a Direct Democracy: The Case of Switzerland." In *Contemporary Political Economy*, edited by D. A. Hibbs and H. Fassbender. Amsterdam: North Holland, 231–248.

Frey, Bruno S. and Alois Stutzer. 2000. "Happiness Prospers in Democracy." *Journal of Happiness Studies* 1 (1): 79–102.

Friemel, Thomas N. (Ed.). 2008. *Why Context Matters: Applications of Social Network Analysis*. Wiesbaden: VS Research.

Gallagher, Michael and Pier Vincenzo Uleri (Eds.). 1996. *The Referendum Experience in Europe*. London: Palgrave–Macmillan.

Gamarra, Eduardo A. 1997. "Hybrid Presidentialism and Democratization: The Case of Bolivia." In *Presidentialism and Democracy in Latin America*, edited by Scott Mainwaring and M. Shugart. Cambridge: Cambridge University Press, 363–393.

Gamble, Barbara S. 1997. "Putting Civil Rights to a Popular Vote." *American Journal of Political Science* 41 (1): 245–269.

Gandhi, Jennifer. 2008. *Political Institutions under Dictatorship*. New York: Cambridge University Press.

Garcé, Adolfo. 2006. *Donde Hubo Fuego. El Proceso de Adaptación del MLN-Tupamaros a la Legalidad y a la Competencia Electoral (1985–2004)*. Montevideo: Fin de Siglo.

Gerber, Elisabeth R. and Arthur Lupia. 1995. "Campaign Competition and Policy Responsiveness in Direct Legislation Elections." *Political Behaviour* 17 (3): 287–306.

Gerber, Elisabeth R. 1999. *The Populist Paradox: Interest Group Influence and the Promise of Direct Legislation*. Princeton: Princeton University Press.

Gerber, Elisabeth R., Arthur Lupia, and Mathew D. McCubbins. 2004. "When Does Government Limit the Impact of Voter Initiatives? The Politics of Implementation and Enforcement." *The Journal of Politics* 66 (1): 43–68.

Gilland, Karin. 2002a. "Ireland's (First) Referendum on the Treaty of Nice." *Journal of Common Market Studies* 40 (3): 527–535.

Gilland, Karin. 2002b. "Ireland's Second Referendum on the Treaty of Nice, October 2002." *Opposing Europe Research Network Referendum Briefing No 1*. www.sussex.ac.uk/sei/documents/irelandno1.pdf.

Gillespie, Charles G. 1991. *Negotiating Democracy: Politicians and Generals in Uruguay*. New York: Cambridge University Press.

Gloger, Andrew M. 2006. "Paid Petitioners after *Prete*." *Initiative & Referendum Institute – Report* 2006-1 (May).

Goertz, Gary. 2005. *Social Science Concepts: A User's Guide*. Princeton: Princeton University Press.

Goldfrank, Benjamin. 2002. "The Fragile Flower of Local Democracy: A Case Study of Decentralization/Participation in Montevideo." *Politics & Society* 30 (1): 51–83.

Goldfrank, Benjamin. 2006. "Los Procesos de "Presupuesto Participativo" en América Latina: Exito, Fracaso y Cambio." *Revista de Ciencia Política* XXVI (2): 3–28.

González-Rissoto, Rodolfo. 2007. "Democracia Directa: El Caso de Uruguay." Presented at the *Direct Democracy in Latin America*, March 14–15, Buenos Aires.

González, Luis E. 1983. "Uruguay, 1980–1981: An Unexpected Opening." *Latin American Research Review* 18 (3): 63–76.

Gosnell, Harold F. 1927. "The German Referendum on the Princes' Property." *American Political Science Review* 21 (1): 119–123.

Gros Espiell, Héctor. 2002. "Uruguay: ¿Presidencialismo o Parlamentarismo?" *Cuestiones Constitucionales* 7 (Julio-Diciembre): 87–108.

Gross, Andreas and Bruno Kaufmann. 2002. *IRI Europe Country Index on Citizenlawmaking 2002: A Report on Design and Rating of the I&R Requirements and Practices of 32 European States*. Amsterdam: IRI Europe.

Grummel, John A. 2008. "Morality Politics, Direct Democracy, and Turnout." *State Politics and Policy Quarterly* 8 (3): 282–292.

Hadenius, Axel. 1992. *Democracy and Development*. Cambridge: Cambridge University Press.

Hadenius, Axel and Jan Teorell. 2005. "Assessing Alternative Indices of Democracy." *Political Concepts, Committee on Concepts and Methods*, Working Paper Series #6.

Hajnal, Zoltan and Paul G. Lewis. 2003. "Municipal Institutions and Voter Turnout in Local Elections." *Urban Affairs Review* 38 (5): 645–668.

Hall, Peter A. and Rosemary C. R. Taylor. 1996. "Political Science and the Three New Institutionalisms." *Political Studies* 44 (5): 936–957.

Hamilton, Alexander, James Madison, and John Jay. 1961. *The Federalist Papers*. Edited by C. Rossiter. New York: Mentor.

Handelman, Howard. 1981. "Politics and Plebiscites: The Case of Uruguay." *Washington: Woodrow Wilson International Center for Scholars*, Working Paper #89.

Hardmeier, Sibylle. 2002. "Switzerland." *European Journal of Political Research* 41 (7–8): 1095–1100.

Haskell, John. 2000. *Direct Democracy or Representative Government? Dispelling the Populist Myth*. Boulder: Westview Press.

Hautala, Heidi, Bruno Kaufmann, and Diana Wallis (Eds.). 2002. *Voices of Europe: IRI Europe Report on the Growing Importance of Initiatives and Referendums in the European Integration Process*. Amsterdam: Initiative & Referendum Institute Europe.

Heiss, Claudia and Patricio Navia. 2007. "You Win Some, You Lose Some: Constitutional Reforms in Chile's Transition to Democracy." *Latin American Politics and Society* 49 (3): 163–190.

Held, David (Ed.). 1993. *Prospects for Democracy*. Stanford: Stanford University Press.

Hibbing, John and Elizabeth Theiss-Morse. 2001. "Process Preferences and American Politics: What the People Want Government to Be." *American Political Science Review* 95 (1): 145–153.

Hibbs, Douglas A. Jr. 1979. "The Mass Public and the Macroeconomic Performance: The Dynamics of Public Opinion towards Unemployment and Inflation." *American Journal of Political Science* 23 (4): 705–731.

Higley, John and Ian McAllister. 2002. "Elite Division and Voter Confusion: Australia's Republic Referendum in 1999." *European Journal of Political Research* 41 (6): 845–861.

Hill, Kim Quaile. 1994. *Democracy in the Fifty States*. Lincoln: University of Nebraska Press.

Hill, Kim Quaile and Jan E. Leighley. 1993. "Party Ideology, Organization, and Competitiveness as Mobilizing Forces in Gubernatorial Elections." *American Journal of Political Science* 37 (4): 1158–1178.

Hill, Lisa. 2003. "Democratic Deficit in the ACT: Is the Citizen Initiated Referendum a Solution?" *Australian Journal of Social Issues* 38 (4): 495–511.

Hinkelammert, Franz. 1994. "Our Project for the New Society in Latin America." In *Latin America Faces the Twenty-First Century*, edited by S. Jonas and E. J. McCaughan. Boulder: Westview Press, 12–27.

Hobolt, Sara B. 2006a. "Direct Democracy and European Integration." *Journal of European Public Policy* 13 (1): 153–166.

Hobolt, Sara B. 2006b. "How Parties Affect Vote Choice in European Integration Referendums." *Party Politics* 12 (5): 623–647.

Hobolt, Sara B. 2008. "How Voters Decide in EU Referendums." Presented at the *Direct Democracy in and around Europe – Integration, Innovation, Illusion and Ideology*, 3–4 October, Congress and Culture Center, Aarau, Switzerland.

Hobolt, Sara B. 2009. *Europe in Question: Referendums on European Integration*. Oxford: Oxford University Press.

Hotelling, Harold. 1929. "Stability in Competition." *Economic Journal* 39 41–57.

Hug, Simon. 2002. *Voices of Europe. Citizens, Referendums and European Integration*. Lanham, MD: Rowman & Littlefield.

Hug, Simon. 2004. "Occurrence and Policy Consequences of Referendums: A Theoretical Model and Empirical Evidence." *Journal of Theoretical Politics* 16 (3): 321–356.

Hug, Simon and Tobias Schulz. 2007. "Referendums and Ratification of the EU Constitution." In *Direct Democracy in Europe: Developments and Prospects*, edited by Z. T. Pállinger, B. Kaufmann, W. Marxer, and T. Schiller. Wiesbaden: VS Verlag für Sozialwissenschaften, 174–188.

Hug, Simon and George Tsebelis. 2002. "Veto Players and Referendums around the World." *Journal of Theoretical Politics* 14 (4): 465–515.

Huneeus, Carlos. 2000. *El Régimen de Pinochet*. Santiago: Editorial Sudamericana.

Huntington, Samuel. 1968. *Political Order in Changing Societies*. New Haven: Yale University Press.

Huntington, Samuel. 1991. *The Third Wave: Democratization in the Late Twentieth Century*. Norman: University of Oklahoma Press.

Ibarra, Luis. 2005. "La Reforma del Agua: Nuevas Alianzas, Nuevas Instituciones y Nuevos Desafíos." In *Las Claves del Cambio: Ciclo Electoral y Nuevo Gobierno 2004/5002*, edited by D. Buquet. Montevideo: Banda Oriental – Instituto de Ciencia Política, 275–293.

Ingberman, Daniel E. 1985. "Running Against the Status Quo: Institutions for Direct Democracy Referenda and Allocations over Time." *Public Choice* 46 (1): 19–44.

Initiative & Referendum Institute. 2007. "Election Results 2007." *Ballotwatch* (2).

Initiative & Referendum Institute. 2008. "Same-Sex Marriage: Breaking the Firewall in California." *Ballotwatch* (2).

Jackman, Robert W. and Ross Miller. 1995. "Voter Turnout in the Industrialized Democracies during the 1980s." *Comparative Political Studies* 27 (4): 467–492.

Karl, Terry Lynn. 1985. "Petroleum and Political Pacts: The Transition to Democracy in Venezuela." In *Transitions from Authoritarian Rule: Latin America*, edited by G. O'Donnell, P. Schmitter, and L. Whitehead. Baltimore and London: The Johns Hopkins University Press, 196–219.

Karl, Terry Lynn. 1995. "The Hybrid Regimes in Central America." *Journal of Democracy* 6 (3): 72–86.

Katz, Richard S. and Peter Mair. 1995. "Changing Models of Party Organization and Party Democracy: The Emergence of the Cartel Party." *Party Politics* 1 (1): 5–28.

Kaufman, Edy. 1979. *Uruguay in Transition: From Civilian to Military Rule*. New Brunswick, NJ: Transaction Books.

Kaufmann, Bruno (Ed.). 2004. *Initiative and Referendum Monitor 2004/2005*. Amsterdam: IRI Europe.

Kaufmann, Bruno, Rolf Büchi, and Nadja Braun. 2007. *Guidebook to Direct Democracy in Switzerland and Beyond. 2007 Edition*. Bern: Benteli Hallwag Druck AG.

Kaufmann, Bruno, Rolf Büchi, and Nadja Braun. 2008. *Guidebook to Direct Democracy in Switzerland and Beyond. 2008 Edition*. Bern: Benteli Hallwag Druck AG.

Kaufmann, Bruno, Diana Wallis, Jo Leinen, Carsten Berg, and Paul Carline (Eds.). 2006. *Initiative for Europe: A Roadmap for Transnational Democracy*. Brussels: The Initiative & Referendum Institute Europe.

Kaufmann, Bruno and Dane Waters (Eds.). 2004. *Direct Democracy in Europe: A Comprehensive Reference Guide to the Initiative and Referendum Process in Europe*. Durham: Carolina Academic Press.

Keesing's Worldwide. (n.d.). "Keesing's Record of World Events Online." *http://www.keesings.com*.

Key, V. O. 1966. *The Responsible Electorate*. Cambridge: Harvard University Press.

Kiewiet, D. Roderick and Mathew D. McCubbins. 1991. *The Logic of Delegation*. Chicago: University of Chicago Press.

King, Gary. 1989. *Unifying Political Methodology: The Likelihood Theory of Statistical Inference*. New York: Cambridge University Press.

King, Gary. 1997. *A Solution to the Ecological Inference Problem: Reconstructing Individual Behavior from Aggregate Data*. Princeton: Princeton University Press.

King, Gary, Robert Keohane, and Sidney Verba. 1994. *Designing Social Inquiry: Scientific Inference in Qualitative Research*. Princeton: Princeton University Press.

King, Gary, Ori Rosen, and Martin A. Tanner. 1999. "Binomial-Beta Hierarchical Models for Ecological Inference." *Sociological Methods and Research* 28 (1) 61–90.

Kirchgässner, Gebhard. 2008. "Direct Democracy: Obstacle to Reform?" *Constitutional Political Economy* 19 (2): 81–93.

Kitschelt, Herbert, Kirk Hawkins, Juan Pablo Luna, Guillermo Rosas, and Elizabeth-Jean Zechmeister. 2010. *Latin American Party Systems*. New York: Cambridge University Press.

Klöti, Ulrigh. 2001. "Consensual Government in a Heterogeneous Polity." *West European Politics* 24 (2): 19–34.

Kobach, Kris. 1993. *The Referendum: Direct Democracy in Switzerland*. Vermont: Dartmouth Publishing Company Limited.

Kobach, Kris. 1994. "Switzerland." In *Referendums Around the World*, edited by D. Butler and A. Ranney. Washington, DC: AEI Press, 98–153.

Kohl, Benjamin. 2002. "Stabilizing Neoliberalism in Bolivia: Popular Participation and Privatization." *Political Geography* 21 (4): 449–472.

Koole, Ruud. 1996. "Cadre, Catch-all or Cartel? A Comment on the Notion of the Cartel Party." *Party Politics* 2 (4): 507–523.

Kornblith, Miriam. 2005. "Elections Versus Democracy." *Journal of Democracy* 16 (1): 124–137.

Kramer, Gerald H. 1971. "Short-Term Fluctuations in U.S. Voting Behavior: 1896–1964." *American Political Science Review* 65 (1): 131–143.

Kriesi, Hanspeter. 2001. "The Federal Parliament: The Limits of Institutional Reform." *West European Politics* 24 (2): 59–76.

Kriesi, Hanspeter. 2002. "Individual Opinion Formation in a Direct Democratic Campaign." *British Journal of Political Science* 32 (1): 171–185.

Kriesi, Hanspeter. 2006. "Role of the Political Elite in Swiss Direct-Democratic Votes." *Party Politics* 12 (5): 599–622.

Kriesi, Hanspeter and Alexander H. Trechsel. 2008. *The Politics of Switzerland: Continuity and Change in a Consensus Democracy*. New York: Cambridge University Press.

Laakso, Markku and Rein Taagepera. 1979. "Effective Number of Parties: A Measure with Application to West Europe." *Comparative Political Studies* 12 (1): 3–27.

Ladner, Andreas and Michael Brändle. 1999. "Does Direct Democracy Matter for Political Parties? An Empirical Test in the Swiss Cantons." *Party Politics* 5 (3): 283–302.

Lagerspetz, Eerik. 2006. "Referenda with Multiple Alternatives." Presented at the *Annual Meeting of the European Public Choice Society*, April 20–23, Turku, Finland.

Lalander, Rickard. 2004. *Suicide of the Elephants? Venezuelan Decentralization between Partyarchy and Chavismo*. Stockholm: Instituto of Latin American Studies.

Laponce, Jean A. 2004. "Turning Votes into Territories: Boundary Referendums in Theory and Practice." *Political Geography* 23 (2): 169–183.

Lassen, David Dreyer. 2005. "The Effect of Information on Voter Turnout: Evidence from a Natural Experiment." *American Journal of Political Science* 49 (1): 103–118.

Lawrence, Steve. 2008. "Wealthy Interests Alter Calif's Initiative Process." *Washington Times*, October 29.

LeDuc, Lawrence. 1993. "Canada's Next Term Constitutional Referendum of 1992: A 'Great Big No'." *Electoral Studies* 12 (3): 257–263.

LeDuc, Lawrence. 2002. "Opinion Change and Voting Behaviour in Referendums." *European Journal of Political Research* 41 (6): 711–732.

LeDuc, Lawrence. 2003. *The Politics of Direct Democracy: Referendums in Global Perspective*. Ontario: Broadview Press.

Lee Van Cott, Donna. 2000. "Party System Development and Indigenous Populations in Latin America: The Bolivian Case." *Party Politics* 6 (2): 155–174.

Lessa, Alfonso. 2002. *La Revolución Imposible: Los Tupamaros y el Fracaso de la Vía Armada en el Uruguay del Siglo XX*. Montevideo: Editorial Fin de Siglo.

Lewis-Beck, Michael. 1988. *Economics and Elections: The Major Western Democracies*. Ann Arbor: The University of Michigan Press.

Li, Quan and Rafael Reuveny. 2003. "Economic Globalization and Democracy: An Empirical Analysis." *British Journal of Political Science* 33 (1): 29–54.

Lijphart, Arend. 1984. *Democracies: Patter of Majoritarian and Consensus Government in Twenty-One Countries*. New Haven and London: Yale University Press.

Lijphart, Arend. 1997. "Unequal Participation: Democracy's Unresolved Dilemma." *American Political Science Review* 91 (1): 1–14.

Lindberg, Staffan I. 2006. *Democracy and Elections in Africa*. Baltimore: The Johns Hopkins University Press.

Linder, Wolf. 1994. *Swiss Democracy: Possible Solutions to Conflict in Multicultural Societies*. New York: St. Martin's Press.

Linton, Martin. 2001. "Options for the Referendum on the Voting System." *The Political Quarterly* 72 (1): 10–17.

Linz, Juan J. 1975. "Totalitarian and Authoritarian Regimes." In *Handbook of Political Science*, vol. 3, *Macropolitical Theory*, edited by N. Polsby and F. Greenstein. Reading: Addison-Wesley Press, 175–411.

Lipset, Seymour Martin, Kyoung-Ryung Seong, and John Charles Torres. 1993. "A Comparative Analysis of the Social Requisites of Democracy." *International Social Science Journal* XLV (2): 155–175.

Lissidini, Alicia. 1998. "Una Mirada Crítica a la Democracia Directa: El Origen y las Prácticas de los Plebiscitos en Uruguay." *Perfiles Latinoamericanos* 7 (12): 169–200.

Lissidini, Alicia. 2007. "La Democracia Directa en Venezuela: ¿Democracia Participativa o Democracia Plebiscitaria?" *C2D – 25/2008*.

Londregan, John and Andrea Vindigni. 2008. "Authoritarian Plebiscites." Presented at the *Seminarios de Macroeconomía y Finanzas del Banco Central de Chile*, June 6, Santiago.

López Maya, Margarita. 2003. "The Venezuelan Caracazo of 1989: Popular Protest and Institutional Weakness." *Journal of Latin American Studies* 35 (1): 117–137.

Luna, Juan Pablo. 2002. "¿Pesimismo Estructural o Voto Económico? Macropolitics en Uruguay." *Revista Uruguaya de Ciencia Política* 13: 123–151.

Luna, Juan Pablo. 2007. "Representación Política en América Latina: El Estado de la Cuestión y una Propuesta de Agenda." *Política y Gobierno* XIV (2): 391–435.

Lupia, Arthur. 1994. "The Effect of Information on Voting Behavior and Electoral Outcomes: An Experimental Study of Direct Legislation." *Public Choice* 78 (1): 65–86.

Lupia, Arthur and John G. Matsusaka. 2004. "Direct Democracy: New Approaches to Old Questions." *Annual Review of Political Science* 7: 463–482.

Lupia, Arthur and Mathew McCubbins. 1998. *The Democratic Dilemma: Can Citizens Learn What They Need to Know?* Cambridge: Cambridge University Press.

Lüthi, Ruth. 2007. "The Parliament." In *Handbook of Swiss Politics*, edited by U. Klöti, P. Knoepfel, H. Kriesi, W. Linder, Y. Papadopoulos, and P. Sciarini. Zurich: Neue Zurcher Zeitung Publishing, 121–144.

Lutz, Georg. 2006. "The Interaction between Representative and Direct Democracy in Switzerland." *Representation* 42 (1): 45–57.

Lutz, Karin Gilland and Simon Hug. 2006. "A Cross-National Comparative Study of the Policy Effects of Referendums." Presented at the *Annual Meeting of the American Political Science Association*, August 31–September 3, Philadelphia, PA.

Machado, Juan Carlos. 2007. "Ecuador: El Derrumbe de los Partidos Tradicionales." *Revista de Ciencia Política* 27 (EE): 129–148.

Machado, Juan Carlos. 2008. "Ecuador:... Hasta que se Fueron Todos." *Revista de Ciencia Política* 28 (1): 189–215.

Magaloni, Beatriz. 2006. *Voting for Autocracy: Hegemonic Party Survival and its Demise in Mexico.* New York: Cambridge University Press.

Magleby, David B. 1984. *Direct Legislation: Voting on Ballot Propositions in the United States.* Baltimore: The Johns Hopkins University Press.

Mainwaring, Scott. 1993. "Presidentialism, Multipartism, and Democracy: The Difficult Combination." *Comparative Political Studies* 26 (4): 198–228.

Mainwaring, Scott, Daniel Brinks, and Aníbal Pérez-Liñán. 2001. "Classifying Political Regimes in Latin America 1945–1999." *Studies in Comparative International Development* 36 (1): 37–65.

Mainwaring, Scott, Daniel Brinks, and Aníbal Pérez-Liñán. 2007. "Classifying Political Regimes in Latin America 1945–2004." In *Regimes and Democracy in Latin America: Theories and Methods,* edited by G. L. Munck. Oxford: Oxford University Press, 123–160.

Mainwaring, Scott and Tim Scully (Eds.). 1995a. *Building Democratic Institutions.* Stanford: Stanford University Press.

Mainwaring, Scott and Tim Scully. 1995b. "Introduction: Party Systems in Latin America." In *Building Democratic Institutions,* edited by S. Mainwaring and T. Scully. Stanford: Stanford University Press, 1–36.

Mainwaring, Scott and Matthew S. Shugart. 1997. "Conclusion: Presidentialism and the Party System." In *Presidentialism and Democracy in Latin America,* edited by S. Mainwaring and M. S. Shugart. Cambridge: Cambridge University Press, 394–439.

Maor, Moshe. 1998. *Parties, Conflicts and Coalitions in Western Europe: Organisational Determinants of Coalition Bargaining.* London: Routledge and LSE.

Maravall, José María. 1999. "Accountability and Manipulation." In *Democracy, Accountability and Representation,* edited by A. Przeworski, S. Stokes, and B. Manin. New York: Cambridge University Press, 131–153.

Marcus, Richard R., Kenneth Mease, and Dan Ottemoeller. 2004. "Popular Definitions of Democracy from Uganda, Madagascar, and Florida, U.S.A." *Journal of African and Asian Studies* 36 (1): 113–132.

Marenco, André. 2006. "*Path-Dependency*, Instituciones Políticas y Reformas Electorales en Perspectiva Comparada." *Revista de Ciencia Política* 26 (2): 53–75.

Margalit, Avishai and Joseph Raz. 1990. "National Self-Determination." *The Journal of Philosophy* 87 (9): 439–461.

Marius, Jorge L. and Juan F. Bacigalupe. 1998. *Sistema Electoral y Elecciones Uruguayas 1925–1998.* Montevideo: Fundacion Konrad Adenauer.

Markarian, Vania. 2004. "De la Lógica Revolucionaria a las Razones Humanitarias: La Izquierda Uruguaya en el Exilio y las Redes Transnacionales de Derechos Humanos (1972–1976)." *Cuadernos del CLAEH* 89 (2): 85–108.

Markoff, John. 1999. "Where and When Was Democracy Invented?" *Comparative Studies in Society and History* 41 (4): 660–690.

Marques, Alvaro and Thomas B. Smith. 1984. "Referendums in the Third World." *Electoral Studies* 3 (1): 85–105.

Marshall, Monty G. and Keith Jaggers. 2001. "Polity IV Project: Political Regime Characteristics and Transitions, 1800–1999." http://www.bsos.umd.edu/cidcm/polity/.

Marshall, Thomas Humphrey. 1992. "Citizenship and Social Class." In *Citizenship and Social Class,* edited by T. H. Marshall and T. Bottomore. London: Pluto Press, 3–51.

Matsusaka, John G. 2004. *For the Many or the Few: The Initiative, Public Policy, and American Democracy*. Chicago: University of Chicago Press.

Mayhew, David. 1974. *Congress: The Electoral Connection*. New Haven: Yale University Press.

Mayorga, René Antonio. 1997. "Bolivia's Silent Revolution." *Journal of Democracy* 8 (1): 142–156.

McCoy, Jennifer L. 2006. "The 2004 Venezuelan Recall Referendum." *Taiwan Journal of Democracy* 2 (1): 61–80.

McCoy, Jennifer L. 2005. "One Act in an Unfinished Drama." *Journal of Democracy* 16 (1): 109–123.

McCubbins, Mathew and Frances Rosenbluth. 1995. "Party Provision for Personal Votes: Dividing the Vote in Japan." In *Structure and Policy in Japan and the United States*, edited by P. Cowhey and M. McCubbins. Cambridge: Cambridge University Press, 35–55.

McDonald, Ronald H. 1982. "The Struggle for Normalcy in Uruguay." *Current History* 81 (472): 69–85.

McKelvey, Richard D. and Norman Schofield. 1986. "Structural Instability of the Core." *Journal of Mathematical Economics* 15 (3): 179–198.

Mendelsohn, Matthew and Fred Cutler. 2000. "The Effect of Referenda on Democratic Citizens: Information, Politicization, Efficacy and Tolerance." *British Journal of Political Science* 30 (4): 669–698.

Mendez, Fernando and Vasiliki Triga. 2009. "Constitution-Making, Constitutional Conventions and Conflict Resolution: Lesson Drawing for Cyprus." *Journal of Balkan and Near Eastern Studies* 11 (4): 363–380.

Méndez, Juan E. 2004. "Fundamental Rights as a Limitation to the Democratic Principle of Majority Will." In *The Quality of Democracy: Theory and Applications*, edited by G. O'Donnell, J. V. Cullell, and O. M. Iazzetta. Notre Dame: University of Notre Dame Press, 196–202.

Mershon, Carol. 1996. "The Cost of Coalition: Coalition Theories and Italian Governments." *American Political Science Review* 90 (3): 534–554.

Michels, Robert. 1999 (1911). *Political Parties: A Sociological Study of the Oligarchical Tendencies of Modern Democracy*. New Brunswick, NJ: Transaction Publishers.

Miller, Kenneth P. 2003. "The Courts and the Initiative Process." In *Initiative and Referendum Almanac*, edited by D. M. Waters. Durham: Carolina Academic Press, 459–467.

Miller, William L. 1988. *Irrelevant Elections? The Quality of Local Democracy in Britain*. Oxford: Clarendon Press.

Milner, Helen V. 2006. "The Digital Divide: The Role of Political Institutions in Technology Diffusion." *Comparative Political Studies* 39 (2): 176–199.

Mittendorf, Volker. 2007. "Databases for (Empirical) Research on 'Direct Democracy.'" In *Direct Democracy in Europe: Developments and Prospects*, edited by Z. T. Pállinger, B. Kaufmann, W. Marxer, and T. Schiller. Wiesbaden: VS Verlag für Sozialwissenschaften, 207–218.

Montalvo, Jose G. and Marta Reynal-Querol. 2005. "Ethnic Diversity and Economic Development." *Journal of Development Economics* 76 (2): 293–323.

Moon, Bruce E., Jennifer Harvey, Sylvia Ceisluk, Lauren M. Garlett, Joshua J. Hermias, Elizabeth Mendenhall, Patrick D. Schmid, and Wai Hong Wong. 2006. "Voting Counts: Participation in the Measurement of Democracy." *Studies in Comparative International Development* 41 (2): 3–32.

Morales Viteri, Juan Pablo. 2008. "Ecuador: Mecanismos de Democracia Directa."
   C2D Working Paper Series 20.
Morgenstern, Scott. 2004. Patterns of Legislative Politics: Roll-Call Voting in Latin
   America and the United States. New York: Cambridge University Press.
Morlino, Leonardo. 2004. "What Is a 'Good' Democracy?" Democratization 11 (5):
   10–32.
Muller, Edward N. 1988. "Democracy, Economic Development, and Income Inequal-
   ity." American Sociological Review 53 (2): 50–68.
Muller, Edward N. 1989. "Democracy and Inequality: Reply to Weede." American
   Sociological Review 54 (5): 868–871.
Muller, Edward N. 1995. "Economic Determinants of Democracy." American Socio-
   logical Review 60 (6): 966–982.
Müller, Wolfgang C. 1999. "Plebiscitary Agenda-Setting and Party Strategies: The-
   oretical Considerations and Evidence from Austria." Party Politics 5 (3): 303–
   315.
Munck, Gerardo. 2003. "Teaching Qualitative Methodology: Rationale, State of the
   Art, and an Agenda." Qualitative Methods-Newsletter of the APSA Organized Sec-
   tion on Qualitative Methods 1 (1): 12–15.
Munck, Gerardo L. 2007. "The Study of Politics and Democracy: Touchstones of
   a Research Agenda." In Regimes and Democracy in Latin America. Theories and
   Methods, edited by G. L. Munck. Oxford: Oxford University Press, 25–38.
Munck, Gerardo L. 2009. Measuring Democracy. A Bridge between Scholarship and
   Politics. Baltimore: The Johns Hopkins University Press.
Munck, Gerardo and Jay Verkuilen. 2002. "Conceptualizing and Measuring Democ-
   racy: Evaluating Alternative Indices." Comparative Political Studies 35 (1): 5–
   34.
Nadeau, Richard, Pierre Martin, and André Blais. 1999. "Attitude Towards Risk-
   Taking and Individual Choice in the Quebec Referendum on Sovereignty." British
   Journal of Political Science 29 (3): 523–539.
Nannestad, Peter and Martin Paldman. 1994. "The VP-Function: A Survey of the
   Literature on Vote and Popularity Functions after 25 Years." Public Choice 79 (3–4):
   213–245.
Nedelmann, Birgitta. 1987. "Individuals and Parties – Changes in Processes of Political
   Mobilization." European Sociological Review 3 (3): 181–202.
Negretto, Gabriel L. 2004. "Government Capacities and Policy Making by Decree in
   Latin America." Comparative Political Studies 37 (5): 531–562.
Nussbaum, Martha. 2000. Women and Human Development: The Capabilities
   Approach. Cambridge: Cambridge University Press.
O'Donnell, Guillermo. 1993. "On the State, Democratization and Some Conceptual
   Problems: A Latin American View with Glances at Some Postcommunist Countries."
   World Development 21 (8): 1355–1369.
O'Donnell, Guillermo. 1994. "Delegative Democracy." Journal of Democracy 5 (1):
   55–69.
O'Donnell, Guillermo. 2001. "Reflections on Contemporary South American Democ-
   racies." Journal of Latin American Studies 33 (3): 599–609.
O'Donnell, Guillermo. 2002. "Acerca de varias Accountabilities y sus Interrelaciones."
   In Controlando la Política: Ciudadanos y Medios en las Nuevas Democracias Lati-
   noamericanas, edited by E. Peruzzotti and C. Smulovitz. Buenos Aires: Temas, 87–
   102.

O'Donnell, Guillermo. 2004a. "Exploración sobre el Desarrollo de la Democracia." In *La Democracia en América Latina: Hacia un Democracia de Ciudadanas y Ciudadanos*, edited by PNUD. New York: PNUD, 47–70.

O'Donnell, Guillermo. 2004b. "Human Development, Human Rights, and Democracy." In *The Quality of Democracy: Theory and Applications*, edited by G. O'Donnell, J. V. Cullell, and O. M. Iazzetta. Notre Dame: University of Notre Dame Press, 9–92.

Olken, Benjamin A. 2008. "Direct Democracy and Local Public Goods: Evidence from a Field Experiment in Indonesia." *National Bureau of Economic Research*, Working Paper Series No. 14123.

Pachano, Simón. 1997. "Bucaram, ¡Fuera! Bucaram, ¿Fuera?" In *¿Y Ahora Qué? Una Contribución al Análisis Político-Histórico Actual*. Quito: Eskeletra Editorial, 229–264.

Panizza, Francisco E. 1990. *Uruguay: Batllismo y Después. Pacheco, Militares y Tupamaros en la Crisis del Uruguay Batllista*. Montevideo: Ediciones de la Banda Oriental.

Panzer, John and Ricardo Paredes. 1991. "The Role of Economic Issues in Elections: The Case of the 1988 Chilean Presidential Referendum." *Public Choice* 71 (1–2): 51–59.

Papadopoulos, Yannis. 1995. "Analysis of Functions and Dysfunctions of Direct Democracy: Top-Down and Bottom-Up Perspectives." *Politics and Society* 23 (4): 421–448.

Papadopoulos, Yannis. 2001. "How Does Direct Democracy Matter? The Impact of Referendum Votes upon Politics and Policy-Making." *West European Politics* 24 (2): 35–58.

Parkinson, John. 2003. "Legitimacy Problems in Deliberative Democracy." *Political Studies* 51 (1): 180–196.

Pateman, Carole. 1970. *Participation and Democratic Theory*. Cambridge: Cambridge University Press.

Patterson, Samuel and Gregory Caldeira. 1983. "Getting Out the Vote: Participation in Gubernatorial Elections." *American Political Science Review* 77 (3): 675–689.

Pérez-Liñán, Aníbal. 2000. "The Institutional Determinants of Impeachment." Presented at the *Latin American Science Association*, March 16–18, Miami, FL.

Pérez-Liñán, Aníbal. 2006. "Evaluating Presidential Runoff Elections." *Electoral Studies* 25 (1): 129–146.

Pérez-Liñán, Aníbal. 2007. *Presidential Impeachment and the New Political Instability in Latin America*. New York: Cambridge University Press.

Pettit, Philip. 2003. "Deliberative Democracy, the Discursive Dilemma and Republican Theory." In *Philosophy, Politics and Society*, edited by J. Fishkin and P. Laslett. New York: Cambridge University Press, 138–162.

Phillips, Anne. 1991. *Engendering Democracy*. University Park: The Pennsylvania State University Press.

Pierson, Paul. 2004. *Politics in Time. History, Institutions, and Social Analysis*. Princeton and Oxford: Princeton University Press.

Pitkin, Hanna Fenichel. 1967. *The Concept of Representation*. Berkeley: University of California Press.

PNUD. 2004. *La Democracia en América Latina: Hacia una Democracia de Ciudadanas y Ciudadanos*. New York: Programa de Naciones Unidas para el Desarrollo.

Pommerehne, Werner W. and Hannelore Weck-Hannemann. 1996. "Tax Rates, Tax Administration and Income Tax Evasion in Switzerland." *Public Choice* 88 (1/2): 161–170.

Porzecanski, Arturo C. 1973. *Uruguay's Tupamaros: The Urban Guerrilla.* New York: Praeger.

Pottie, David. 2003. "The Presidential Elections in Zimbabwe, March 2002." *Electoral Studies* 22 (3): 516–523.

Pottie, David. 2002. "Parliamentary Elections in Zimbabwe, 2000." *Electoral Studies* 21 (3): 485–492.

Powell, G. Bingham Jr. 1986. "American Voter Turnout in Comparative Perspective." *American Political Science Review* 80 (1): 17–43.

Powell, G. Bingham Jr. 2004. "Political Representation in Comparative Politics." *Annual Review of Political Science* 7: 273–296.

Preston, Matthew. 2004. *Ending Civil War: Rhodesia and Lebanon in Perspective.* New York: Tauris Academic Studies.

Pribble, Jennifer. 2008. "Protecting the Poor: Welfare Politics in Latin America's Neoliberal Era." Department of Political Science, University of North Carolina at Chapel Hill. Ph.D. Thesis.

Przeworski, Adam. 1986. "Some Problems in the Study of the Transition to Democracy." In *Transitions from Authoritarian Rule: Comparative Perspectives*, vol. III, edited by G. O'Donnell, P. C. Schmitter, and L. Whitehead. Baltimore and London: The Johns Hopkins University Press, 47–63.

Przeworski, Adam. 1988. "Democracy as a Contingent Outcome of Conflicts." In *Constitutionalism and Democracy*, edited by J. Elster and R. Slagstad. Cambridge: Cambridge University Press, 59–80.

Przeworski, Adam, Michael Alvarez, José Antonio Cheibub, and Fernando Limongi. 1996. "What Makes Democracies Endure?" *Journal of Democracy* 7 (1): 39–55.

Przeworski, Adam, Michael E. Alvarez, José Antonio Cheibub, and Fernando Limongi. 2000. *Democracy and Development: Political Institutions and Well-Being in the World, 1950–1990.* Cambridge: Cambridge University Press.

Przeworski, Adam and Fernando Limongi. 1997. "Modernization: Theories and Facts." *World Politics* 49 (2): 155–183.

Qvortrup, Mads. 1999. "A.V. Dicey: The Referendum as the People's Veto." *History of Political Thought* XX (3): 531–546.

Qvortrup, Mads. 2005. *A Comparative Study of Referendums: Government by the People.* 2nd ed. Manchester: Manchester University Press.

Ragin, Charles. 2000. *Fuzzy-Set, Social Science.* Chicago: University of Chicago Press.

Ragin, Charles and John Sonnett. 2004. "Between Complexity and Parsimony: Limited Diversity, Counterfactual Cases, and Comparative Analysis." In *Vergleichen in der Politikwissenschaft*, edited by S. Kropp and M. Minkenberg. Wiesbaden: VS Verlag für Sozialwissenschaften, 180–197.

Ranney, Austin. 1965. "Parties in State Politics." In *Politics in the American States: A Comparative Analysis*, edited by H. Jacob and K. N. Vines. Boston and Toronto: Little, Brown and Company, 51–92.

Rasler, Karen. 1996. "Concessions, Repression, and Political Protest in the Iranian Revolution." *American Sociological Review* 61 (1): 132–152.

Reif, Karlheinz. 1984. "National Electoral Cycles and European Elections." *Electoral Studies* 3 (3): 244–255.

Reif, Karlheinz and Hermann Schmitt. 1980. "Nine Second Order National Elections: A Conceptual Framework for the Analysis of European Election Results." *European Journal of Political Research* 8 (1): 3–44.

Remmer, Karen. 1989. *Military Rule in Latin America*. Boston: Unwin Hyman.

Réti, Pál. 2009. "Hungary: Direct Democracy in an Antagonistic Society." In *Global Citizens in Charge: How Modern Direct Democracy Can Make Our Representative Democracies Truly Representative*, edited by J.-O. Lee and B. Kaufmann. Seoul: Korea Democracy Foundation, 211–220.

Reynal-Querol, Marta. 2002. "Ethnicity, Political Systems, and Civil Wars." *Journal of Conflict Resolution* 46 (1): 29–54.

Rial, Juan. 2000. "Instituciones de Democracia Directa en América Latina." *National Democratic Institute* (October). www.ndipartidos.org/pdf/gobernando/democraciadirecta.pdf.

Riker, William. 1982. *Liberalism against Populism*. San Francisco: W.H. Freeman and Co.

Rilla, José. 1997. "Uruguay 1980: Transición y Democracia Plebiscitaria." *Nueva Sociedad* 150 (Julio-Agosto): 77–83.

Rius, Andrés. 1992. "El Gobierno, la Economía y el Hombre de la Calle." *SUMA* 7 (13): 7–35.

Rodríguez Raga, Juan Carlos and Felipe Botero. 2006. "Ordenando el caos. Elecciones legislativas y reforma electoral en Colombia." *Revista de Ciencia Política* 26 (1): 138–151.

Rosenstone, Steven J. and John Mark Hansen. 1993. *Mobilization, Participation, and Democracy in America*. New York: MacMillan.

Rotberg, Robert I. 2000. "Africa's Mess, Mugabe's Mayhem." *Foreign Affairs* 79 (5): 47–61.

Rotberg, Robert I. 2007. "The Challenge of Weak, Failing, and Collapsed States." In *Leashing the Dogs of War: Conflict Management in a Divided World*. Washington, DC: United States Institute of Peace Press, 83–94.

Rourke, John T., Richard P. Hiskes, and Cyrus Ernesto Zirakzadeh. 1992. *Direct Democracy and International Politics: Deciding International Issues Through Referendums*. Colorado: Lynne Rienner Publishers.

Rousseau, Jean-Jacques. 1988. *The Social Contract*. London: Penguin Books.

Royston, Patrick and Douglas G. Altman. 1997. "Approximating Statistical Functions by Using Fractional Polynomial Regression." *Journal of the Royal Statistical Society: Series D (The Statistician)* 46 (3): 411–422.

Rueschemeyer, Dietrich, Evelyne Huber, and John Stephens. 1992. *Capitalist Development and Democracy*. Chicago: University of Chicago Press.

Rummel, Rudolph J. 1997. "Is Collective Violence Correlated with Social Pluralism?" *Journal of Peace Research* 34 (2): 163–175.

Rustow, Dankwart. 1970. "Transitions to Democracy." *Comparative Politics* 2 (3): 337–363.

Rydgren, Jens. 2005. "Is Extreme Right-Wing Populism Contagious? Explaining the Emergence of a New Party Family." *European Journal of Political Research* 44 (3): 413–437.

Sartori, Giovanni. 1970. "Concept Misformation in Comparative Politics." *American Political Science Review* 64 (4): 1033–1046.

Sartori, Giovanni. 1976. *Parties and Party Systems: A Framework for Analysis*. New York: Cambridge University Press.

Sartori, Giovanni. 1987. *The Theory of Democracy Revisited*. New Jersey: Chatham House Publishers.

Sartori, Giovanni. 1997. *Comparative Constitutional Engineering: An Inquiry into Structures, Incentives and Outcomes*. New York: New York University Press.

Scarrow, Susan. 1999. "Parties and the Expansion of Direct Democracy: Who Benefits?" *Party Politics* 5 (3): 341–362.

Scarrow, Susan E. 2001. "Direct Democracy and Institutional Change: A Comparative Investigation." *Comparative Political Studies* 34 (6): 651–665.

Schattschneider, Elmer Eric. 1960. *The Semisovereign People: A Realist's View of Democracy in America*. New York: Holt, Rinehart and Winston.

Schlozman, Daniel and Ian Yohai. 2008. "How Initiatives Don't Always Make Citizens: Ballot Initiatives in the American States, 1978–2004." *Political Behavior* 30 (4): 469–489.

Schmidt, Manfred G. 2002. "Political Performance and Types of Democracy: Findings from Comparative Studies." *European Journal of Political Research* 41 (1): 147–163.

Schneider, Friedrich and Jorg Naumann. 1982. "Interest Groups in Democracies – How Influential Are They? An Empirical Examination for Switzerland." *Public Choice* 38 (3): 281–303.

Schofer, Evan and Marion Fourcade-Gourinchas. 2001. "The Structural Contexts of Civic Engagement. Voluntary Association Membership, Comparative Perspective." *American Sociological Review* 66 (6): 806–828.

Schuck, Andreas R. T. and Claes H. de Vreese. 2008. "The Dutch No to the EU Constitution: Assessing the Role of EU Skepticism and the Campaign." *Journal of Elections, Public Opinion and Parties* 18 (1): 101–128.

Schumpeter, Joseph. 1950. *Capitalism, Socialism, and Democracy*. New York: Harper and Brother Publishers.

Sen, Amartya. 1997. "Maximization and the Act of Choice." *Econometrica* 65 (4): 745–779.

Sen, Amartya. 1999. *Development as Freedom*. New York: Anchor Books.

Serdült, Uwe. 2007. "Direct Democracy in Switzerland and its Discontents." Presented at the *Direct Democracy in Latin America*, March 14–15, Buenos Aires.

Setälä, Maija. 1999a. *Referendums and Democratic Government: Normative Theory and the Analysis of Institutions*. London: Palgrave – MacMillan.

Setälä, Maija. 1999b. "Referendums in Western Europe – A Wave of Direct Democracy?" *Scandinavian Political Studies* 22 (4): 327–340.

Setälä, Maija. 2006a. "National Referendums in European Democracies: Recent Developments." *Representation* 42 (1): 13–23.

Setälä, Maija. 2006b. "On the Problems of Responsibility and Accountability in Referendums." *European Journal of Political Research* 45 (4): 699–721.

Silva, Fred. 2003. "The Indirect Initiative Process." In *Initiative and Referendum Almanac*, edited by D. M. Waters. Durham: Carolina Academic Press, 13–29.

Skidmore, Thomas E. and Peter H. Smith. 2001. *Modern Latin America*. New York and Oxford: Oxford University Press.

Slaughter, Barbara and Stuart Nolan. 2000. "Zimbabwe: Referendum Defeat for Mugabe Shakes Zanu-PF Government." *World Socialist Web Site*. http://www.wsws .org/articles/2000/feb2000/zimb-f22.shtml.

Smith, Daniel A. and Caroline J. Tolbert. 2004. *Educated by Initiative: The Effects of Direct Democracy on Citizens and Political Organizations in the American States*. Ann Arbor: University of Michigan Press.

Smith, Mark A. 2002. "Ballot Initiatives and the Democratic Citizen." *The Journal of Politics* 64 (3): 892–903.

Smith, Peter H. 2004. "Los Ciclos de Democracia Electoral en América Latina 1900–2000." *Política y Gobierno* XI (2): 189–228.

Sondrol, Paul C. 1991. "Totalitarian and Authoritarian Dictators: A Comparison of Fidel Castro and Alfredo Stroessner." *Journal of Latin American Studies* 23 (3): 599–620.

Sotelo Rico, Mariana. 1999. "La Longevided de los Partidos Tradicionales Uruguayos desde una Perspectiva Comparada." In *Los Partidos Políticos Uruguayos en Tiempos de Cambio*, edited by L. E. González. Montevideo: Fundación de Cultura Universitaria, 131–158.

Stallings, Barbara and Phillip Brock. 1993. "The Political Economy of Adjustment: Chile, 1973–1990." In *Political and Economic Interactions in Economic Policy Reform: Evidence of Eight Countries*, edited by R. Bates and A. Krueger. Cambridge: Blackwell, 78–121.

Starr, Harvey. 1991. "Democratic Dominoes: Diffusion Approaches to the Spread of Democracy in the International System." *Journal of Conflict Resolution* 35 (2): 356–381.

Stepan, Alfred C. 1978. *The State and Society: Peru in Comparative Perspective*. Princeton: Princeton University Press.

Stimson, James. 1985. "Regression in Space and Time: A Statistical Essay." *American Journal of Political Science* 29 (4): 914–947.

Stokes, Susan C. 1996. "Economic Reform and Public Opinion in Peru, 1990–1995." *Comparative Political Studies* 29 (5): 544–565.

Stokes, Susan C. 1999. "What Do Policy Switches Tell Us about Democracy?" In *Democracy, Accountability and Representation*, edited by A. Przeworski, S. C. Stokes, and B. Manin. New York: Cambridge University Press, 98–130.

Stokes, Susan C. 2001. *Mandates and Democracy: Neoliberalism by Surprise in Latin America*. Cambridge: Cambridge University Press.

Stone, Walter J. and Monti Narayan Datta. 2004. "Rationalizing the California Recall." *PS: Political Science & Politics* 37 (1): 19–21.

Suksi, Markku. 1993. *Bringing in the People: A Comparison of Constitutional Forms and Practices of the Referendums*. Dordrecht: Martinus Nijhoff Publishers.

Svensson, Palle. 2002. "Five Danish Referendums on the European Community and European Union: A Critical Assessment of the Franklin Thesis." *European Journal of Political Research* 41 (6): 733–750.

Svensson, Palle. 2007. "Direct and Representative Democracy – Supplementing, Not Excluding Each Other." Presented at the *ECPR Joint Sessions*, 7–12 May, Helsinki.

Szczerbiak, Aleks and Paul Taggart. 2004. "The Politics of European Referendum Outcomes and Turnout: Two Models." *West European Politics* 27 (4): 557–583.

Teixeira, Ruy. 1987. *Why Americans Don't Vote: Turnout Decline in the United States, 1960–1984*. New York: Greenwood Press.

The National Conference of State Legislatures. 2008. Available at http://www.ncsl.org/ncsldb/elect98/irsrch.cfm.

Thomas Acuña, Evaristo. 2007. "Colombia: Entre la crisis de la representatividad y la democracia directa." *C2D – 16/2008*.

Tolbert, Caroline J. and Daniel Bowen. 2008. "Direct Democracy, Engagement and Turnout." In *Democracy in the States: Experiments in Election Reform*, edited by

B. E. Cain, T. Donovan, and C. Tolbert. Washington, DC: Brookings Institution Press, 99–113.

Tolbert, Caroline J. and Daniel A. Smith. 2005. "The Educative Effects of Ballot Initiatives on Voter Turnout." *American Politics Research* 33 (2): 283–309.

Tolbert, Caroline J. and Daniel A. Smith. 2006. "Representation and Direct Democracy in the United States." *Representation* 42 (1): 25–44.

Torres Rivas, Edelberto. 1997. "La Gobernabilidad Centroamericano en las Noventa: Consideraciones sobre las Posibilidades Democráticas en la Postguerra." *América Latina Hoy* 8 (June): 27–34.

Tranter, Bruce. 2003. "The Australian Constitutional Referendum of 1999: Evaluating Explanations of Republican Voting." *Electoral Studies* 22 (4): 677–701.

Trechsel, Alexander H. and Hanspeter Kriesi. 1996. "Switzerland: The Referendum and Initiative as a Centerpiece of the Political System." In *The Referendum Experience in Europe*, edited by M. Gallagher and P. V. Uleri. London: Macmillan, 185–208.

Trechsel, Alexander H. and Pascal Sciarini. 1998. "Direct Democracy in Switzerland: Do Elites Matter?" *European Journal of Political Research* 33 (1): 99–124.

Tsebelis, George. 1990. *Nested Games: Rational Choice in Comparative Politics*. Berkeley: University of California Press.

Tsebelis, George. 1995. "Decision Making in Political Systems: Veto Players in Presidentialism, Parliamentarism, Multicameralism and Multipartyism." *British Journal of Political Science* 25 (3): 289–325.

Tyler, Tom R. 1997. "Procedural Fairness and Compliance with the Law." *Swiss Journal of Economics and Statistics* 133 (2/2): 219–240.

Uggla, Fredrik. 2008. "Bolivia: Referéndums como Armas Políticas." Presented at the *¿Hacia dónde va la democracia en América Latina?* October 20–21, Montevideo.

Uleri, PierVincenzo. 1996. "Italy: Referendums and Initiatives from the Origins to the Crisis of a Democratic Regime." In *The Referendum Experience in Europe*, edited by M. Gallagher and P. V. Uleri. London: Macmillan, 106–125.

Uleri, PierVincenzo. 2002. "On Referendum Voting in Italy: YES, NO or Non–Vote? How Italian Parties Learned to Control Referendums." *European Journal of Political Research* 41 (6): 863–883.

Ullman, Jodie B. 1996. "Structural Equation Model." In *Using Multivariate Statistics*, edited by B. Tabachnick and L. Fidell. Needham Heights, MA: Allyn and Bacon, 653–771.

Valenzuela, Arturo. 1991. "The Military in Power: The Consolidation of One-Man Rule." In *The Struggle for Democracy in Chile, 1982–1990*, edited by P. Drake and I. Jaksic. Lincoln and London: University of Nebraska Press, 21–72.

Valenzuela, Samuel J. 1992. "Democratic Consolidation in Post-Transitional Settings: Notion, Process and Facilitating Conditions." In *Issues in Democratic Consolidation: The New South American Democracies in Comparative Perspective*, edited by S. Mainwaring, Guillermo O'Donnell, and S. Valenzuela. Notre Dame: University of Notre Dame Press, 57–73.

Vanhanen, Tatu. 1999. "Domestic Ethnic Conflict and Ethnic Nepotism: A Comparative Analysis." *Journal of Peace Research* 36 (1): 55–73.

Vanhanen, Tatu. 2000. "A New Dataset for Measuring Democracy, 1810–1998." *Journal of Peace Research* 37 (2): 251–265.

Vargas Cullell, Jorge. 2007. "Costa Rica: Fin de una Era Política." *Revista de Ciencia Política* 27 (EE): 113–128.

Vargas Cullell, Jorge. 2008. "Costa Rica: Una Decisión Estratégica en Tiempos Inciertos." *Revista de Ciencia Política* 28 (1): 147–169.

Vatter, Adrian. 2000. "Consensus and Direct Democracy: Conceptual and Empirical Linkages." *European Journal of Political Research* 38 (2): 171–192.

Vatter, Adrian. 2007. "Three Dimensions of Democracy? Lijphart's Typology and Direct Democracy. A Cross-National Analysis of Forms of Government in 23 Advanced Democracies between 1997 and 2006." Presented at the *35th Joint Sessions of Workshops of the European Consortium for Political Research*, May 7–12, Helsinki.

Vatter, Adrian. 2008. "Swiss Consensus Democracy in Transition: A Re-analysis of Lijphart's Concept of Democracy for Switzerland from 1997 to 2007." *World Political Science Review* 4 (2): Article 1.

Vatter, Adrian. 2009. "Lijphart Expanded: Three Dimensions of Democracy in Advanced OECD Countries?" *European Political Science Review* 1 (1): 125–153.

Venter, Denis. 2005. "Zimbabwe Before and After the June 2000 Elections: An Assessment." *EISA*. Available at http://www.eisa.org.za/WEP/zim2000election1.htm.

Venturini, Angel R. 1989. *Estadísticas Electorales 1917–1989*. Montevideo: Ediciones de la Banda Oriental.

Vergara, Pilar. 1985. *Auge y Caída del Neoliberalismo en Chile*. Santiago: FLACSO-Salesianos.

Vergara, Pilar. 1986. "Changes in the Economic Functions of the Chilean State under the Military Regime." In *Military Rule in Chile: Dictatorship and Oppositions*, edited by A. Valenzuela and S. Valenzuela. Baltimore: Johns Hopkins University Press.

Verhulst, Jos and Arejen Nijeboer. 2007. *Direct Democracy: Facts and Arguments about the Introduction of Initiative and Referendum*. Brussels: Democracy International.

Voss, Stephen and David Lublin. 1998. "Ecological Inference and the Comparative Method." *American Political Science Association – Comparative Politics Newsletter*. Winter 25–31.

Wald, Kenneth D., James W. Button, and Barbara A. Rienzo. 1996. "The Politics of Gay Rights in American Communities: Explaining Antidiscrimination Ordinances and Policies." *American Journal of Political Science* 40 (4): 1152–1178.

Walton, John and David Seddon. 1994. *Free Markets and Food Riots. The Politics of Global Adjustments*. Cambridge: Cambridge University Press.

Walzer, Michael. 2004. *Politics and Passion: Toward a More Egalitarian Liberalism*. New Haven and London: Yale University Press.

Ward, Michael D. 2002. "Green Binders in Cyberspace: A Modest Proposal." *Comparative Political Studies* 35 (1): 46–51.

Warren, Mark E. 2001. *Democracy and Association*. Princeton: Princeton University Press.

Wernli, Boris. 1998. "Die Bestimmungsfaktoren der Wahlbeteiligung. Eine vergleichende Analyse von 10 Schweizer Kantonen." In *Selects. Die Schweizer Wahlen 1995*, edited by H. Kriesi, W. Linder, and U. Klöti. Bern: Haupt, 73–100.

Weyland, Kurt. 1998. "The Politics of Corruption in Latin America." *Journal of Democracy* 9 (2): 108–121.

Weyland, Kurt. 2002. *The Politics of Market Reform in Fragile Democracies: Argentina, Brazil, Peru, and Venezuela*. Princeton: Princeton University Press.

Weyland, Kurt. 2005. "Theories of Policy Diffusion: Lessons from Latin American Pension Reform." *World Politics* 57 (2): 262–295.

Wheatley, Jonathan. 2008. "Direct Democracy in the Commonwealth of Independent States: The State of the Art." *C2D Working Paper Series* 28.

Whitehead, Laurence. 1992. "The Alternatives to 'Liberal Democracy': A Latin American Perspective." *Political Studies* 40 (1): 146–159.

Wintrobe, Ronald. 1998. *The Political Economy of Dictatorship.* New York: Cambridge University Press.

Wolfinger, Raymond and Steven Rosenstone. 1980. *Who Votes?* New Haven: Yale University Press.

Zimmerman, Joseph F. 1986. *Participatory Democracy: Populism Revived.* New York: Praeger.

Zovatto, Daniel. 2001. "La Práctica General de las Instituciones de Democracia Directa en América Latina. Un Balance Comparado: 1978–2000." Presented at the *Primer Encuentro Multidisciplinario sobre Democracia y Formación Ciudadana*, Diciembre 6–8, México.

Zovatto, Daniel, Iván Marulanda, Antonio Lizarazo, and Rodolfo González. 2004. *Democracia Directa y Referéndum en Amércia Latina.* La Paz: Corte Nacional Electoral.

Index

CPSIA information can be obtained
at www.ICGtesting.com
Printed in the USA
LVOW07s0211031217
558397LV00006B/475/P